AI Solutions for the United Nations Sustainable Development Goals (UN SDGs)

A Practical Approach Using JavaScript

Tulsi Pawan Fowdur
Lavesh Babooram

Apress®

AI Solutions for the United Nations Sustainable Development Goals (UN SDGs): A Practical Approach Using JavaScript

Tulsi Pawan Fowdur
Department of Electrical and Electronic
Engineering, University of Mauritius, Reduit,
Mauritius

Lavesh Babooram
Department of Electrical and Electronic
Engineering, University of Mauritius, Reduit,
Mauritius

ISBN-13 (pbk): 979-8-8688-0538-7
https://doi.org/10.1007/979-8-8688-0536-3

ISBN-13 (electronic): 979-8-8688-0536-3

Copyright © 2024 by Tulsi Pawan Fowdur and Lavesh Babooram

This work is subject to copyright. All rights are reserved by the Publisher, whether the whole or part of the material is concerned, specifically the rights of translation, reprinting, reuse of illustrations, recitation, broadcasting, reproduction on microfilms or in any other physical way, and transmission or information storage and retrieval, electronic adaptation, computer software, or by similar or dissimilar methodology now known or hereafter developed.

Trademarked names, logos, and images may appear in this book. Rather than use a trademark symbol with every occurrence of a trademarked name, logo, or image we use the names, logos, and images only in an editorial fashion and to the benefit of the trademark owner, with no intention of infringement of the trademark.

The use in this publication of trade names, trademarks, service marks, and similar terms, even if they are not identified as such, is not to be taken as an expression of opinion as to whether or not they are subject to proprietary rights.

While the advice and information in this book are believed to be true and accurate at the date of publication, neither the authors nor the editors nor the publisher can accept any legal responsibility for any errors or omissions that may be made. The publisher makes no warranty, express or implied, with respect to the material contained herein.

Managing Director, Apress Media LLC: Welmoed Spahr
Acquisitions Editor: Celestin Suresh John
Development Editor: James Markham
Editorial Assistant: Kripa Joseph

Cover designed by eStudioCalamar

Distributed to the book trade worldwide by Springer Science+Business Media New York, 1 New York Plaza, Suite 4600, New York, NY 10004-1562, USA. Phone 1-800-SPRINGER, fax (201) 348-4505, e-mail orders-ny@springer-sbm.com, or visit www.springeronline.com. Apress Media, LLC is a California LLC and the sole member (owner) is Springer Science + Business Media Finance Inc (SSBM Finance Inc). SSBM Finance Inc is a **Delaware** corporation.

For information on translations, please e-mail booktranslations@springernature.com; for reprint, paperback, or audio rights, please e-mail bookpermissions@springernature.com.

Apress titles may be purchased in bulk for academic, corporate, or promotional use. eBook versions and licenses are also available for most titles. For more information, reference our Print and eBook Bulk Sales web page at http://www.apress.com/bulk-sales.

Any source code or other supplementary material referenced by the author in this book is available to readers on GitHub. For more detailed information, please visit https://www.apress.com/gp/services/source-code.

If disposing of this product, please recycle the paper

Table of Contents

About the Authors ix

About the Contributors xi

Chapter 1: Introduction to Machine Learning Applications Development and the UN SDGs 1

    1.1 The UN SDGs and Machine Learning 2

    1.2 AI and Machine Learning Concepts 15

        1.2.1 Artificial Intelligence 15

        1.2.2 Machine Learning 16

        1.2.3 Data Types 26

        1.2.4 Data Preprocessing Steps 29

        1.2.5 Data Preprocessing Program in JavaScript 34

    1.3 Implementation of ML-Based Prediction and Classification Algorithms in JavaScript 39

        1.3.1 Simple Linear Regression (SLR) 39

        1.3.2 Polynomial Regression (PLR) 45

        1.3.3 Multiple Linear Regression (MLR) 49

        1.3.4 K-Nearest Neighbor 55

    1.4 Summary 57

Chapter 2: Utilizing Machine Learning Algorithms for Power Generation Prediction and Classification in Wind Farms 59

    2.1 Introduction 60

    2.2 AI Use Cases for SDG 7 63

    2.3 Data Processing and Application Design 68

TABLE OF CONTENTS

    2.3.1 Data Collection Process and Description of Dataset 68

    2.3.2 Data Preprocessing Steps 70

    2.3.3 Wind Turbine Modeling 71

    2.3.4 Program Structure 72

  2.4 Application Testing and Analysis 82

    2.4.1 Application Testing... 82

    2.4.2 Polynomial Regression Results 86

    2.4.3 KNN Regression 88

    2.4.4 Multilinear Regression... 90

    2.4.5 KNN Classification 90

    2.4.6 Comparative Analysis of Regression Models: Polynomial Regression vs. KNN Regression vs. Multilinear Regression 93

  2.5 Benefits of Classification in Wind Power Prediction 96

    2.5.1 Accurate Energy Generation Forecasting 96

    2.5.2 Optimized Energy Distribution 96

    2.5.3 Cost Reduction 97

    2.5.4 Grid Stability 97

    2.5.5 Enhanced Energy Planning 97

  2.6 Summary.. 98

Chapter 3: A Crop Recommendation System Using Machine Learning Algorithms for Achieving SDGs 2, 9, and 12 101

  3.1 Introduction.. 102

  3.2 AI Use Cases for SDGs 2, 9, and 12 104

  3.3 Data Processing and Application Design 108

    3.3.1 Data Collection Process and Description of the Datasets.............. 108

    3.3.2 Data Preprocessing Steps 110

    3.3.3 Program Structure 111

    3.3.4 Layout of Web Application 112

TABLE OF CONTENTS

3.4 Application Testing and Analysis 118
    3.4.1 Application Testing 119
    3.4.2 K-NN Classification Results 121
    3.4.3 Decision Trees Classification Results 126
    3.4.4 Random Forest 128
    3.4.5 Multilayer Perceptron 130
    3.4.6 Discussion 134
3.5 Summary 136

Chapter 4: Aligning Manufacturing Emissions with SDGs 9 and 13 Using Machine Learning Algorithms 139

4.1 Introduction 141
4.2 Use Cases for SDGs 9 and 13 143
4.3 Data Processing and Application Design 148
    4.3.1 Data Collection Process and Description of Datasets 148
    4.3.2 Data Preprocessing Steps 149
4.4 Program Structure for Analysis 151
    4.4.1 Simple Linear Regression (SLR) 155
    4.4.2 Multiple Linear Regression (MLR) 157
    4.4.3 k-Nearest Neighbor (k-NN) 159
4.5 Application Testing and Analysis 162
    4.5.1 Simple Linear Regression (SLR) 162
    4.5.2 Multiple Linear Regression (MLR) 165
    4.5.3 k-Nearest Neighbors (k-NN) 169
    4.5.4 Discussion 172
4.6 Recommendations 174
4.7 Improvements 175

TABLE OF CONTENTS

4.8 Summary 176
4.9 Appendix 176
    4.9.1 Dataset 176

Chapter 5: Potability Analysis of Water Using Machine Learning 179

5.1 Introduction 181
5.2 AI Use Cases for SDGs 3, 6, and 12 183
5.3 Data Processing and Application Design 188
    5.3.1 Data Collection Process and Description of the Datasets 188
    5.3.2 Data Preprocessing Steps 190
    5.3.3 General Layout of Web Application 190
    5.3.4 Water Potability System 192
    5.3.5 Machine Learning Algorithms 193
5.4 Application Testing and Analysis 200
    5.4.1 Application Testing 200
    5.4.2 k-NN 201
    5.4.3 Decision Tree 204
    5.4.4 Random Forest 208
    5.4.5 Naïve Bayes 212
5.5 Summary 220

Chapter 6: Air Quality Monitoring: A Case Study for the Application of Machine Learning in Meeting SDGs 3 and 13 221

6.1 Introduction 223
6.2 AI Use Cases for SDGs 3 and 13 224
    6.2.1 SDG 3: Good Health and Well-Being 224
    6.2.2 SDG 13: Climate Action 226
6.3 Data Processing and Application Design 228
    6.3.1 Data Collection Process and Dataset Description 228
    6.3.2 Program Structure 230

6.3.3 Layout of Website 231
6.3.4 Implementation of Linear Regression..................................232
6.3.5 Implementation of Polynomial Regression 233
6.3.6 Implementation of LSTM/MLP 234
6.3.7 Displaying Regression Graphs..234
6.3.8 AQI Classification...235

6.4 Application Testing and Analysis 236
6.4.1 Testing of Web Application..236
6.4.2 Performance of Regression Algorithms...............................241
6.4.3 Performance of SLR..241
6.4.4 Performance of PR 242
6.4.5 Performance of MLP...244
6.4.6 Performance of LSTM...246
6.4.7 Performance of Classification Algorithms 248

6.5 Summary...249

Chapter 7: Clustering the Development of Worldwide Internet Connectivity for SDGs 7, 9, and 11 251

7.1 Introduction..252
7.2 AI Use Cases for SDGs 7, 9, and 11 255
7.3 Data Processing and Application Design 259
7.3.1 Collection and Description of Dataset 259
7.3.2 Data Preprocessing 262
7.3.3 Scatter Plots..263
7.3.4 Application System Model 268
7.3.5 Application Layout 272
7.3.6 Program Structure 273

TABLE OF CONTENTS

> 7.4 Application Testing and Analysis 279
>   7.4.1 Application Testing..279
>   7.4.2 Discussions 283
> 7.5 Benefits of Global Internet Connectivity Analysis..286
> 7.6 Summary...289

References..291

Index..327

About the Authors

Dr. Tulsi Pawan Fowdur received his bachelor of engineering degree in electronic and communication engineering with honors from the University of Mauritius in 2004. He was also the recipient of a gold medal for having produced the best degree project at the Faculty of Engineering in 2004. In 2005 he obtained a full-time PhD scholarship from the Tertiary Education Commission of Mauritius and was awarded his PhD degree in electrical and electronic engineering in 2010 by the University of Mauritius. He is also a registered chartered engineer of the Engineering Council of the UK, a fellow of the Institute of Telecommunications Professionals of the UK, and a senior member of the IEEE. He joined the University of Mauritius as an academic in June 2009 and is presently an associate professor at the Department of Electrical and Electronic Engineering of the University of Mauritius. His research interests include mobile and wireless communications, multimedia communications, networking and security, telecommunications applications development, the Internet of Things, and AI. He has published several papers in these areas and is actively involved in supervising research, reviewing papers, and organizing international conferences.

ABOUT THE AUTHORS

Lavesh Babooram received his bachelor of engineering degree in telecommunications engineering with networking with honors from the University of Mauritius in 2021. He was also awarded a gold medal for having produced the best degree project at the Faculty of Engineering in 2021. Since 2022, he has been a graduate research student at the University of Mauritius. With in-depth knowledge of telecommunications applications design, analytics, and network infrastructure, he aims to pursue research in networking, multimedia communications, Internet of Things, artificial intelligence, and mobile and wireless communications. He joined Mauritius Telecom in 2022 and is currently working in the Customer Experience and Service Department as a pre-registration trainee engineer.

About the Contributors

Chapter 2

Mr. Lalitesh recently graduated with a BEng Telecommunications Engineering with Networking degree from the University of Mauritius. He is currently working at Orange Business, delving into modern networking infrastructure, including MPLS networks, customer VPNs, and public clouds such as Azure, AWS, and SAP among others.

—Lalitesh Dobee
Camp Fouquereaux, Phoenix, 73606, Mauritius
laliteshdobee2016@outlook.com

Mr. Ashven Sanghan is a final-year student pursuing a Bachelor's Degree in Telecommunications Engineering with Networking at the University Of Mauritius.

—Ashven Sanghan
Shivala Lane, L'Escalier, 61412, Mauritius
sanghanashven@gmail.com

Miss Gyaneeta Luchmunparsad holds a Bachelor's Degree in Telecommunications Engineering with Networking. She currently works at Talan Mauritius as a SAP consultant.

—Gyaneeta Luchmunparsad
Clairfond 2, Vacoas, 73412, Mauritius
lgyaneeta@gmail.com

ABOUT THE CONTRIBUTORS

Mr. Mohammad Adnaan Kurmally graduated with a Bachelor's Degree in Telecommunications Engineering with a focus on Networking. Currently employed at Emtel Ltd as a Network Engineer, he specializes in technical support, network design, and optimization. His role includes ensuring the continuous and effective operation of Emtel Ltd's MPLS network in real time. His professional interests span machine learning and real-time systems, complemented by his expertise in networking and network security.

—Mohammad Adnaan Kurmally
Morcellement Prud'homme. Riviere des Anguilles, 60604, Mauritius
ad8kurmally@hotmail.com

Chapter 3

Mr. Avishaye Domah holds a Bachelor's Degree in Telecommunications Engineering with Networking. He is currently working at Orange Business as a Network Engineer. His research interests embed artificial intelligence and networking.

—Avishaye Domah
Seebundhun Road, Plaine Des Papayes, 21211, Mauritius
avishaye.domah@outlook.com

Mr. Dheeraj Radjoo holds a Bachelor's Degree in Telecommunications Engineering with Networking. He is currently working at Emtel Ltd as a Network Engineer. His research interests embed routing protocols for WSNs and networking.

—Dheeraj Radjoo
New Sainte Marie Street, Sainte Croix, 11706, Mauritius
Dheerajradjoo@gmail.com

ABOUT THE CONTRIBUTORS

Miss Vandana Hanumunthadu is a final-year student pursuing a Bachelor's Degree in Telecommunications Engineering with Networking. Her research interests include artificial intelligence, the Internet of vehicles, and cybersecurity measures.

—Vandana Hanumunthadu
Domaine du Moulin, Goodlands, 30407, Mauritius
vandana.hanumunthadu@gmail.com

Chapter 4

Miss Sai Maadhavee Mohadeb graduated with first class honors in Telecommunications Engineering with Networking. She is currently working as a cybersecurity consultant in technology consulting at EY. Her main engagements evolve around MENA and SA clients, and she is growing within the offensive cyber stream. Her research interests include PAPR reduction and BER analysis of MIMO OFDM systems, focusing on a preferred air interface used for 4G/5G broadband wireless communications.

—Sai Maadhavee Mohadeb
Charles Regnaud Street, Curepipe, 7425, Mauritius
neermahmohadeb@gmail.com

Miss Aishani Radhakeesoon is currently a final-year student pursuing BEng (Hons) Telecommunications Engineering with Networking. Her research interests encompass artificial intelligence, Internet of things, and networking.

—Aishani Radhakeesoon
Shamlall Road, Laventure, Flacq, 41001, Mauritius
aishaniradh@gmail.com

ABOUT THE CONTRIBUTORS

Miss Oushna Seeballack holds a Bachelor's Degree in Telecommunications Engineering with Networking. Currently, she works at Emtel Ltd as a Network Architect. She is responsible for designing and provisioning enterprise solutions tailored to the specific needs of clients. She is involved in testing last-mile technologies on the client's premises. Her research interests include designing and optimizing PIFA antennas for 5G mobile phones.

—Oushna Seeballack
Engrais Martial, Curepipe, 74124, Mauritius
seeballackoushna@gmail.com

Chapter 5

Miss Leena Soodhoo holds a Bachelor's Degree in Telecommunications Engineering with Networking. She is currently working as a Management Support Officer in the Ministry of Finance, Economic Planning and Development.

—Leena Soodhoo
Royal Road, Lesur, Sebastopol, 42105, Mauritius
leena.soodhoo@gmail.com

Miss Diteesha Ramdin holds a Bachelor's Degree in Telecommunications Engineering with Networking. Her research interests include the performance analysis of massive MIMO systems, particularly with ZF receivers. She is currently employed as a Network Engineer at Orange Business and has expertise in networking and network security.

—Diteesha Ramdin
Savanne Road, Nouvelle France, 51312, Mauritius
diteesharamdin01@gmail.com

ABOUT THE CONTRIBUTORS

Mr. Roshwar Ramjansing holds a Bachelor's Degree in Telecommunications Engineering with Networking. He is currently working as a Network Engineer at Emtel Ltd. His research interests include the analysis and optimization of massive MIMO systems to enhance wireless communications.

—Roshwar Ramjansing
Royal Road Chamouny, 61301, Mauritius
yanishramjansing@gmail.com

Chapter 6

Mr. Mohammed Fayez Hawseea holds a Bachelor's Degree in Telecommunications Engineering with Networking with first class honours. He is presently working as an Engineer at Emtel Ltd. His research interests include machine learning and real-time systems. He has expertise in fiber optics and wireless communication systems.

—Mohammed Fayez Hawseea
JSS Road Goodlands, 30418, Mauritius
fayezunknown@gmail.com

Mr. Navish Kumar Ragoo graduated with first class honors in Telecommunications Engineering with Networking. He currently works as an Engineer at Emtel Ltd. His research interests are focused on machine learning and real-time systems, and he has expertise in networking and network security.

—Navish Kumar Ragoo
Cooperative Road, La flora, 61702, Mauritius
navisragoo@gmail.com

ABOUT THE CONTRIBUTORS

Mr. Appadoo holds a Bachelor's Degree in Telecommunications Engineering with Networking. He is currently working at the University of Mauritius as a Research Assistant with interests in artificial intelligence, Internet of things, and real-time systems.

—Appadoo Sarvesh Sanjeevi
St Paul Rd, Vacoas, 73449, Mauritius
sarvesh.appadoo1@gmail.com

Mr. Kwok Hin holds a Bachelor's Degree in Telecommunications Engineering with Networking. He is currently working at IT SOLVZ in an IoT department where his responsibilities include installing and configuring sensors in corporate environments for monitoring purposes.

—Kwok Hin John Darren Joshua
Volcy Pougnet Street, Port Louis, 11310, Mauritius
darrenkwok2000@gmail.com

Mr. Munisamy Sodiyen holds a Bachelor's Degree in Telecommunications Engineering with Networking. He is currently working at Emtel Ltd as a Trainee Network Architect where his responsibilities include the planning, deployment, and optimization of radio access technologies. His research interests include designing and optimizing antennas for various applications.

—Munisamy Sodiyen
Valton Road, Long-Mountain, 20814, Mauritius
munisamysodiyen@gmail.com

Mr. Aunowar holds a Bachelor's Degree in Telecommunications Engineering with Networking. He is currently working at Emtel Ltd as an Engineer. His research interests include optimization and design of 5G networks for a wide variety of industrial applications.

—Aunowar Mohammad Farhaan Jeelany
La Caverne 2, Vacoas, 73325, Mauritius
farhaanaunowar@gmail.com

CHAPTER 1

Introduction to Machine Learning Applications Development and the UN SDGs

Chapter authors:
Tulsi Pawan Fowdur, `p.fowdur@uom.ac.mu`
Lavesh Babooram, `lavesh.babooram1@umail.uom.ac.mu`
Department of Electrical and Electronic Engineering, University of Mauritius

The 17 United Nations Sustainable Development Goals (UN SDGs) are a global blueprint for addressing social, economic, and environmental challenges. They aim to transform our world by providing standards to address pressing global challenges such as poverty, hunger, inequality, education, economic growth, and climate change, while ensuring the welfare of the inhabitants of this planet.

CHAPTER 1   INTRODUCTION TO MACHINE LEARNING APPLICATIONS DEVELOPMENT AND THE UN SDGS

Artificial intelligence (AI) and machine learning (ML) aim to help achieve the SDGs by harnessing vast amounts of data, making predictions, and uncovering patterns from large and complex datasets to enable proactive decision-making and optimizations within core systems and distribution channels. ML is indeed a very potent and innovative approach in addressing all 17 SDGs.

In this chapter, we give an overview of the SDGs and the applications of AI and ML to achieve these goals. Moreover, we cover some fundamental concepts of the most common ML-based prediction and classification algorithms along with the implementation details of these algorithms using JavaScript.

1.1 The UN SDGs and Machine Learning

The Sustainable Development Goals were created in Rio de Janeiro at the United Nations Conference on Sustainable Development in 2015 by the UN General Assembly through resolution 70/1 on the 2030 Agenda. The UNSDG is a group of 193 states established to provide a better future and a better quality of life. The SDGs were developed as a response to the pressing global challenges in the environmental, economic, and political domains. These goals replaced the Millennium Development Goals (MDGs), which were started in 2000 to reduce poverty. The SDGs builds upon the MDGs and addresses more urgent global challenges.

The 17 interconnected goals encompass a wide range of issues, where success in one area influences progress in others. The 17 SDG goals aim at three significant community development aspects: protecting the environment, fostering social diversity, and promoting economic growth. These SDGs have been established by governments, academia, and the private sector and are one of the most recognized standards to attain sustainable community development [1], [2], [3].

Figure 1-1 shows the 17 SDGs.

CHAPTER 1   INTRODUCTION TO MACHINE LEARNING APPLICATIONS DEVELOPMENT AND THE UN SDGS

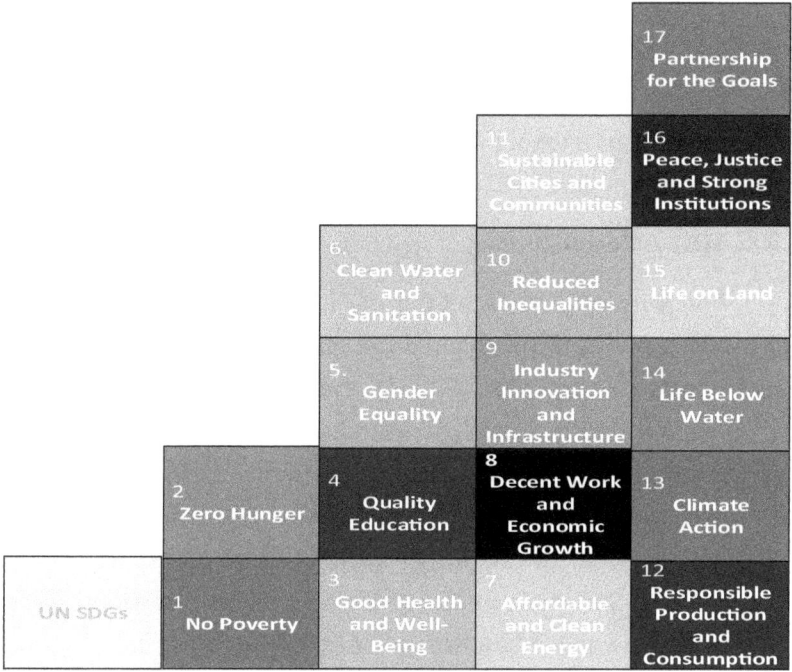

Figure 1-1. *The UN SDGs*

AI and machine learning provide a powerful means of achieving the UN SDGs, and several studies have reported their effectiveness. The following list is a review of some of the works where AI and ML have been employed to SDGs 1, 2, 3, 6, 7, 9, 11, 12, and 13:

- **SDG 1: No Poverty**

    The objective of this SDG is the worldwide eradication of extreme poverty by 2030 and to ensure equal rights to economic resources to all people. Extreme poverty is characterized by people with a daily wage of less than $1.25 [4]. According to the Decentralized AI Alliance (DAIA) [5], it is possible to extract vital information such as the closest water sources, agricultural fields, and marketplaces using AI [6]. Moreover, high-tech satellite-based image analysis was used to identify poverty in Nigeria, Tanzania, Uganda, Malawi, and Rwanda by a team of researchers at Stanford University using sophisticated machine learning algorithms [7].

- **SDG 2: Zero Hunger**

  The primary purpose of this SDG is to eradicate hunger, improve nutrition, ensure food security, and promote sustainable agriculture [8]. At present, up to half of the world's food is wasted. An increase in poverty will lead to food insecurity and, as a consequence, an increase in diseases. AI can be of a major help in dealing with food wastage and security issues. Take the case of the TOMRA Sorting Solutions, which is powered by AI. It analyzes and categorizes food as either good or bad. The algorithm can analyze a tomato and determine if it can be used in a salad. If not, it can be better suited for tomato juice [9]. Several machine learning algorithms such as decision trees, k-NN, multivariate logistic regression, and random forest have also been used in crop prediction and classification of soil types in countries such as India and Bangladesh [10, 11, 12, 13].

- **SDG 3: Good Health and Well-Being**

  The aim of SDG 3 is to guarantee healthy lifestyles and promote well-being for all individuals, regardless of their age, race, and religion. This includes a wide range of objectives, such as lowering the global maternal mortality rate and putting an end to preventable infant and child deaths under five years of age. Moreover, it aims to minimize or put an end to AIDS, tuberculosis, malaria, and other communicable disease epidemics and to lower premature mortality from non-communicable diseases through prevention and treatment, stepping up the prevention and treatment of substance abuse, and ensuring universal access to sexual and reproductive health services [14]. However, the worldwide threats from pandemics like COVID-19 have emphasized the pressing requirement for readiness. The UNDP emphasized the contrasting capabilities of nations to cope with the COVID-19 problem. Investments in vital public services and health emergency preparation witnessed a turning point in the 21st century due to the pandemic.

The following are some of the targets by 2030:

- To decrease the global maternal mortality rate to less than 70 for every 100,000 live births.

- To eliminate the death of newborns and children younger than 5 years old. The aims of all nations are to lower neonatal mortality to at least 12 per 1,000 live births and under-5 mortality to at least 25 per 1,000 live births.

- To significantly lower the number of fatalities and diseases caused by contaminated air, toxic chemicals, water, and soil.

CHAPTER 1 INTRODUCTION TO MACHINE LEARNING APPLICATIONS DEVELOPMENT AND THE UN SDGS

With regard to the application of ML to help achieve this SDG, in [15], the use of the deep learning approach (DLA) in medical image analysis has emerged as a rapidly advancing research domain where DLA is extensively applied in medical imaging to discern the presence or absence of diseases. This work focused on the evolution of artificial neural networks and conducted an extensive examination of DLA, which exhibits promising applications within the realm of medical imaging. Moreover, in the work carried out in [16], an approach for distinguishing autism traits using machine learning was presented. An existing prediction model was enhanced by combining two different algorithms, namely, CART and ID3 within random forest.

- **SDG 6: Clean Water and Sanitation**

  SDG 6 holds a pivotal role within the United Nation's 2030 Agenda for Sustainable Development [17]. It makes sure that there is a worldwide commitment to ensure that everyone has access to safe and affordable drinking water and sanitation by the year 2030. SDG 6 addresses several significant challenges. First, it focuses on ensuring access to safe and uncontaminated potable water, acknowledging that billions of individuals globally still lack this fundamental necessity. Second, it places emphasis on sanitation by aiming to eradicate open defecation and ensuring proper wastewater treatment to prevent water pollution.

CHAPTER 1 INTRODUCTION TO MACHINE LEARNING APPLICATIONS DEVELOPMENT AND THE UN SDGS

- Machine learning, especially k-Nearest Neighbors (k-NN) can serve as a valuable tool in confronting these challenges. k-NN is a supervised learning algorithm that can be utilized for classification and regression tasks. It has pertinent applications within the context of SDG 6:

    - **Monitoring water quality:** k-NN can be employed to scrutinize data on water quality collected from various sources such as sensors and monitoring stations. This analysis aids in identifying patterns and irregularities in water quality, facilitating early detection of contamination or pollution incidents.

    - **Proactive maintenance:** Machine learning algorithms such as k-NN can predict when maintenance or repair is needed for water infrastructure. This proactive approach ensures that there is an interrupted provision of clean water.

In [18] researchers addressed SDG 6 by exploring AI-driven water quality anomaly detection (WQAD). They conducted an extensive review of ML and deep learning (DL) applications in smart water systems. Additionally, in [19] the study contributed to SDG 6 by using machine learning to forecast Escherichia coli (E. coli) contamination in Ethiopian drinking water sources. They employed risk mapping algorithms like Random Forest (RF) and Extreme Gradient Boosting (XGBoost), combining geographical and household data. Furthermore, the work in [20] employed machine learning, specifically a modified Faster R-CNN (convolutional neural network), to detect and categorize algae in water, addressing both SDGs 6 and 14. Manually identifying diverse, microscopic algae is time-consuming and error-prone. In [21], the work indirectly supported SDGs 3 and 6 by using machine learning to predict water quality, a critical aspect of ensuring access to safe drinking water. It focused on classifying water as potable or nonpotable, vital for public health. Effective algorithms like Support Vector Machine (SVM) and k-NN achieved high F1-scores and accuracy.

- **SDG 7 – Affordable and Clean Energy**

    Implementing renewable energy options is becoming increasingly affordable and reliable and is therefore a prospective solution to ensure sustainability. Our heavy dependence on unrenewable sources such as fossil fuels is not only harmful to the environment but also leaves future generations with limited options to carry out their activities. The main objective of this SDG is to reach accessible, eco-friendly, and sustainable energy for all. Despite that energy holds an important position in both environmental and economic aspects, one-fifth of the global population still did not have access to electricity in 2021 [22]. There are several targets that should be met to achieve this SDG and some of them are listed here:

- **Target 7.1 – To ensure that everyone across the globe is able to access state-of-the-art and reliable energy services by 2030.**

  As stated in [22], 1 out of 10 people do not have access to electricity to fulfil basic requirements. It is also stated that around 2.6 billion people make use of biomass energy resources such as charcoal, coal and animal waste; 80% of countries globally do not have access to green energy. The SDGs can be achieved by making use of greener energy alternatives. SDG 7.1 aims at closing those energy gaps by 2030.

- **Target 7.2 – Focus on clean energy technologies and energy sources to increase the use of renewable energy for daily purposes by 2030.**

  SDG 7.2 aims to encourage more countries in approaching renewable energy methods. It is stated in [22] that around 17% of the world's energy consumption comes from renewable sources. Industries across the world have started investing in sustainable resources that aim at producing green energy and causing less harm to the planet.

- **Target 7.3 – Increase global energy efficiency by twofold and improve international cooperation to facilitate access to renewable energy services by 2030.**

It aims at improving the ratio of the total energy output to the energy input into a system producing energy. This can be done by minimizing the total amount of waste, by improving the technologies involved and by approaching sustainable approaches. Target 7.3 aims at doubling the rate at which energy is being now by 2030.

By employing machine learning algorithms on historical turbine data and weather forecasts on a 700 megawatts wind power grid, DeepMind and Google could generate 36-hour forecasts of the wind power output, thus promoting SDG 7. It was thus possible to optimally plan the hourly delivery commitments to the power grid, one day in advance. A 20 % gain in wind energy management was obtained with this scheme compared to a conventional system that does not take into consideration the predicted wind power output [23].

- **SDG 9: Industry, Innovation, and Infrastructure**

    This SDG targets the setting up of durable infrastructure, support inclusive and sustainable industrialization and foster innovation as per the motto of the United Nations [24]. Investment in infrastructure and innovation are essential for economic growth and development while also improving and expanding new industries and infrastructure, especially in developing countries. Moreover, SDG 9 accounts for the advancement of economic growth by creating employment opportunities, promoting sustainable development such as energy-efficiency and sustainable industries, and investing in scientific research and innovation.

Some key targets and areas of focus are as follows:

- Developing reliable, sustainable, and resilient infrastructure affordable and accessible to all
- Promoting inclusive and sustainable industrialization to increase the employment and GDP rate
- Expanding access to financial resources, particularly for small and medium-sized enterprises (SMEs) in developing countries
- Upgrading industries to employ resilient, sustainable, and environment-friendly resources
- Promoting research and development, technological advancement, and innovation to drive economic growth and find solutions to global challenges [25]

In [26], the impact of digitization to achieve SDGs was studied by focusing on the competitiveness of the Ha'il region of Saudi Arabia. An ML technique, a vector auto-regressive model, and impulse response functions were used. Results suggested that digitization promoted a rise in sustainable development of the Ha'il region, mainly SDG 9, which pertains to industry, innovation, and infrastructure. In [27], the opportunities offered by the acceleration of the Internet of Things (IoT) and advances in AI in reaching SDGs, related to health, energy, and cities have been studied. A system model combining IoT and AI to facilitate mobility in cities, thus targeting SDGs 9, 11, and 13, was proposed.

CHAPTER 1 INTRODUCTION TO MACHINE LEARNING APPLICATIONS DEVELOPMENT AND THE UN SDGS

- **SDG 11: Sustainable Cities and Communities**

    This SDG aims to build safe, sustainable, inclusive, and resilient cities and human habitats [28]. Technological advances are expected to have a major impact on smart cities. According to the UN, by 2050, smart cities will accommodate nearly 66% of the world's population [29]. Socio-economic concerns in areas such as energy, healthcare, and security are being addressed by countries where fast-growing urban areas are being converted into smart cities.

    Real-time location, video, and biometric data analysis can be achieved by combining AI with the ultra-reliable 5G networks. Self-driving cars are also an outcome of the combination of ultra-fast 5G networks with AI. Furthermore, high-resolution surveillance cameras can be connected to cloud-based facial recognition systems to recognize and spot potential law breakers in real time [30].

- **SDG 12: Responsible Consumption and Production**

    SDG 12 promotes the reduction of chemical usage and waste generation in industries. This activity relates to water treatment and testing processes. By optimizing chemical usage and minimizing waste generation, water treatment processes can be carried out more effectively and in an environment friendly manner [31].

CHAPTER 1 INTRODUCTION TO MACHINE LEARNING APPLICATIONS DEVELOPMENT AND THE UN SDGS

In water potability testing, the SDG 12 ensures efficient use of water resources by verifying the safety of water for consumption purposes. In addition, the water potability testing aids in analyzing the environmental impacts of water treatment and ensures that these treatments are eco-friendly. Water potability testing can be improvised by the use of innovative technologies such as sensor networks, IOT, and machine learning. This improves the accuracy and efficiency of testing.

SDG12 emphasizes on managing water resources and assure safe and clean drinking water for the public. The purpose of this SDG is to promote a sustainable means of consumption and production whereby resources are widely being used. This objective can be achieved by minimizing the ecological footprint. This meets the consumption needs of people without exploiting the natural resources and without causing harm to the environment such as discharge of toxic chemicals in water, air, or land.

Again, machine learning can prove to be very efficient in achieving SDG 12. For example, in [32], short-term water demand was predicted, and pumping schedules were optimized to reduce electricity costs by optimizing water supply systems through machine learning.

CHAPTER 1 INTRODUCTION TO MACHINE LEARNING APPLICATIONS DEVELOPMENT AND THE UN SDGS

- **SDG 13 – Climate Action**

    SDG 13 aims to alleviate the impact of climate change by decreasing greenhouse gas emissions, improving resilience to climate-related disasters, and promoting sustainable practices. SDG 13 recognizes that climate change poses significant threats to ecosystems, economies, and communities worldwide, emphasizing the need for immediate and coordinated efforts to protect the planet for a sustainable and climate-resilient future [1, 2].

    - Some of their targets are as follows:
        - To increase global adaptability and immunity to climate-related threats and natural disasters
        - To add climate change mitigation actions in national planning, strategy, and policies
        - To increase educational and awareness campaigns on climate change, institutional and human capacity for impact reduction, early warning, and adaptation

Some ML techniques that have been used for SDG 13 include the work in [33] in which the authors proposed a real-time multistep multi-output multivariate ML model to forecast the concentrations of the different air pollutants in Ho Chi Minh City (HCMC), which is located in Vietnam. The model proposed by the authors took as input various parameters, including meteorological conditions and air quality data from urban, residential, and industrial areas as well as hourly NO_2, SO_2, O_3, and CO concentrations. The concentration of each air pollutant was predicted using the proposed model, and the results demonstrated that the Mean Absolute Percentage Error (MAPE) value obtained, when predicting the concentration of each pollutant, ranged from 0.18 to 0.23. Moreover, in [34], deprived urban areas in Philippines were monitored over a four-year period, following the impact of 2013's super Typhoon Haiyan. Both satellite imagery and ML methods were employed for the purpose. Due to the increase in gravity and impact of natural disasters in such areas, effective disaster risk mitigation strategies are required. A support vector machine classification technique supported by a local binary pattern feature extraction model initially detected slum areas in pre- and post-disaster imageries. Afterward, a dense conditional random fields model produced final slum areas maps. The developed method detected slum areas with high accuracy. The results revealed that the city returned to the pre-existing vulnerability level.

1.2 AI and Machine Learning Concepts

In this section, we describe some basic concepts of AI and machine learning.

1.2.1 Artificial Intelligence

The discipline of AI was founded by Alan Turing, who defines it as: "AI is the science and engineering of making intelligent machines, especially intelligent computer programs. It is usually defined as the science of making computers do things that require intelligence when done by humans" [35, 36, 37]. AI can be classified based on capabilities and functionalities as per Figure 1-2 [38].

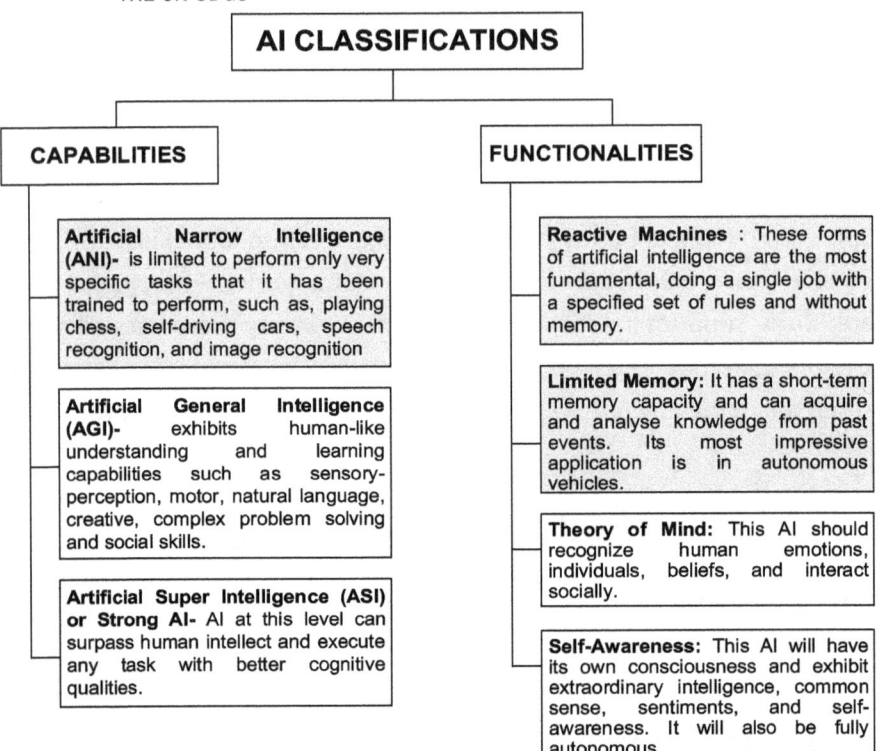

Figure 1-2. AI classifications

In Figure 1-2, the shaded boxes represent AI capabilities and functionalities that have been developed so far. The others are hypothetical and are currently being actively researched by different AI companies and researchers [39, 40, 41, 42, 43].

1.2.2 Machine Learning

Machine learning is a subfield of artificial intelligence, which allows machines to learn from previous data or processes without the need of explicit programming. Machine learning is essentially a well-defined process that allows a refined or optimized "model" to be derived from data, as shown in Figure 1-3.

CHAPTER 1 INTRODUCTION TO MACHINE LEARNING APPLICATIONS DEVELOPMENT AND THE UN SDGS

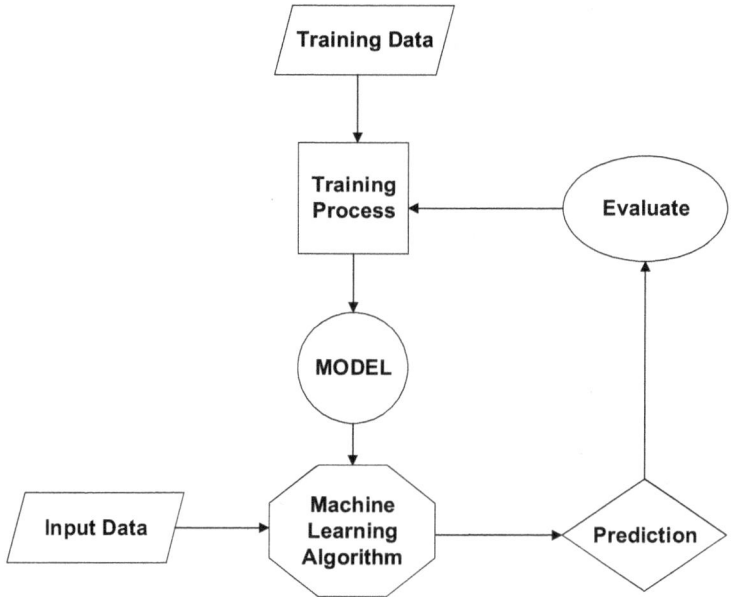

Figure 1-3. *Generic view of the machine learning process*

The data can be structured, semi-structured, or unstructured as will be defined in the next subsection. The optimized/trained model can then be used to make predictions, perform classification, or even gain more knowledge from new data. The mathematical models of ML algorithms are mainly derived from statistics' theories [44, 45]. Figure 1-4 shows the interrelationship between AI and the different types of machine learning [46].

CHAPTER 1 INTRODUCTION TO MACHINE LEARNING APPLICATIONS DEVELOPMENT AND THE UN SDGS

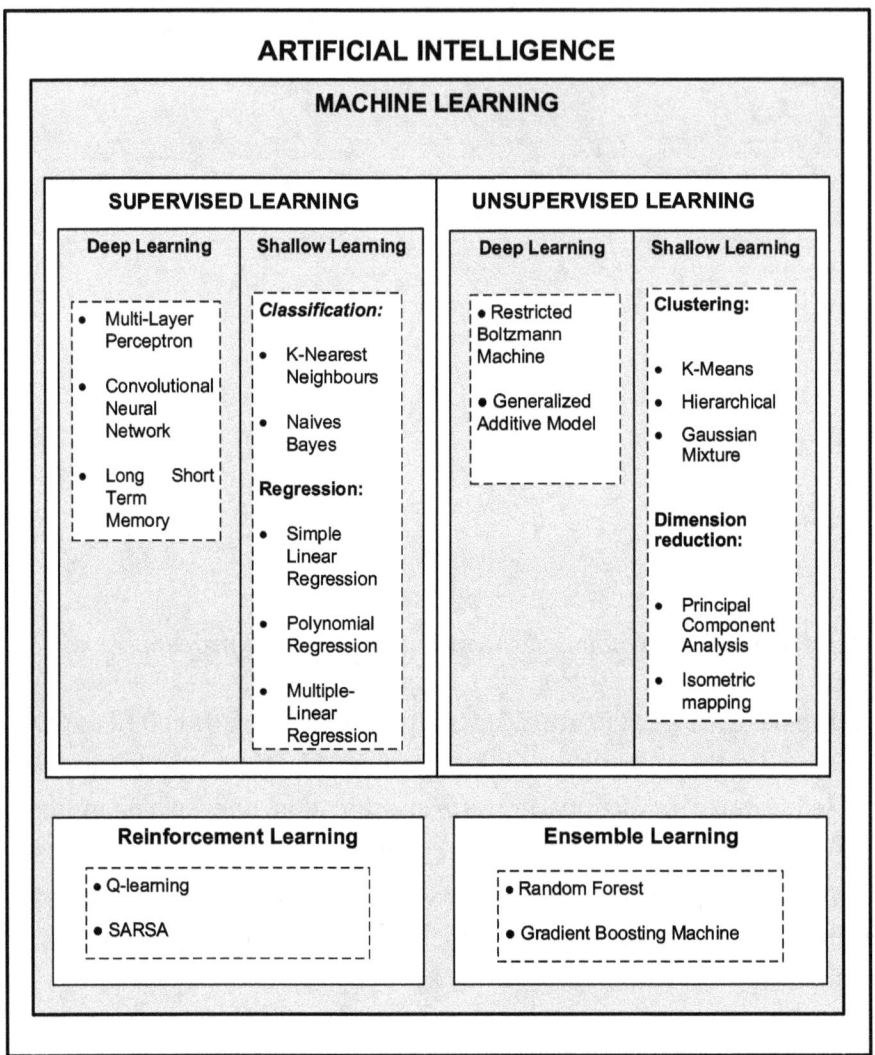

Figure 1-4. *Interrelationship between AI and machine learning*

- **Supervised Learning:** It employs a set of unique labeled data to develop the learning model via a training process. The two categories of supervised learning are classification and regression.

CHAPTER 1 INTRODUCTION TO MACHINE LEARNING APPLICATIONS DEVELOPMENT AND THE UN SDGS

The objective of classification analysis is to provide a categorical label to each input sample. The main classification algorithms include decision trees (DT), naïve Bayes, and k-Nearest Neighbors (k-NN).

Regression analysis consists of algorithms such as linear, polynomial, and multiple-linear regression. Based on the statistical characteristics of the independent and dependent data sequences, regression aims at predicting continuous values of the dependent variable.

Supervised learning is also used to train an artificial neural network (ANN) by presenting an input vector to the network, which will generate an output vector. The difference between this output vector and the target output vector is used to produce an error signal. This error signal is then used to adjust the weights of the ANN until the actual output is matched with the target output [46,47].

A generic illustration of supervised learning for classification problems is shown in Figure 1-5 (a) and for the training of an ANN in Figure 1-5 (b).

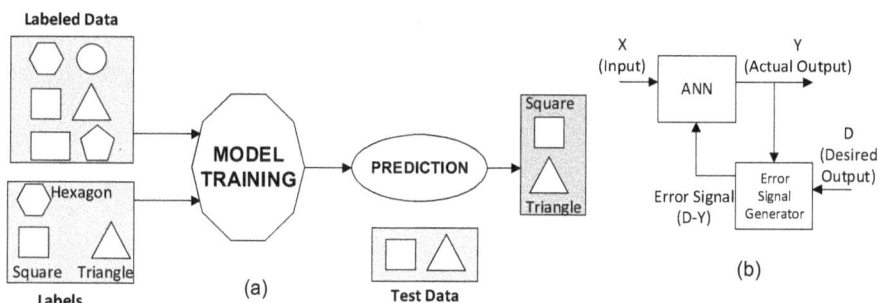

Figure 1-5. *Supervised learning*

CHAPTER 1 INTRODUCTION TO MACHINE LEARNING APPLICATIONS DEVELOPMENT AND THE UN SDGS

- **Unsupervised Learning**

    Unsupervised learning allows the discovery of hidden patterns and the extraction of useful features from unlabelled data. It is generally classified into clustering and dimensionality reduction techniques. Clustering essentially groups a set of samples into distinct clusters based on their similarities, and two of the most common algorithms are K-means and hierarchical clustering. A generic illustration is given in Figure 1-6 (a) [44, 45, 46, 47].

    In the case of ANNs, with unsupervised learning, training is performed by combining similar input vectors to form clusters. When a new input pattern is applied, then the neural network gives an output response indicating the class to which the input pattern belongs. There is no feedback from the environment as to what should be the desired output and if it is correct or incorrect. Hence, in this type of learning, the network itself must discover the patterns and features from the input data, and the relation for the input data over the output. Figure 1-6(b) illustrates this process.

CHAPTER 1   INTRODUCTION TO MACHINE LEARNING APPLICATIONS DEVELOPMENT AND THE UN SDGS

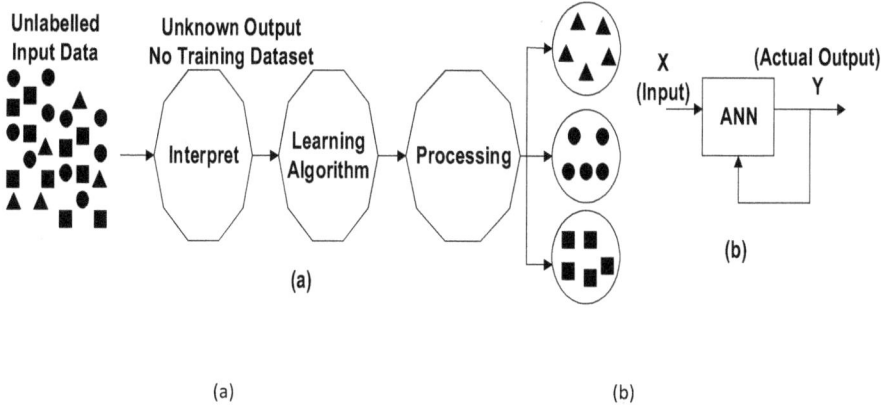

(a)   (b)

Figure 1-6. *Unsupervised learning*

- **Shallow Learning**

    It is a form of machine learning in which knowledge is gained from data whose characteristics have been predefined. The features extraction in Shallow It takes domain knowledge of the data we are learning from perform machine learning. Shallow learning algorithms include three main learning steps: data collection, manual feature selection/reduction, and classification/regression. Figure 1-7(a) illustrates this process [46, 47].

CHAPTER 1　INTRODUCTION TO MACHINE LEARNING APPLICATIONS DEVELOPMENT AND THE UN SDGS

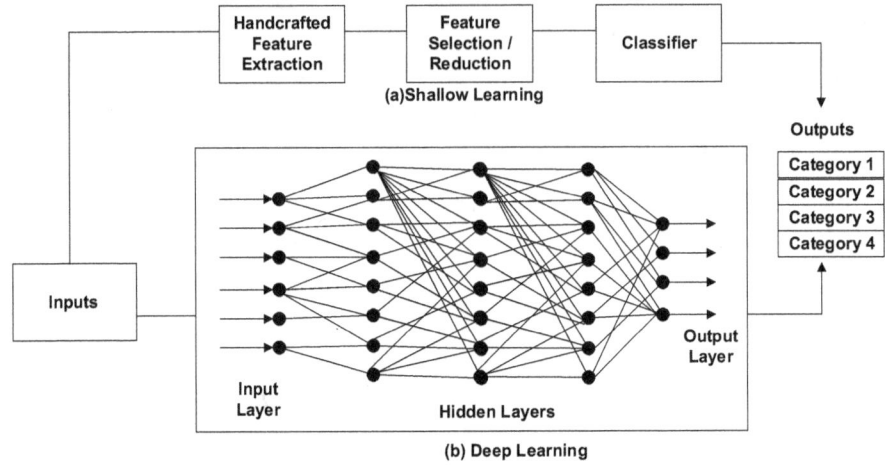

Figure 1-7. Shallow and deep learning

- **Deep Learning**

    It is a specialized form of machine learning, in which a machine learns from experience rather than through a human operator. Thus, with minimal input from humans, DL algorithms can easily be applied to problems, and they generally provide highly accurate performances and may sometimes exceed human-level performance.

    Deep learning algorithms include only two steps. Similar to shallow learning algorithms, they require the same data collection step, but then they combine the feature extraction/selection and classification/ regression steps, as shown in Figure 1-7(b).

    One important class of DL algorithm is the convolutional neural network (CNN), which consists mainly of convolutional layers and pooling layers. The convolutional layers are mainly responsible for feature extraction while the pooling layers perform data reduction and preprocessing. In CNNs, there are fully connected neuron layers with neurons linked to all activation functions in the previous layer to perform predictions and classifications [46, 47].

- **Reinforcement Learning**

    In reinforcement learning, the learner is given no directives about the actions to take. Instead, they are allowed to train themselves in their training environment by taking random actions on their own and are allocated rewards upon performing the correct expected actions. Eventually, they learn the best course of action leading to the maximum reward and thus act as an intelligent system. In contrast, the feedback in supervised learning furnishes the agent with the precise sequence of actions to execute. Such an answer key does not exist in RL. The agent independently determines the procedure to execute the task accurately. Contrary to unsupervised learning, RL has distinct objectives. Unsupervised learning seeks to discern distinctions or commonalities among data items. Finding the optimal action model that maximizes the RL agent's total cumulative reward is the objective of RL. The RL problem is resolved through the agent's actions in conjunction with environmental input in the absence of a training dataset. Figure 1-8 illustrates the typical reinforcement learning process [46, 47, 48].

CHAPTER 1   INTRODUCTION TO MACHINE LEARNING APPLICATIONS DEVELOPMENT AND THE UN SDGS

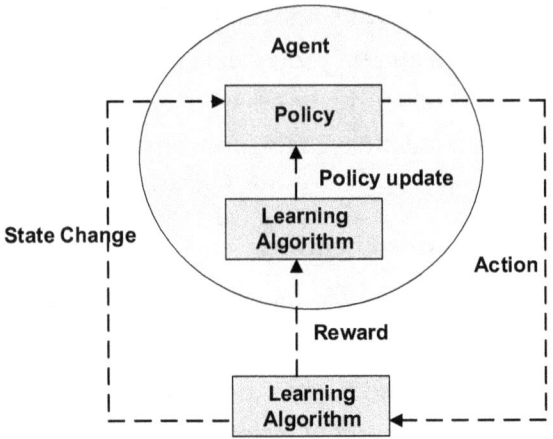

Figure 1-8. *Reinforcement learning*

The following are fundamental components of reinforcement learning:

- **Environment:** The operating environment of a computer application. This can take the form of a real structure or a virtual one, such as a simulation.

- **Agent:** Denotes the computer software functioning as the learner or decision-maker within the given environment. An agent investigates and engages with the environment.

- **Action:** Denotes the actions performed by an agent in its environment.

- **State:** The current conditions of the agent at a specific instant in time. A state change results from every action performed.

- **Reward:** The agent obtains feedback from its surroundings in response to a certain activity. It can be positive, which serves to encourage a desired outcome, or negative, which discourages an undesired one.

- **Policy:** It specifies the activities the agent should perform next in accordance with its present state, establishing a path or mapping between various states or situations and actions.

- **Value:** Indicates the agency's ability to evaluate the attractiveness of various states or actions by representing the long-term benefits of a specific state.

- **Ensemble Learning**

    Ensemble learning essentially involves combining the outcomes of several machine learning models to enhance a classification decision or prediction value [49]. Figure 1-9(a) shows a typical illustration of this type of learning for classification, and Figure 1-9(b) shows it for prediction.

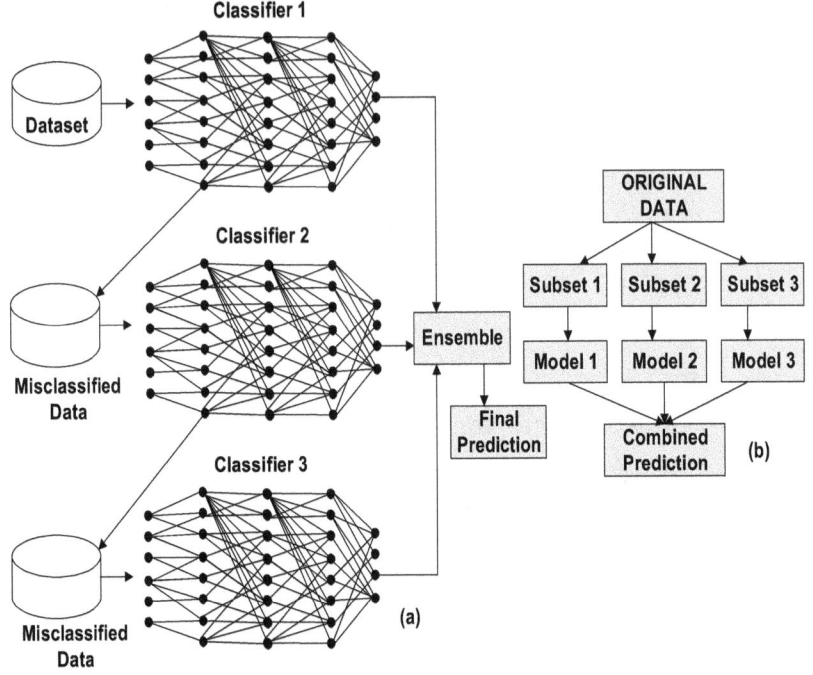

***Figure 1-9.** Ensemble learning*

In Figure 1-9(a), three different classifiers have been employed in a configuration also known as *boosting* whereby the outcome of one classifier is fed to the next classifier along with misclassified data. Eventually, the outputs of all classifiers are combined to provide the best possible prediction. It is also possible to split the dataset into, for example, three different subsets and perform predictions with three different models to obtain an enhanced combined prediction, as shown in Figure 1-9(b). This type of configuration is also referred to as *bagging* [46. 47].

1.2.3 Data Types

All measurements, numbers, words, observations, object descriptions, photographs, and so forth are collectively referred to as *data*. They are a representation of the numbers, letters, or symbols that a computer uses

CHAPTER 1 INTRODUCTION TO MACHINE LEARNING APPLICATIONS DEVELOPMENT AND THE UN SDGS

to carry out tasks. On magnetic, optical, or solid-state recording medium, data can be recorded, stored, and communicated as electrical impulses. A collection of attribute-value pairs is the most popular method for displaying the data, for example [50]:

```
Bob = {
            height: 185cm,
            eye color: blue,
            Body temperature: 98.6°F
            Grade: A
      }
```

Such data can be represented simply as structured data in the form of a table, with rows denoting specific data types and columns denoting properties or features, as shown in Table 1-1.

Table 1-1. *Structured Data*

Name	Height (cm)	Eye Color	Body Temperature [°F]	Grade
Bob	185	Blue	98.6	A
Anna	160	Brown	97.7	B

The different types of measurement scales shown in Table 1-1 can be categorized as follows:

(i) **Nominal:** Unordered and mutually exclusive, for example, eye color.

(ii) **Ordinal:** (Categorical data.) Relates to categories in which the order is significant, but not the variation in values, for e.g., student letter grade, service quality rating, etc.

(iii) **Interval:** Where the idea of zero does not exist but the difference between two numbers is meaningful; i.e., these variables lack a zero value, which signifies the absence of the corresponding attribute. For e.g., 0°F represents a temperature rather than a lack of temperature.

(iv) **Ratio:** Possesses all the characteristics of an interval variable and a precise definition of zero, which is reached when the variable equals zero, e.g., Height [50].

Data can also be classified as structured, unstructured, and semi-structured.

(i) **Structured data:** Information in a set format that is capable of storage, access, and processing as in Table 1-1 is termed *structured* data. While this type of data is very convenient to analyze, when the size of such data grows to a huge extent, in the rage of multiple zettabytes, it becomes difficult to manage.

(ii) **Unstructured data:** Unstructured data is defined as any type of data that lacks a known form or structure. Unstructured data is enormous in quantity and presents several processing difficulties when trying to extract value from it. A typical example of unstructured data is a heterogeneous data source containing a combination of simple text files, images, videos, etc., such as a Google search.

CHAPTER 1 INTRODUCTION TO MACHINE LEARNING APPLICATIONS DEVELOPMENT AND THE UN SDGS

(iii) **Semi-structured:** Both types of data can be found in semi-structured data. Semi-structured data may appear to be structured in appearance, but it lacks explicit definitions such as tables in relational database management systems. Data contained in an XML file is an example of semi-structured data as given here:

```
<rec><name>P.Jones</name><sex>Male</sex><age>35</age></rec>
<rec><name>E.Smith</name><sex>Female</sex><age>41</age></rec>
```

1.2.4 Data Preprocessing Steps

Because not all algorithms can handle missing data, extra attributes, or denormalized values, the objective of data preprocessing jobs is to enhance the data's suitability for a machine learning algorithm. Figure 1-10 shows the main aspects of data preprocessing.

CHAPTER 1 INTRODUCTION TO MACHINE LEARNING APPLICATIONS DEVELOPMENT AND THE UN SDGS

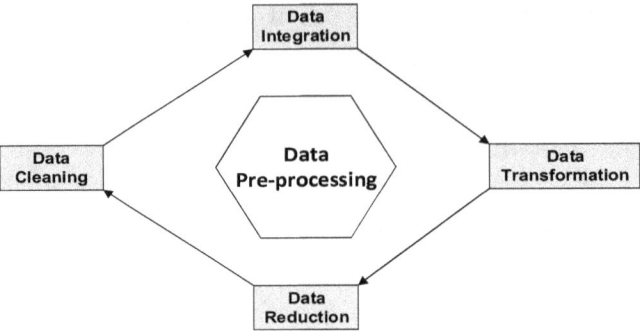

Figure 1-10. Data preprocessing

> A. **Data cleaning:** Also known as data cleansing or data scrubbing, this includes the following processes:
>
> (i) **Fill missing values:** When missing values are present, machine learning algorithms typically perform poorly. Decision trees, the naïve Bayes classifier, and certain rule-based learners are examples of rare exceptions. The reason behind a missing value must be understood. There are numerous potential causes for its absence, including random error, systematic error, and sensor noise. Multiple approaches exist for handling missing values once the cause has been established.
>
> - **Remove the instance:** The few non-relevant cases with missing values can be removed if there is enough data.
>
> - **Remove the attribute:** If the majority of values are absent, the values remain constant, or if an attribute exhibits a strong correlation with another property, it is logical to eliminate that attribute.

- **Assign a special value N/A:** Values may be absent for justifiable reasons, or their acquisition or measurement may be impossible.

- **Take the average attribute value:** Assigning the average value of an attribute or the average value over instances that are comparable is one way to approximate the missing values.

- If an attribute has time dependencies, predict its value from prior entries.

(ii) **Remove outliers:** Values that are outliers in data deviate significantly to the rest of the series and have varying degrees of impact on all learning approaches. Confidence intervals and thresholds help detect and eliminate such extreme values. Figure 1-11 shows a typical outlier in a dataset.

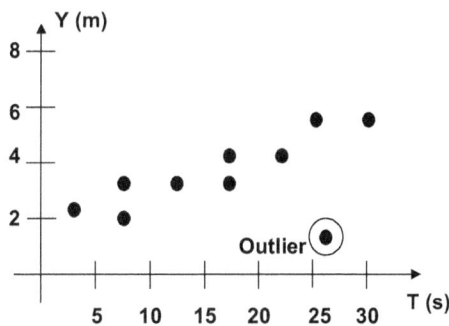

Figure 1-11. *Outlier in a dataset*

(iii) **Parsing data:** Validating the format of a string of data or extracting pertinent information is an example of this process.

(iv) **Formatting data:** Normalizing the range or temporal scale of the data or encoding it in a standard encoding format (e.g., UTF-8 or int32) is an example. Additionally, this entails the conversion of data into a standardized data schema. For example, in the case of aggregating temperature values from several sensor types, it may be desirable for them to possess an identical format.

B. **Data transformation**

By converting the dataset to the format expected by a machine-learning algorithm as input, data transformation techniques might potentially accelerate the system's learning process and improve its overall performance.

By way of example, standardization converts the values such that the mean is equal to zero and the deviation is equal to one, under the assumption that the data follows a Gaussian distribution as per equation (1.1):

$$X_{std} = \frac{X - \underline{X}}{\sigma_X} \qquad (1.1)$$

Where,
X is the original dataset.
X_{std} is the standardized dataset.
$\underline{X}$ is the mean of the dataset.
σ_X is the standard deviation of the dataset.

CHAPTER 1 INTRODUCTION TO MACHINE LEARNING APPLICATIONS DEVELOPMENT AND THE UN SDGS

In contrast, normalization reduces the magnitudes of attribute values to a narrow, predetermined interval, often spanning from zero to one:

$$X_{norm} = \frac{X - X_{min}}{X_{max} - X_{min}} \tag{1.2}$$

Where,

X_{min} and X_{max} are the minimum and maximum values in the dataset, respectively.

C. Data integration

Data integration is the procedure of amalgamating and synchronizing information from numerous sources to produce a cohesive and uniform structure suitable for a wide range of operational, decision-making, and analytical objectives.

In the contemporary digital environment, it is generally impossible for enterprises to operate without collecting data from several sources, such as databases, applications, spreadsheets, cloud services, APIs, and more. Data discrepancies and silos result from the fact that this information is typically stored in many locations and formats with variable degrees of quality.

Integrating data from several sources into a uniform format and making it available for analysis and decision-making helps solve these problems [51].

CHAPTER 1　INTRODUCTION TO MACHINE LEARNING APPLICATIONS DEVELOPMENT AND THE UN SDGS

D. **Data and dimensionality reduction**

Data reduction is concerned with a multitude of instances and attributes. In our dataset, the number of dimensions is equivalent to the number of attributes. Aside from making a negligible contribution to the entire model, dimensions with low prediction power also have a negative impact. For example, a machine learning algorithm may detect random patterns introduced by an attribute containing arbitrary values. Dimensionality reduction strategies eliminate certain characteristics, or, alternatively stated, prioritize the most promising ones, to address this issue.

An excessive number of instances constitutes the second challenge in data reduction. These instances may be duplicates or originate from a data stream that is extremely frequent.

Critically, the objective is to choose a subset of examples whose distribution closely fits that of the original data and the process being monitored.

1.2.5 Data Preprocessing Program in JavaScript

In the following example we will look at a JavaScript program that performs data cleaning on a dataset shown partially in Table 1-2.

Table 1-2. *Temperature Dataset with Outliers*

Temp	Time
19.73	0
20.4	1
19.71	2
19.98	3
20.32	4
39.74	5
20.48	6
19.79	7
20.09	8
19.68	9
20.02	10
20.46	11
19.96	12
20.51	13
19.98	14
-3.5	15
19.79	16

In this dataset there are two outliers: one with value 39.74 and another one with value -3.5. We are now going to perform some pre-processing steps, namely, removing the outliers, standardization, and normalization.

The HTML/JavaScript program for data preprocessing on this dataset is available on the GitHub page for this book. It starts with codes for prompting a user to browse to the location of the CSV file, which holds this dataset. It then asks the user to enter the number of rows to be displayed. The Display Data and Analyse button will perform basic statistical analysis such as computing the mean, mode, median, and standard deviation on the dataset as well as removing the outliers, standardization, normalization, and plotting. It uses the papaparse.min.js [52] and plotly-latest.min.js [53] libraries. It is to be noted that all the code in this chapter can be found in the folder Chapter 1 - Codes hosted on the GitHub page for this book.

The main HTML file of this application is called DataCollection.html. The application also needs two JavaScript libraries, namely, papaparse.min and ploty-latest.min, which are placed in the same folder as the HTML file. The dataset in this case is a CSV file named Regression_Weather-outliers.

When the application is run, the layout shown in Figure 1-12 is displayed. A user first enters the number of rows to be displayed and then click the Browse button to select the CSV file. Finally, when the Display Data and Analyse button is clicked, the first five rows of the CSV file are displayed, followed by some basic statistics on the Temperature attribute. Additionally, the graphs in Figures 1-13 and 1-14 are displayed.

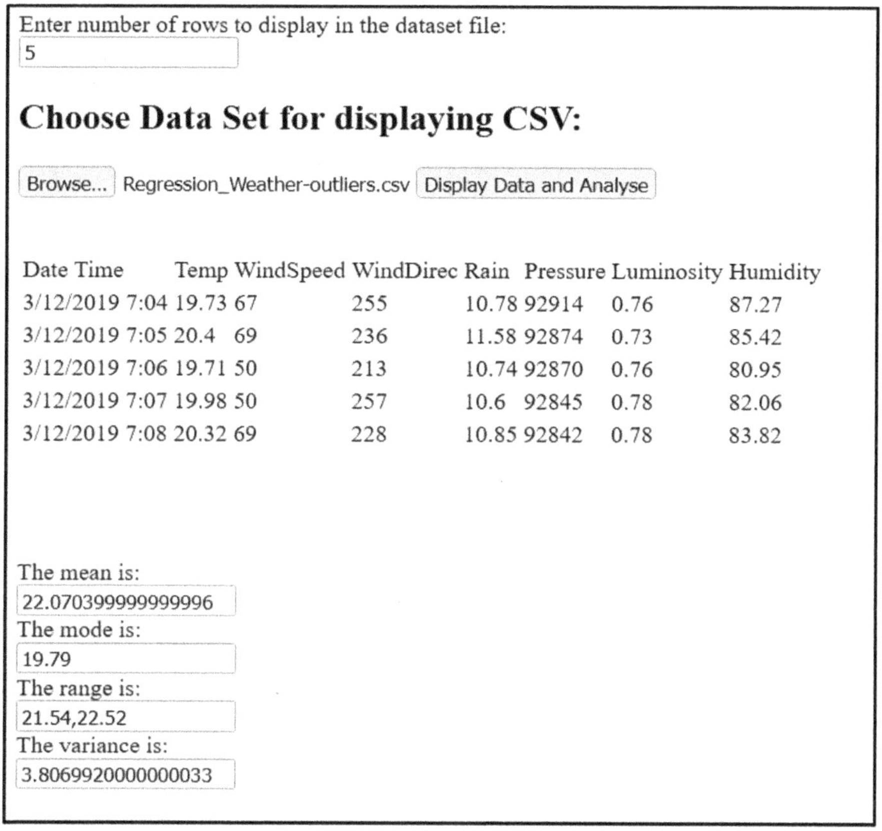

CHAPTER 1   INTRODUCTION TO MACHINE LEARNING APPLICATIONS DEVELOPMENT AND
             THE UN SDGS

Enter number of rows to display in the dataset file:
5

Choose Data Set for displaying CSV:

Browse... Regression_Weather-outliers.csv Display Data and Analyse

Date Time	Temp	WindSpeed	WindDirec	Rain	Pressure	Luminosity	Humidity
3/12/2019 7:04	19.73	67	255	10.78	92914	0.76	87.27
3/12/2019 7:05	20.4	69	236	11.58	92874	0.73	85.42
3/12/2019 7:06	19.71	50	213	10.74	92870	0.76	80.95
3/12/2019 7:07	19.98	50	257	10.6	92845	0.78	82.06
3/12/2019 7:08	20.32	69	228	10.85	92842	0.78	83.82

The mean is:
22.070399999999996
The mode is:
19.79
The range is:
21.54,22.52
The variance is:
3.8069920000000033

Figure 1-12. *Layout of data collection and preprocessing*

Figure 1-13 shows the graphs of the original dataset and the corrected dataset for 50 data samples. It is observed that in the corrected dataset the outliers have been replaced by values within the range.

Figure 1-14 shows the graphs of the standardized and normalized dataset after correcting the outliers.

CHAPTER 1 INTRODUCTION TO MACHINE LEARNING APPLICATIONS DEVELOPMENT AND
         THE UN SDGS

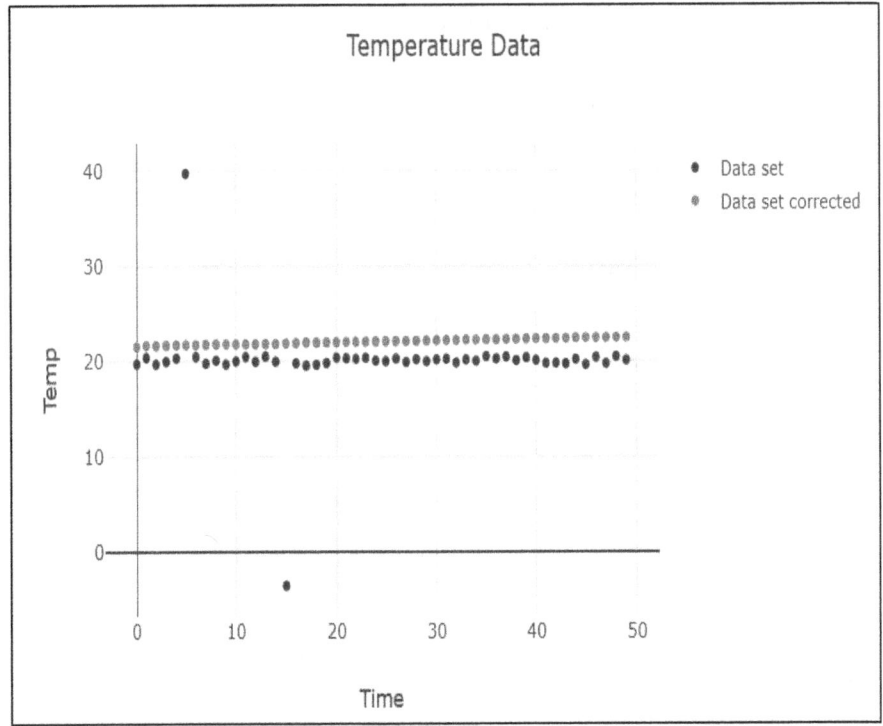

Figure 1-13. *Original temperature dataset versus corrected dataset*

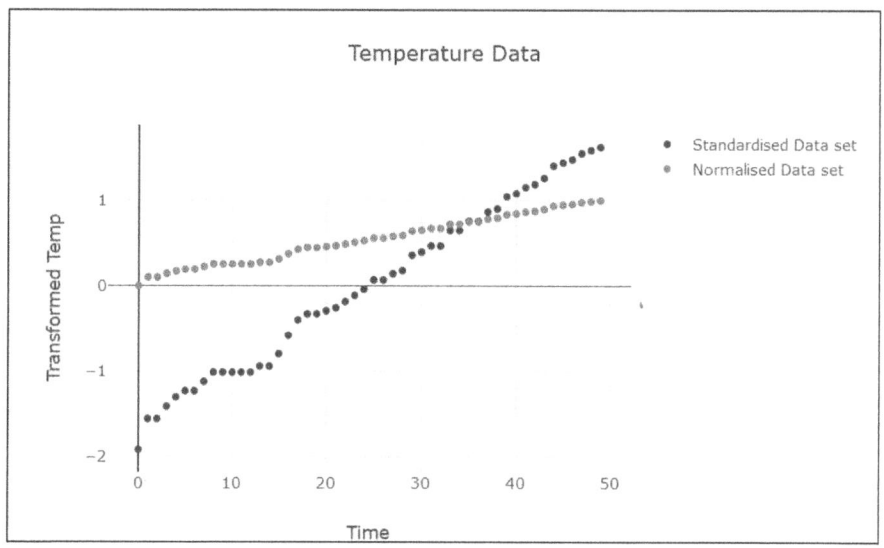

Figure 1-14. *Original temperature dataset versus corrected dataset*

1.3 Implementation of ML-Based Prediction and Classification Algorithms in JavaScript

In this section, we give an overview of some common regression and classification algorithms, along with their implementation in JavaScript.

1.3.1 Simple Linear Regression (SLR)

SLR is a statistical technique that analyzes the relationship between two quantitative variables and predicts the value of a dependent variable at a certain value of the independent variable. The correlation between the dependent and independent variables can be determined by the regression line, which follows a straight line of best fit across the dataset. Additionally, regression is utilized to assess the relationship between changes in the independent variable and the dependent variable.

CHAPTER 1 INTRODUCTION TO MACHINE LEARNING APPLICATIONS DEVELOPMENT AND THE UN SDGS

The formula for a simple linear regression is as follows [46]:

$$Y = \beta_0 + \beta_1 X + \epsilon \tag{1.3}$$

Where,

Y is the dependent variable or predicted output.
β_0 is the y-intercept of the regression line.
β_1 is the gradient of the regression line or regression coefficient.
X is the independent variable or targeted input.
ϵ is the error of the estimated value, a measure of the variation between the predicted and actual value.

SLR finds the line of best-fit through the dataset by computing the regression coefficient (β_1) and y-intercept (β_0) that minimizes the total error (ϵ) of the model. Using the least squares method the coefficients are calculated as follows:

$$\beta_0 = M_Y - \beta_1 M_X = \frac{1}{N}\left(\sum_{i=1}^{N} Y_i - \beta_1 \sum_{i=1}^{N} X_i\right) \tag{1.4}$$

$$\beta_1 = \frac{SC_{XY}}{SS_X} = \frac{\sum_{i=1}^{N}(Y_i - M_Y)(X_i - M_X)}{\sum_{i=1}^{N}(X_i - M_X)^2} \tag{1.5}$$

Where,

SC_{XY} is the sum of the co-deviate of XY.
SS_X is the sum of the squared deviate of X.
M_Y is the mean of Y.
M_X is the mean of X.
N is the total number of values in X and Y.

Two versions of a JavaScript implementation of SLR will be provided whereby the first version allows users to enter values directly on the web page for prediction and the second version allows users to upload a dataset for prediction.

CHAPTER 1 INTRODUCTION TO MACHINE LEARNING APPLICATIONS DEVELOPMENT AND THE UN SDGS

When the first version of the application is run, the user will have to populate the input fields, and when the Read and Analyse button is clicked, the outputs shown in Figure 1-15(a) are displayed.

Enter the independent variable X: Enter the dependent variable Y:

```
1,3,4,5,8
```

```
2,5,2,7,9
```

Enter X Value for which Y has to be predicted:
```
10
```

Read Data and Analyse

The gradient (b1) is:
```
1.007462686567164
```
The intercept (b0) is:
```
0.7686567164179108
```
The correlation coefficient (r) is:
```
0.9641202591480795
```
The predicted value of y is:
```
10.843283582089551
```
SSx:
```
26.799999999999997
```
SSy:
```
38
```
SCxy:
```
27
```
Mx:
```
4.2
```
My:
```
5
```

Figure 1-15(a). *Inputs and outputs for SLR version 1*

CHAPTER 1 INTRODUCTION TO MACHINE LEARNING APPLICATIONS DEVELOPMENT AND
         THE UN SDGS

The application also outputs the equation of the line, the mean absolute percentage error (MAPE), and the graph of the dataset and regression line with the predicted point, as shown in Figure 1-15(b). The MAPE is computed as follows:

$$MAPE = \frac{\sum_{i=1}^{N} \frac{(Y_i - \underline{Y_i})}{Y_i}}{N} \times 100 \qquad (1.6)$$

Where,

$\underline{Y_i}$ is the predicted value of Y_i.

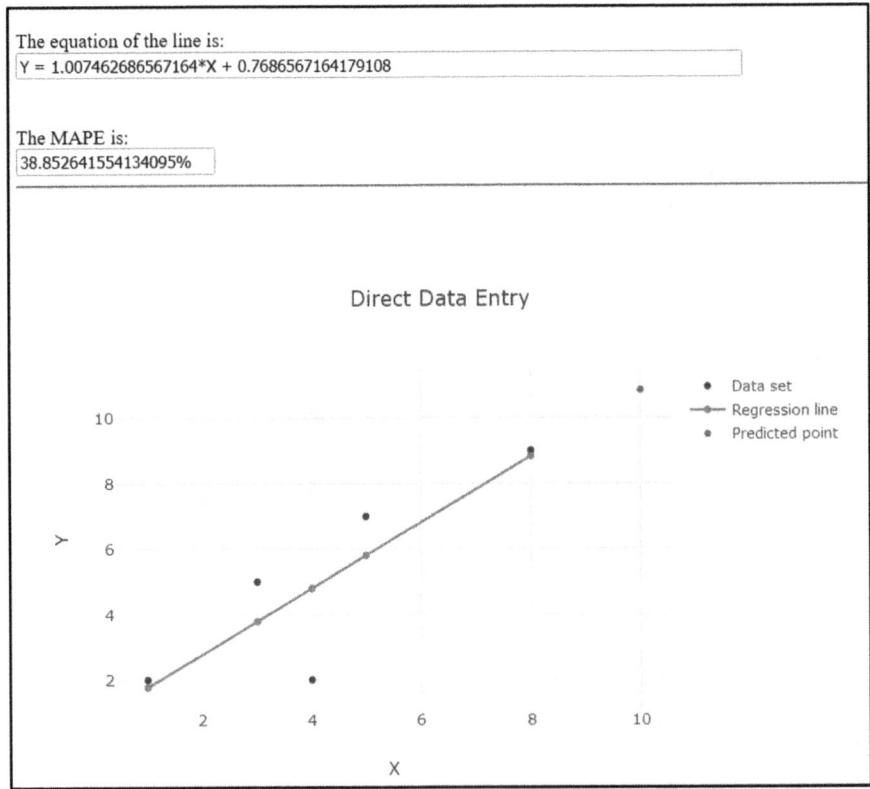

Figure 1-15(b). *MAPE and Graph for SLR version 1*

42

CHAPTER 1 INTRODUCTION TO MACHINE LEARNING APPLICATIONS DEVELOPMENT AND THE UN SDGS

For the second version of the SLR implementation, the dataset is obtained from a CSV file named Regression_Weather.csv. Part of this dataset is shown in Table 1-3.

Table 1-3. *Weather Dataset*

Temp	WindSpeed	WindDirection	Rain	Pressure	Luminosity	Humidity
19.73	67	255	10.78	92914	0.76	87.27
20.4	69	236	11.58	92874	0.73	85.42
19.71	50	213	10.74	92870	0.76	80.95
19.98	50	257	10.6	92845	0.78	82.06
20.32	69	228	10.85	92842	0.78	83.82
39.74	58	252	9.63	92884	0.78	90.44
20.48	52	247	11.34	92887	0.79	79.57
19.79	63	269	10.09	92866	0.74	84.48
20.09	49	213	10.51	92916	0.76	74.6
19.68	54	223	10.1	92870	0.75	77.05
20.02	62	240	11.19	92918	0.74	75.69
20.46	56	257	10.14	92948	0.76	85.43
19.96	59	212	11.24	92964	0.76	87.5
20.51	67	262	10.02	93002	0.77	77.25
19.98	68	249	9.72	92983	0.77	89.98

When the application is run, the user will have to enter the number of rows to display from the dataset and browse the CSV file. When the Display Data and Analyse button is pressed, the outputs shown in Figure 1-16(a) are displayed.

CHAPTER 1 INTRODUCTION TO MACHINE LEARNING APPLICATIONS DEVELOPMENT AND THE UN SDGS

Enter number of rows to display in the dataset file:
5

Enter X Value for which Y has to be predicted:
100

Choose Data Set for displaying CSV:

Browse... Regression_Weather.csv   Display Data and Analyse

Date Time	Temp	WindSpeed	WindDirec	Rain	Pressure	Luminosity	Humidity
03/12/2019 07:04	19.73	67	255	10.78	92914	0.76	87.27
03/12/2019 07:05	20.4	69	236	11.58	92874	0.73	85.42
03/12/2019 07:06	19.71	50	213	10.74	92870	0.76	80.95
03/12/2019 07:07	19.98	50	257	10.6	92845	0.78	82.06
03/12/2019 07:08	20.32	69	228	10.85	92842	0.78	83.82

The gradient (b1) is:
-0.00150834762480153336

The intercept (b0) is:
20.206490881664042

The correlation coefficient (r) is:
0.9980214583949835

The predicted value of y is:
20.055656119183887

SSx:
1279.0048979999847

SSy:
3.8390719999988505

SCxy:
-1.9291840000078082

Mx:
82.79979999999999

My:
20.081599999999998

Figure 1-16(a). *Inputs and outputs for SLR version 1*

The application also outputs the equation of the line, the MAPE, and the graph of the dataset and regression line with the predicted point, as shown in Figure 1-16(b).

CHAPTER 1 INTRODUCTION TO MACHINE LEARNING APPLICATIONS DEVELOPMENT AND THE UN SDGS

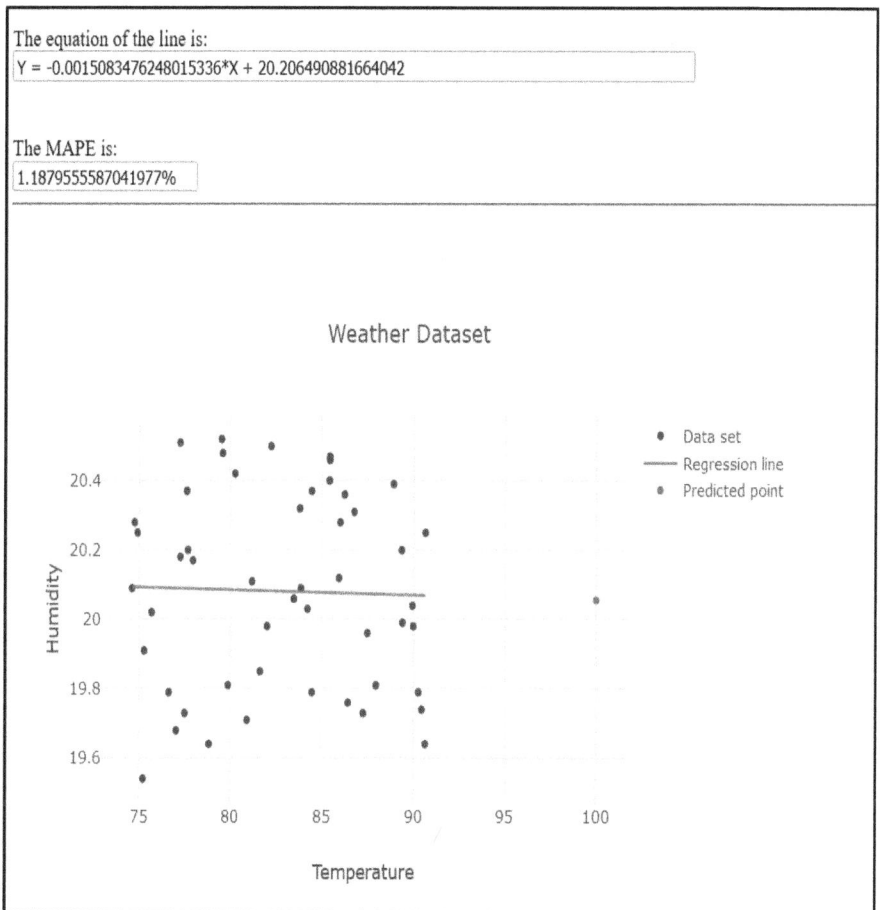

Figure 1-16(b). *MAPE and graph for SLR version 2*

1.3.2 Polynomial Regression (PLR)

PLR extends the concept of SLR to situations where predictors may be more accurately related to their responses using a polynomial function. In other words, PLR is preferred when the relationship between the predictor and the response are curvilinear. The simple linear regression model may be modified by adding polynomial terms to obtain the polynomial regression model as follows [46]:

CHAPTER 1 INTRODUCTION TO MACHINE LEARNING APPLICATIONS DEVELOPMENT AND THE UN SDGS

$$y = \beta_0 + \beta_1 x + \beta_2 x^2 + \beta_3 x^3 + \ldots + \beta_n x^k + \varepsilon \tag{1.7}$$

Where,

y is the dependent variable.

β_0 is the Y-intercept.

k is the order of the polynomial (highest degree).

β_1 is the $\beta_2, \beta_3, \ldots, \beta_n$ coefficients.

x is the independent variable.

ε is the error.

The regression line can be obtained using the least square method, which requires solving a system of linear equations in the following form [46]:

$$\begin{aligned} &\left[N \sum_{i=1}^{N} x_i \ldots \sum_{i=1}^{N} x_i^k \sum_{i=1}^{N} x_i \sum_{i=1}^{N} x_i^2 \ldots \sum_{i=1}^{N} x_i^{k+1} \vdots \right. \\ &\left. \sum_{i=1}^{N} x_i^k \sum_{i=1}^{N} x_i^{k+1} \ldots \sum_{i=1}^{N} x_i^{2k} \right] \\ &\left[\beta_0 \, \beta_1 \vdots \beta_k \right] = \left[\sum_{i=1}^{N} y_i \sum_{i=1}^{N} x_i y_i \vdots \sum_{i=1}^{N} x_i^k y_i \right] \end{aligned} \tag{1.8}$$

Two versions of a JavaScript implementation of PLR will be provided whereby the first version allows users to enter values directly on the web page for prediction, while the second version allows users to upload a dataset for prediction.

When the application is run, the user will have to populate the input fields, and when the Read Data and Analyse button is click, the outputs shown in Figure 1-17(a) are displayed.

CHAPTER 1   INTRODUCTION TO MACHINE LEARNING APPLICATIONS DEVELOPMENT AND THE UN SDGS

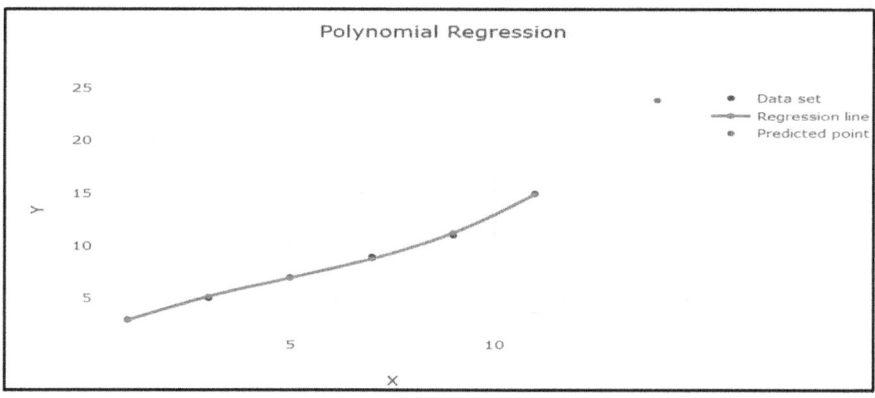

Figure 1-17(a). Inputs and outputs for PLR version 1

The regression curve alongside the dataset and predicted point are shown in Figure 1-17(b).

Figure 1-17(b). Regression curve for the PLR version 1

CHAPTER 1 INTRODUCTION TO MACHINE LEARNING APPLICATIONS DEVELOPMENT AND
         THE UN SDGS

For the second version of the PLR implementation, the dataset is obtained from a CSV file named Regression_Weather.csv. Part of this dataset is shown in Table 1-3.

The next listing, i.e., Listing 1-5(b), is similar to Listing 1-3(c), which shows the reading of the data from the CSV file. Moreover, Listings 1-5(c) and 1-5(d) are equivalent to Listings 1-4(d) and 1-4(e), respectively.

When the application is run, the user will have to enter the number of rows to display from the dataset and browse the CSV file. When the Display Data and Analyse button is clicked, the outputs shown in Figure 1-18(a) are displayed.

Enter number of rows to display in the dataset file:
5

Enter X Value for which Y has to be predicted:
94

Enter polynomial degree:
3

Choose Data Set for displaying CSV:

Browse... Regression_Weather.csv   Display Data and Analyse

Date Time	Temp	WindSpeed	WindDirec	Rain	Pressure	Luminosity	Humidity
03/12/2019 07:04	19.73	67	255	10.78	92914	0.76	87.27
03/12/2019 07:05	20.4	69	236	11.58	92874	0.73	85.42
03/12/2019 07:06	19.71	50	213	10.74	92870	0.76	80.95
03/12/2019 07:07	19.98	50	257	10.6	92845	0.78	82.06
03/12/2019 07:08	20.32	69	228	10.85	92842	0.78	83.82

Figure 1-18(a). *Inputs and outputs for PLR version 2*

The application also outputs the equation of the line, the MAPE, and the graph of the dataset and regression line with the predicted point, as shown in Figure 1-18(b).

CHAPTER 1 INTRODUCTION TO MACHINE LEARNING APPLICATIONS DEVELOPMENT AND THE UN SDGS

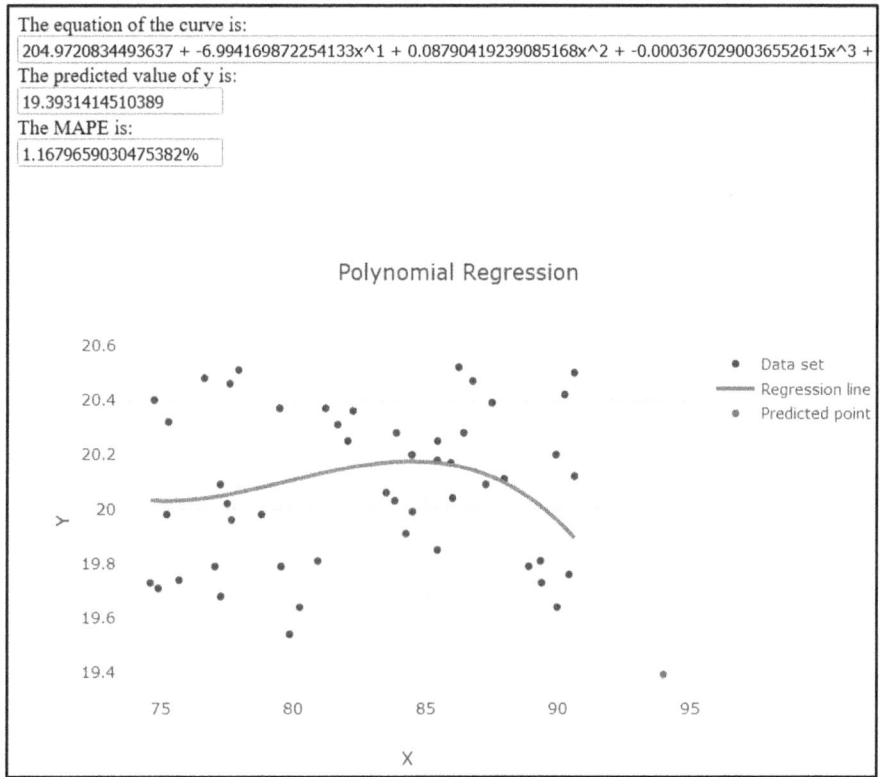

Figure 1-18(b). *MAPE and graph for PLR version 2*

1.3.3 Multiple Linear Regression (MLR)

MLR is a statistical technique that helps us understand how several independent variables influence a dependent variable. It is an extension of simple linear regression (SLR), which examines only a single independent variable. By analyzing multiple variables, MLR can make more accurate predictions and forecasts. For example, MLR may be used to forecast the CO_2 emissions of a car depending on its engine size and the number of cylinders available.

The following are some key characteristics of MLR:

- The dependent variable or output (Y) should be a continuous or real value, while the independent variables or predictors can take continuous or categorical values.

- A linear relationship exists between the independent variables and the dependent variable.

- MLR endeavours to establish a regression line within a multidimensional dataset.

The multiple linear regression model can be expressed as follows [46]:

$$Y = \beta_0 + \beta_1 X_1 + \beta_2 X_2 + \ldots + \beta_k X_k + \varepsilon \qquad (1.9)$$

Where,
y denotes the dependent variables or output.
k denotes the number of predictors available in the model.
$X_1, X_2, \ldots, X_k$ represent the independent variables.
β_0 denotes the y-intercept (constant term) of the regression line.
$\beta_1, \beta_2, \ldots, \beta_k$ represent the slope coefficients of each independent variable.
ε represents the error term in the model that occurs between the predicted value of Y and its actual value.

The primary objective of performing MLR is to determine the coefficients ($\beta_0, \beta_1, \beta_2, \ldots, \beta_k$) that reduce the sum of squared differences between the observed values of the dependent variable and the values predicted by the linear equation. This approach is known as the least squares method [46]. The model can also be written in the following matrix form as follows:

$$y = X\beta + \varepsilon \qquad (1.10)$$

Where,

$\beta = \{\beta\_0, \beta\_1, \ldots, \beta\_(k-1)\}'$.

The design matrix X is built in the following form:

$$X = \begin{bmatrix} 1\, x_{1,1}\, x_{1,2} \ldots x_{1,k-1}\, 1\, x_{2,1}\, x_{2,2} \ldots x_{2,k-1} \vdots 1\, x_{n,1}\, x_{n,2} \ldots x_{n,k-1} \end{bmatrix} \qquad (1.11)$$

Where,

n is the total number of observations.

An estimate of the β matrix, $\hat{\beta}$, can be obtained using the following equation:

$$\hat{\beta} = (X'X)^{-1} X'y \qquad (1.12)$$

Two versions of a JavaScript implementation of MLR will be provided whereby the first version allows users to enter values directly on the web page for prediction, while the second version allows users to upload a dataset for prediction.

When the application is run, the user will have to populate the input fields, and when the Read Data and Analyse button is clicked, the outputs shown in Figure 1-19(a) are displayed.

CHAPTER 1 INTRODUCTION TO MACHINE LEARNING APPLICATIONS DEVELOPMENT AND
THE UN SDGS

> Enter the independent variables: Enter the dependent variable:
>
> X1 X2 Y
>
> | 1,2,1,3 | 2,5,0,1 | 5,3,17,4 |
>
> Enter value of X1 for which Y has to be predicted:
> 4
> Enter value of X2 for which Y has to be predicted:
> 3
>
> [Analyse]
>
> The equation of the curve is:
> Y = -3.24x1 + -1.8400000000000003x2 + 16.599999999999998
> The predicted value of y is:
> -1.880000000000006
> The MAPE is:
> 52.58627450980392%

Figure 1-19(a). *Inputs and outputs for PLR version 1*

The regression plots are shown in Figure 1-19(b).

CHAPTER 1   INTRODUCTION TO MACHINE LEARNING APPLICATIONS DEVELOPMENT AND
            THE UN SDGS

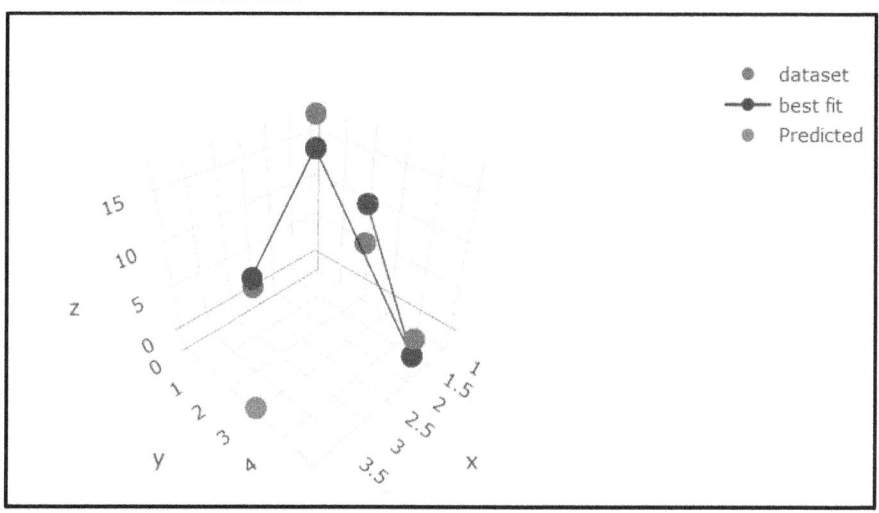

Figure 1-19(b). *Regression plots of MLR version 1*

For the second version of the MLR implementation, the dataset is obtained from a CSV file named `Regression_Weather.csv`. Part of this dataset is shown in Table 1-3.

When the application is run, the user will have to enter the number of rows to display from the dataset and browse the CSV file. When the Display Data and Analyse button is clicked, the outputs shown in Figure 1-20(a) are displayed.

53

CHAPTER 1   INTRODUCTION TO MACHINE LEARNING APPLICATIONS DEVELOPMENT AND
            THE UN SDGS

Enter number of rows to display in the dataset file:
5
Enter Humidity:
95
Enter Rain:
12

Choose Data Set for displaying CSV:

Browse... Regression_Weather.csv   Display Data and Analyse

Date Time	Temp	WindSpeed	WindDirec	Rain	Pressure	Luminosity	Humidity
03/12/2019 07:04	19.73	67	255	10.78	92914	0.76	87.27
03/12/2019 07:05	20.4	69	236	11.58	92874	0.73	85.42
03/12/2019 07:06	19.71	50	213	10.74	92870	0.76	80.95
03/12/2019 07:07	19.98	50	257	10.6	92845	0.78	82.06
03/12/2019 07:08	20.32	69	228	10.85	92842	0.78	83.82

The equation of the curve is:
$z = 0.0487879008547214x + 20.92778139734685y + 0.16816182315846362$
The predicted value of y is:
37.48860940765755

Figure 1-20(a). *Inputs and outputs for MLR version 2*

Figure 1-20(b) shows the regression plots along with the predicted point.

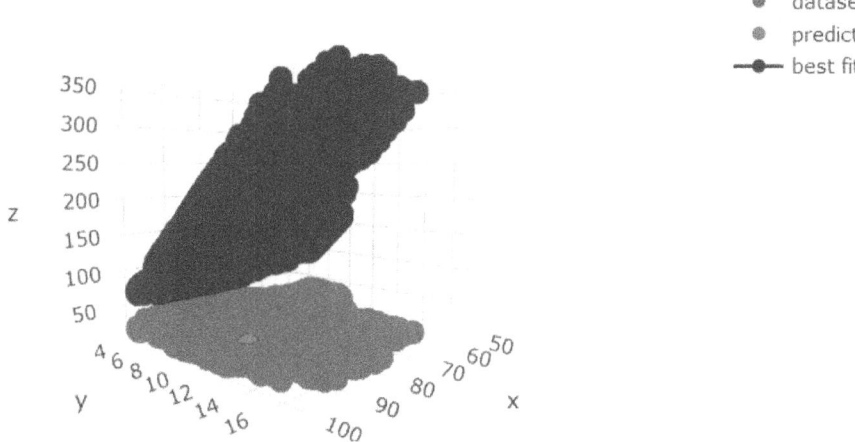

Figure 1-20(b). *Plot of MLR version 2*

1.3.4 K-Nearest Neighbor

K-Nearest Neighbor (k-NN) is a well-known simple supervised learning algorithm that may be used for both classification and regression.

In this technique, k represents the number of nearest neighbors. It categorizes an object based on the majority vote of its nearest neighbors. The object is then classified into the most common class based on its k closest neighbors, where k is a positive integer [46].

The Euclidean distance is one of the most common distance metrics used to calculate the distances between the objects to determine their k nearest neighbors. The Euclidean distance between two objects with n features is given as follows:

$$d(x,y) = \sqrt{\sum_{i=1}^{n}(x_i - y_i)^2} \qquad (1.13)$$

We will be using the Diabetes.csv dataset obtained from [52]. A section of the dataset is shown in Table 1-4.

CHAPTER 1   INTRODUCTION TO MACHINE LEARNING APPLICATIONS DEVELOPMENT AND THE UN SDGS

Table 1-4. *Diabetes Dataset [56]*

Glucose	BloodPressure	SkinThickness	Insulin	BMI	Age	Outcome
148	72	35	0	33.6	50	1
85	66	29	0	26.6	31	0
183	64	0	0	23.3	32	1
89	66	23	94	28.1	21	0
137	40	35	168	43.1	33	1
116	74	0	0	25.6	30	0
78	50	32	88	31	26	1
115	0	0	0	35.3	29	0
197	70	45	543	30.5	53	1
125	96	0	0	0	54	1
110	92	0	0	37.6	30	0
168	74	0	0	38	34	1
139	80	0	0	27.1	57	0
189	60	23	846	30.1	59	1
166	72	19	175	25.8	51	1
100	0	0	0	30	32	1
118	84	47	230	45.8	31	1
107	74	0	0	29.6	31	1
103	30	38	83	43.3	33	0

The KNN program, KNN.html, is given on the GitHub page of this book. Figure 1-21 shows a snapshot of the output of the program.

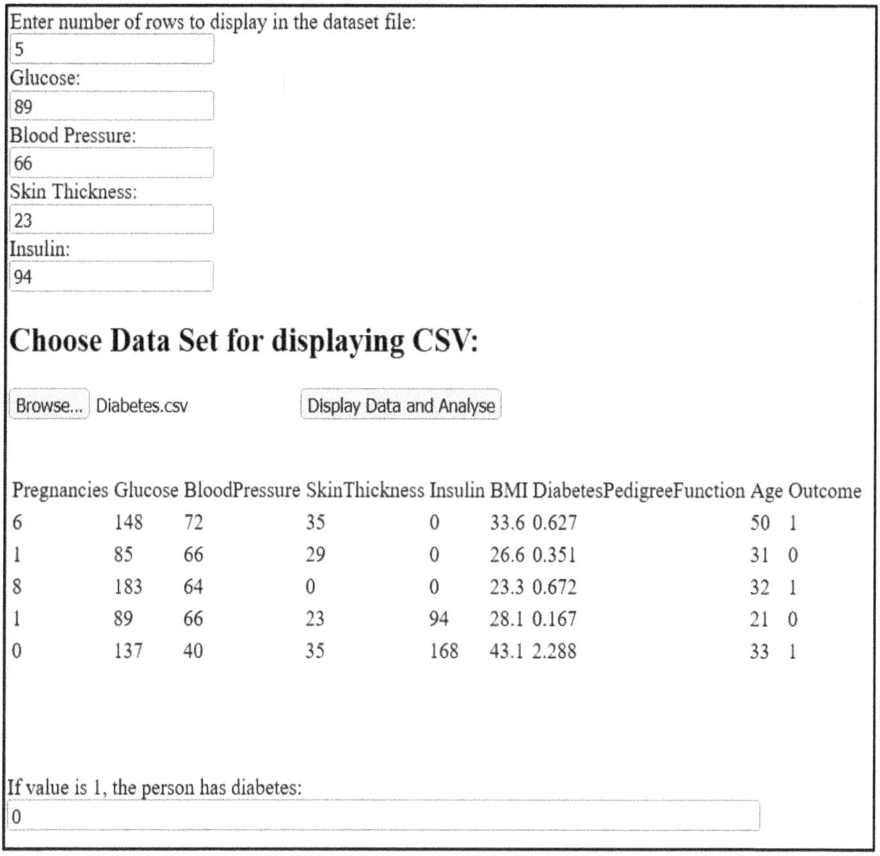

CHAPTER 1 INTRODUCTION TO MACHINE LEARNING APPLICATIONS DEVELOPMENT AND THE UN SDGS

```
Enter number of rows to display in the dataset file:
5
Glucose:
89
Blood Pressure:
66
Skin Thickness:
23
Insulin:
94
```

Choose Data Set for displaying CSV:

Browse... Diabetes.csv   [Display Data and Analyse]

Pregnancies	Glucose	BloodPressure	SkinThickness	Insulin	BMI	DiabetesPedigreeFunction	Age	Outcome
6	148	72	35	0	33.6	0.627	50	1
1	85	66	29	0	26.6	0.351	31	0
8	183	64	0	0	23.3	0.672	32	1
1	89	66	23	94	28.1	0.167	21	0
0	137	40	35	168	43.1	2.288	33	1

If value is 1, the person has diabetes:
0

Figure 1-21. *Output of the KNN classification program with diabetes dataset*

1.4 Summary

This chapter gave an overview of the UN SDGs along with their importance in addressing several challenges such as climate change, education, renewable energy, economic growth, etc. A review of research carried out on the application of AI and machine learning techniques to support the implementation of the UN SDGs has also been conducted. These techniques can definitely provide a significant boost in achieving the SDG targets. Moreover, the fundamental concepts of AI and ML have been introduced by providing a clear distinction between the different categories of AI and ML. Finally, some basic regression and classification algorithms have been discussed along with their JavaScript implementations. These will form the basis of several other applications that will be discussed in the subsequent chapters of the book.

CHAPTER 2

Utilizing Machine Learning Algorithms for Power Generation Prediction and Classification in Wind Farms

Chapter authors:
Dobee Lalitesh, lalitesh.dobee@umail.uom.ac.mu
Kurmally Mohammad Adnaan, mohammad.kurmally4@umail.uom.ac.mu
Luchmunparsad Gyaneeta, gyaneeta.luchmunparsad@umail.uom.ac.mu
Sanghan Ashven, ashven.sanghan@umail.uom.ac.mu

CHAPTER 2   UTILIZING MACHINE LEARNING ALGORITHMS FOR POWER GENERATION PREDICTION AND CLASSIFICATION IN WIND FARMS

The Sustainable Development Goals (SDGs) aim at transforming our world by putting an end to poverty and inequality, while ensuring the welfare of the inhabitants of this planet. Machine learning aims to help achieve these SDGs by offering prediction capabilities and patterns identification from large and complex datasets.

In this chapter, three machine learning algorithms, namely, polynomial regression, k-nearest neighbors (k-NN) regression, and multilinear regression are used to predict and classify wind power from a dataset found on Kaggle. The JavaScript language is used to code the machine learning algorithms and HTML is used to create a web page so the user can input the independent variables to obtain the predicted wind power for the wind turbines.

This chapter addresses SDG Targets 7.1, 7.2, and 7.3. SDG Target 7.1 ensures that everyone has access to reliable energy sources by 2030. SDG Target 7.2 aims at increasing the use of renewable technologies to produce energy, and SDG Target 7.3 aims at improving the access to renewable energies technologies by 2030. The application of machine learning within energy production by making use of wind power aims at improving the accuracy of energy generation forecasting and optimizing energy distribution within energy production companies compared to traditional techniques, which are less accurate and more memory intensive.

2.1 Introduction

Machine learning has become an invaluable tool for optimizing the production efficiency of green energy. The energy industry has approached clean energy technologies in recent years so as to reduce the impact of pollution on the environment and human health.

However, the problem associated with renewable resources is that they generate most of their power at a certain time of the day and the generation power is related to other environmental factors such as wind, pressure, or temperature. The production of renewable energy is also sustainable and eco-friendly and It is the dependence on fossil fuels which causes more harm. It also aims at achieving SDG Target 7.1, which ensures that everyone has access to reliable energy sources by 2030; SDG Target 7.2, which aims at increasing the use of renewable technologies to produce energy; and SDG Target 7.3, which aims at improving the access to renewable energy technologies by 2030.

This chapter aims to use different machine learning algorithms to predict wind power generated by wind turbines by using the following independent variables: wind speed, wind direction, pressure, and air temperature. In the chapter, the wind power generated was also classified as low, medium, or high by making use of the same independent variables. Polynomial regression, k-nearest neighbors (k-NN) regression, k-NN classification, and multilinear regression were used in the chapter, and the accuracy of the three machine learning algorithms was then compared. A dataset from Kaggle, which contains values for wind direction, wind speed, temperature, pressure, and the corresponding power generated, was downloaded and used within the program (Esapour et al., 2022).

The dataset was first preprocessed so that it can be processed by the different machine learning algorithms, and a new attribute, which is the category of power was also added. JavaScript and HTML were used to build a web page for the user to enter the corresponding independent variable, and the predicted value along with the accuracy was displayed on the web page. The different machine learning algorithms were developed using JavaScript, and the mean absolute percentage error (MAPE) was calculated. Some optimization of the hyper-parameters was also made to obtain better accuracy.

Moreover, a classification of wind power prediction, which involves categorizing wind power into low, medium, or high levels, has been performed. One of the primary benefits of classification models in wind power prediction is their ability to provide precise and reliable forecasts of expected wind power output. By categorizing wind power into these

CHAPTER 2 UTILIZING MACHINE LEARNING ALGORITHMS FOR POWER GENERATION PREDICTION AND CLASSIFICATION IN WIND FARMS

three levels, energy providers gain valuable insights into the availability of energy resources. This information is instrumental in scheduling energy production and distribution. For instance, when wind power is predicted to be high, energy providers can allocate resources and plan to harness this clean and renewable energy source optimally.

This is the main novelty of the chapter compared to previous works, which aim only at predicting the power output level. Predicting wind power levels in low, medium, or high categories empowers energy grid operators to make well-informed decisions regarding the balance of electricity supply and demand. Grid operators can allocate resources more efficiently, adjust energy generation according to forecasted wind power levels, and strategically activate or deactivate power plants to meet consumer needs without overloading or underutilizing the grid. This optimization enhances the overall reliability and efficiency of energy distribution. Classification models play a pivotal role in cost reduction within the energy sector. By accurately predicting wind power levels, energy providers can minimize their reliance on backup power sources, such as fossil fuels, during periods of low wind power generation. This reduction not only results in cost savings by reducing fuel expenses but also decreases operational costs associated with conventional power generation. In essence, it fosters a more cost-effective and sustainable energy production process. Wind power generation is inherently variable due to fluctuations in wind speed and direction. Classification models offer early warnings and insights into potential fluctuations in wind power output and aims at stabilizing the grid. Armed with this information, grid operators can proactively manage the energy grid, ensuring a stable and consistent energy supply.

By preemptively addressing variations in wind power, these models help prevent power outages and maintain grid stability, especially during periods of rapidly changing weather conditions. Classification-based wind power predictions significantly benefit energy infrastructure planning. Energy providers and stakeholders can make informed decisions about the construction, expansion, and maintenance of wind farms and related infrastructure. This level of foresight ensures that energy infrastructure aligns with current and future energy demands efficiently. By investing in the right projects at the right time, energy providers can maximize the utilization of wind energy resources and bolster the overall sustainability of their operations.

2.2 AI Use Cases for SDG 7

Several previous works have used machine learning techniques to address SDG 7, which highlights the significance of accessible, clean, and reliable energy.

For example, in Liu, Zhang, and Baziar (2023), the goal was to close the gap left by the most recent publication by Esapour et al. (2022) by focusing on the area of smart city communication and energy management. In particular, the authors wanted to overcome the restrictions of the aforementioned work and simultaneously improved the accuracy of predicting values and optimum solutions. To do this, a unique heuristic strategy was employed for optimizing solutions while utilizing the benefits that machine learning techniques have to offer in order to increase accuracy. The work sought to improve responsible consumption patterns and production practices to reduce waste, promote resource efficiency, and foster a more sustainable approach to consumption and production in smart cities.

Shahzad et al. (2023) applied machine learning technologies such as long short-term memory (LSTM), artificial neural networks (ANNs), support vector regression (SVR), and multiple linear regression (MLR) to daily data on natural gas futures prices, crude oil futures prices, carbon futures prices, and Dow Jones energy commodity futures prices from January 2018 to October 2021. Two major conclusions are drawn from the machine learning investigation. To establish links between future oil prices (crude oil and heating oil) and the pricing of carbon emission futures, nonlinear frameworks perform better than linear models. Second, the machine learning results show that carbon emission futures prices respond nonlinearly to severe movements in oil and natural gas prices. Understanding the nonlinear dynamics of extreme movements can aid in the development of environmental and climate policies as well as the revaluation of natural gas and oil futures. We talk about significant consequences for the SDGs, especially SDGs 7 and 12.

The purpose of the research conducted in Asadikia, Rajabifard, and Kalantari (2020) was to find synergistic SDGs using the machine learning and data mining approach known as *boosted regression trees*. This study identifies the contributions of each SDG to the SDG index and does a "what-if" analysis to determine the importance of target scores. Findings indicate that SDGs 3, 4, and 7, "Quality education," "Good health and well-being," and "Affordable and clean energy" are the most synergistic objectives when their scores are over 60%. "Good health and well-being" was one of the most crucial synergetic aims, according to the findings of this research. There have been several disease outbreaks throughout history that have had a terrible effect on society and the economy because they were so deadly, broad, and expensive to contain. SDG breakouts like COVID-19 could have a significant influence on the likelihood of attaining the objectives since they strived to balance social, economic, and environmental factors. The SDG 3 score could be lowered by a rise in death rates and detrimental effects on healthcare.

It has been demonstrated in Nwokolo, Obiwulu, and Ogbulezie (2023) that the primary difficulties faced by the authors consisted of creating a hybridized machine learning with the Gumbel probabilistic functional model, which were inherent in the mathematical transformation process and necessitated a significant amount of repeated mathematical science knowledge to produce the final transformed and effective model for forecasting the potential of solar PV output. The hybrid model using solely the quantifiable solar radiation parameter was the most accurate representation of the observed PV energy production of all technologies, with a comprehensive coefficient of determination (R2) of 0.9998% and a root mean square error (RMSE) of 0.0063 kwh. To investigate the possible effects of climate change on the various solar PV systems, the most effective hybridized model was utilized. This research examined the implications of climate change on the potential for solar PV energy generation in the near future (2015-2049), the distant future (2050-2099), the all-future (2015-2099), the 2020s (2015-2040), the 2050s (2041-2070), and the 2080s (2071-2099), in line with the UN's SDG 7 and 13. The best hybrid model (MLP-CARIMA-GPM) was used to investigate the possible effects of climate change on various solar PV systems.

Additionally, the assessment made use of energy simulations from the Australian Community Climate and Earth System Simulator (ACCESS-CM2), a participant in Coupled Model Intercomparison Project Phase 6 (CMIP6), based on three different shared socioeconomic pathways (SSPs): SSP126, SSP245, and SSP585.

In Anastasiadou, Santos and Dias (2021), the authors' study presented a conceptual and theoretical framework that could be used to analyze literature studies that leveraged statistical or machine learning techniques to address the issue of a building's energy performance. More specifically, by locating and assessing the most recent and suitable machine learning or statistical techniques as a baseline for future research and by developing a conceptual and theoretical framework based on a systematic literature review using PRISMA guidelines, this work aims to contribute to the improvement of the energy performance (EP) of existing buildings, one of the key objectives of the EU Green Deal. The European Green Deal is closely related to several SDGs established by the United Nations.

While it particularly aligns with SDG 13 (Climate Action), its impact and objectives also have implications for several other SDGs. A "double the global rate of improvement in EE" might also be achieved by measuring, monitoring, and increasing the energy efficiency (EE) of buildings. This would result in less energy being spent while preserving or even improving the quality of services offered by such buildings, hence contributing to SDGs 7 and 8.

The study carried out by Chen et al. (2022) offered a technique to assess trends and major drivers of SDG7 in the Aral Sea Basin from 2000–2020 by combining nighttime light indices, population distribution data, and statistics. In this work, the optimal combination of two linear regression methods and three machine learning methods, together with four light indices, was chosen to mimic the geographical distribution of GDP in the Aral Sea Basin. The prediction utilizing the XGBoost model with TNL performed better than other models, according to the findings.

From 2000 to 2020, the Aral Sea Basin's GDP demonstrated an uneven pattern of growth (+101.73 billion, +585.5%), with the GDP of the lower Aral Sea and the Amu Darya River increasingly converging in the middle Aral Sea and Syr Darya River basins, respectively. The GDP of the Aral Sea Basin has a high negative association with the area of water bodies at the same time. SDG 7 is challenging to accomplish by 2030, despite a little improvement in the Aral Sea Basin's score (+6.57) and ranking (+9) from 2000 to 2020. The achievement of SDG 7 depends on strengthening inter-basin energy cooperation, boosting investment in renewable energy, and raising energy intensity.

Sarkodie et al. (2020) conducted a study on the connections between energy consumption (SDG 7), climate (SDG 13), economic growth, and population in Kenya, Senegal, and Eswatini. It is motivated by the SDGs and its influence by 2030. They made use of econometric techniques including Dynamic Ordinary Least Squares (DOLS), Fully Modified Ordinary Least Squares (FMOLS) regression, the Mean-Group (MG) and Pooled Mean-Group (PMG) estimation models, as well as the Kernel Regularized Least Squares (KRLS) machine learning methodology. While the machine learning method supported the scale effect hypothesis, econometric techniques support the Environmental Kuznets Curve (EKC) hypothesis between income level and CO_2 emissions. It was discovered that while population, income level, and CO_2 emissions all influence energy demand and usage, energy consumption and population dynamics were the main forces behind economic growth. It showed how income, population growth, energy use, and CO_2 emissions were all interrelated yet need to be decided together in order to reach the SDGs.

The objective in the article by Boza and Evgeniou (2021) was to examine the value that AI can add in terms of controlling variable renewable energy sources VRE integration expenses. The authors gave a comprehensive evaluation of how AI may significantly reduce integration costs using an economic model of variable renewable integration cost from the literature. They have also gone over many use scenarios and talked about difficulties in calculating the value that AI solutions would add to the power industry. The use of AI and data-intensive technologies to reduce integration costs for variable renewable energy (VRE), in line with the overarching objective of developing clean and sustainable energy systems, are considered as key elements in achieving SDG 7. The latter is concerned with ensuring that everyone has access to affordable, dependable, sustainable, and modern energy.

In the research conducted by Chen et al. (2021), the artificial intelligence-based useful evaluation model (AIEM) has been put out as a forecasting tool for the economic effects of renewable energy and energy efficiency. The goal of this work was to evaluate, contrast, and develop a model using artificial intelligence and certain economic variables important for predicting the economic viability of renewable energy sources. The best customer to respond to qualities and wishes, competitive pricing, scheduling, and facility management, as well as motivating demand response participants and fairly rewarding them, may all be accomplished using AI methodologies. The suggested approach may increase energy efficiency to 97.32% and increase the use of renewable energy sources. The main components of artificial intelligence in renewable energy technology are energy forecasting, energy efficiency, and energy accessibility. The work explains how artificial intelligence may be used to anticipate renewable energy and increase energy efficiency, thus advancing SDG 7's goal of clean and efficient energy sources.

The wide range of novel issues presented by the developing Internet of Things and the difficulty in addressing these challenges with current computing and networking models are the starting points of the study conducted in Chiang and Zhang (2016). The article also covered the need for a new architecture, which is referred to as fog computing, fog networking, fog storage, and fog control and how it may close technological gaps and open up new commercial prospects.

Along the cloud-to-Things continuum, fog is an emergent architecture for computing, storage, control, and networking that distributes these services closer to end users. By optimizing the processing and storage of data closer to the source, fog computing reduces the energy consumption associated with data transmission and processing, aligning with SDG 7. The Internet of Things (IoT) has its importance in a variety of sustainability-related applications, including environmental monitoring, smart agriculture, and energy management, and which supports SDG 13, is made possible by fog computing. It supports an increasing number of applications as an architecture, such as those found on the Internet of Things, Fifth Generation (5G) wireless systems, and embedded artificial intelligence.

2.3 Data Processing and Application Design

2.3.1 Data Collection Process and Description of Dataset

During the data collection process, various existing datasets were investigated, and the one that would achieve the best-targeted SDGs was selected. This dataset was retrieved from Kaggle and uses the National Renewable Energy Laboratory software to simulate the time-series data of a particular region in Texas, for one whole year In 2021.

CHAPTER 2   UTILIZING MACHINE LEARNING ALGORITHMS FOR POWER GENERATION PREDICTION AND CLASSIFICATION IN WIND FARMS

The data that was collected focused mainly on obtaining the amount of power generated by a wind turbine system under varying environmental conditions at different times of the day. These environmental conditions, which will act as predictors, include wind speed, wind direction, atmospheric pressure, and air temperature and were collected on an hourly basis from 12 a.m. to 11 p.m. Finally, all the data was recorded in the form of a CSV file and named TexasTurbine.csv. Table 2-1 displays a few instances of this CSV file.

Table 2-1. *TexasTurbine.csv*

Timestamp	System Power Generated/ (kW)	Wind Speed/ (m/s)	Wind Direction/ (deg)	Pressure/ (atm)	Air Temperature/ (°C)
Jan 1, 12:00 am	1766.64	9.926	128	1.00048	18.263
Jan 1, 01:00 am	1433.83	9.273	135	0.99979	18.363
Jan 1, 02:00 am	1167.23	8.66	142	0.999592	18.663
Jan 1, 03:00 am	1524.59	9.461	148	0.998309	18.763
Jan 1, 04:00 am	1384.28	9.184	150	0.998507	18.963
Jan 1, 05:00 am	1293.93	8.996	149	0.998507	19.063
Jan 1, 06:00 am	1301.63	9.016	151	0.998211	19.113
Jan 1, 07:00 am	1308.13	9.036	154	0.997815	19.163

This original dataset contains all the relevant attributes that would allow for the prediction of the power generated by the wind turbines in kW.

2.3.2 Data Preprocessing Steps

Once the original dataset is obtained, it was prepared so that it can be processed by the designated machine learning algorithm. The main steps involved in the data preprocessing is hence listed and discussed next.

1. Checking for missing values and filling them if there are any.

   The first step in the data preprocessing procedure was to check for any missing data or instances in the dataset and assign a value to these data or remove any row which have too many missing values. However, the dataset that was chosen did not contain any such values or instances and was already in a complete format.

2. Removing unnecessary attributes.

   In the original dataset, the timestamps were removed as this data will not be used by the KNN machine learning algorithm. The aim is to use the different environmental attributes to be able to predict the power generated by the wind turbines.

3. Adding a new attribute.

   Since the algorithm will also perform classification in addition to predicting a value of the power, a new attribute called PowerCategory was inserted in the dataset. The category assigns a label such as High, Medium, and Low given the value of the generated power.

CHAPTER 2 UTILIZING MACHINE LEARNING ALGORITHMS FOR POWER GENERATION PREDICTION AND CLASSIFICATION IN WIND FARMS

2.3.3 Wind Turbine Modeling

The classification of the wind power was done by considering predictors including the wind speed, pressure, and temperature. This can be modeled by the following formula:

$$Wind\ Power = \frac{1}{2} \times \rho \times A \times V^3 \quad (2.1)$$

where

V is the wind speed and ρ is the air density and is given by the following formula:

$$\rho = \frac{Pressure}{Gas\ Constant \times Air\ Temperature}$$

$$and\ the\ gas\ constant = 8.314 \frac{\frac{J}{mol}}{K} \quad (2.2)$$

Also, A is the swept area, which is given by the following equation:

$$A = \pi \left(\frac{D}{2}\right)^2 \quad (2.3)$$

where D is twice the blade diameter of the tubine.

The radius of the wind turbine is assumed to be 1.5 m in length, which results in a diameter of 3 m. The model is based on the principles of kinetic energy of the wind turbines and is mainly defined by the wind speed to provide its corresponding mechanical wind power. Also, it is being assumed that the losses to the turbines are negligible, such that the all the mechanical power gets converted to electrical power (Salih Mohammed Salih, 2012).

The classification is therefore represented as shown in Table 2-2 (Yiannis A. Katsigiannis, 2013).

Table 2-2. *Power Classification*

Wind Speed | ms^{-1}	Classification
0 – 7.5	Low
7.5 – 8.5	Medium
8.5 and above	High

After the introduction of the category attribute, the new dataset was saved and used for training the machine learning model.

The final CSV file, which will be fed to the model will thus be of the form shown in Table 2-3.

Table 2-3. *Final CSV File*

SystemPower	Windspeed	Wind Direction	Pressure	Temperature	PowerCategory
2036.19	10.608	136	0.984488	21.163	High
2288.37	11.171	142	0.986561	20.563	High
1762.46	9.995	150	0.986856	21.063	Medium
1202.84	8.518	155	0.987152	21.563	Medium
461.536	6.426	159	0.992483	21.363	Low
530.497	6.723	165	0.991792	21.163	Low

2.3.4 Program Structure

Figure 2-1 shows the overall program structure including all the HTML and JavaScript files. It is to be noted that all the code of this chapter is found in the folder Chapter 2 - Codes hosted on the GitHub page for this book.

CHAPTER 2   UTILIZING MACHINE LEARNING ALGORITHMS FOR POWER GENERATION
PREDICTION AND CLASSIFICATION IN WIND FARMS

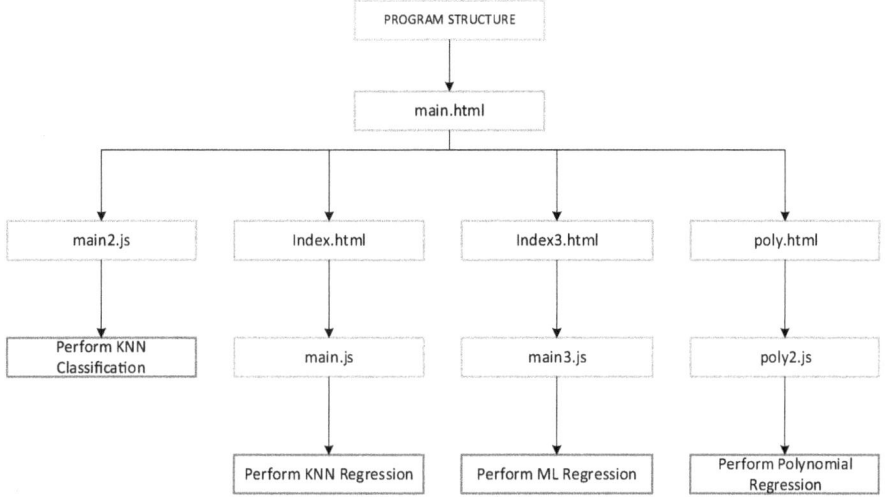

Figure 2-1. *Overall program structure*

Layout of Web Application

Figure 2-2 shows the layout of the web application with the different buttons and text fields.

CHAPTER 2   UTILIZING MACHINE LEARNING ALGORITHMS FOR POWER GENERATION
            PREDICTION AND CLASSIFICATION IN WIND FARMS

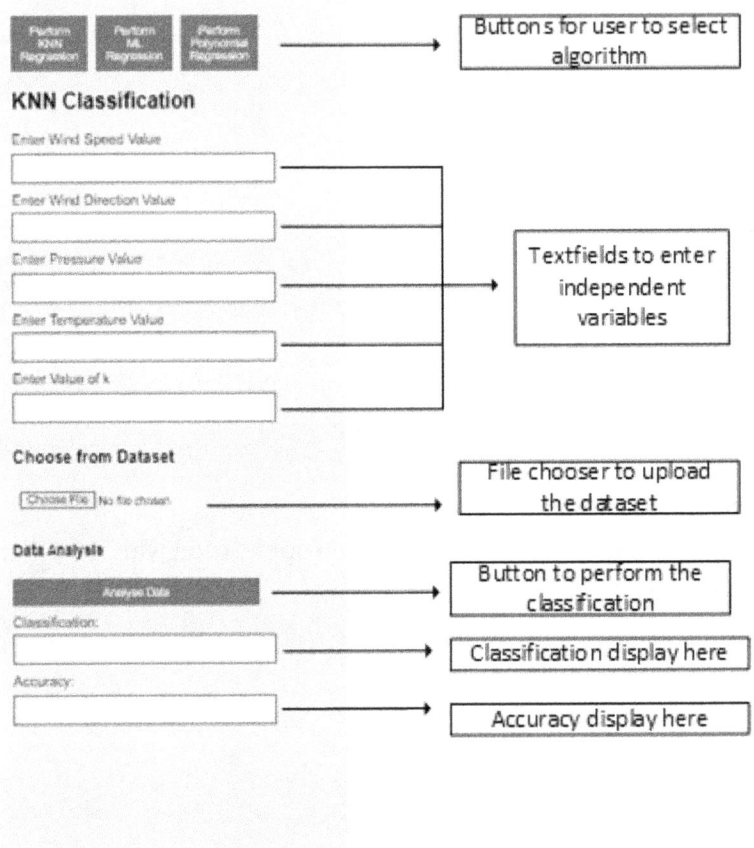

Figure 2-2. Layout of website

KNN

The program is based on the KNN machine learning algorithm (where k=3), which will accept a training dataset, which is the preprocessed CSV file, and will perform both classification and regression of the power generated by wind turbines. Classification of the power category is more suitable before the establishment of the wind turbines, especially during the planning process, and can be helpful in determining what size of wind farm can be mounted so that the wind energy is used in the most efficient manner possible. On the other hand, regression allows for more accurate predictions of the power given an already established wind farm. Figure 2-3 illustrates the program workflow of the model.

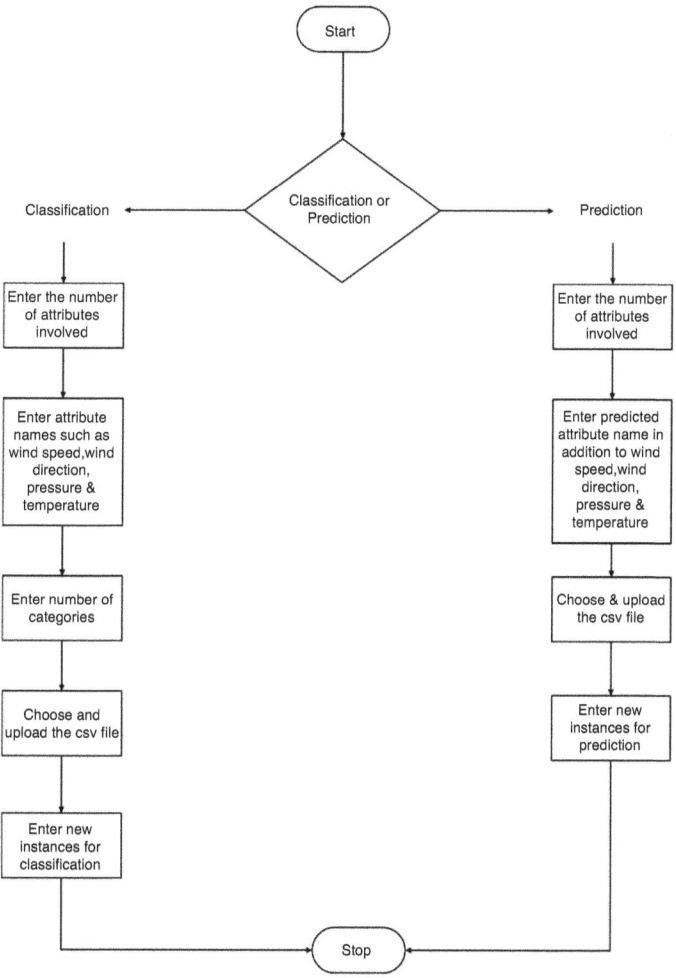

Figure 2-3. *Program workflow, KNN*

CHAPTER 2   UTILIZING MACHINE LEARNING ALGORITHMS FOR POWER GENERATION
            PREDICTION AND CLASSIFICATION IN WIND FARMS

Figure 2-4 gives the program structure of the main.js file. The program consists of a main JavaScript class called main.js, which is primarily responsible for the prediction tasks. This class has a main method, namely, the getKNNRegression() and function, where the latter allows prediction of the system power based on the three nearest neighbors.

The pseudocode in Listing 2-1 provides a broad overview of how main.js works.

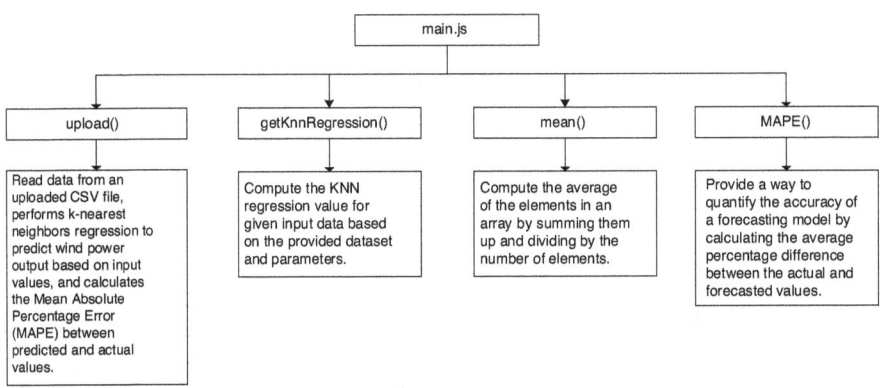

Figure 2-4. *Program structure: main.js*

Listing 2-1. Reading and Processing Selected CSV File to Perform KNN Regression

```
function upload() {
// Read CSV file chosen by the user
// Process the dataset

function getKnnRegression(x, y, k, inputs):
// Compute distances between inputs and existing data points
// Find the k nearest neighbors
// Compute the regression based on the k nearest neighbors

function MAPE(array1, array2):
```

```
// Calculate the Mean Absolute Percentage Error between two arrays
}

// Upon a button click, invoke the upload function to read and
   process the CSV file
// Compute k-NN regression based on user-provided inputs
// Display the prediction and MAPE on the webpage
```

The main.js file is embedded within the index.html layout. The web page will first prompt the user to enter the values of the attributes to be predicted. Additionally, the user will be required to upload the appropriate dataset that will be used by the model. Once the user gets new environmental data, the latter can perform regression, which will be based on conditions such as wind speed, wind direction, pressure, and temperature. The same operation is carried out for the classification of the power category of the system and is embedded within another class called main2.js. The structure of main2.js is illustrated in Figure 2-5.

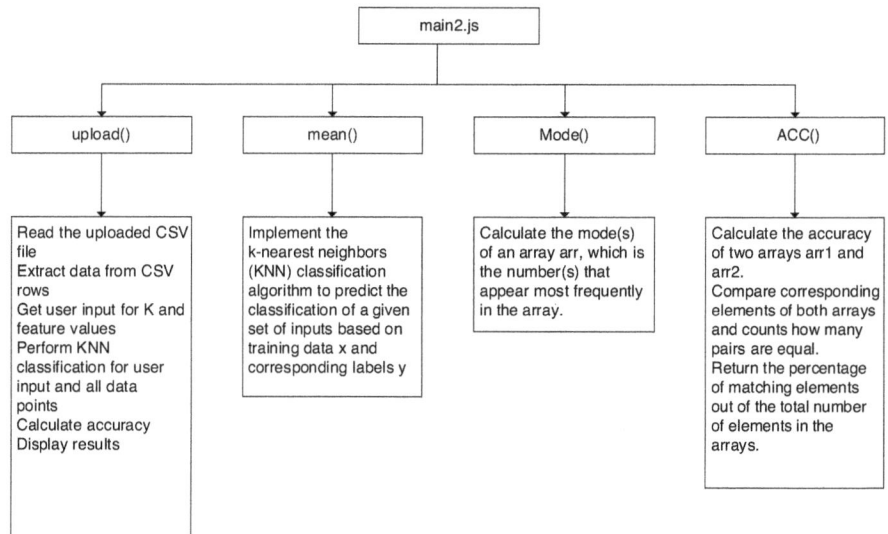

Figure 2-5. Program structure, main2.js

The pseudocode in Listing 2-2 shows the main actions performed by main2.js.

Listing 2-2. Reading and Processing Selected CSV File to Perform KNN Classification

```
function processData() {
    // Read CSV file chosen by the user
    // Process the dataset
}
function kNNClassification(dataArray, categoriesArray, k,
inputValues) {
    // Compute distances between input values and existing
      data points
    // Find the k nearest neighbors
    // Determine the classification based on the k nearest
      neighbors

function calculateAccuracy(predictedArray, actualArray) {
    // Calculate the accuracy between the predicted and
      actual values
}
// Upon clicking a button, invoke the processData function to
  read and process the CSV file
// Compute k-NN classification based on user-provided inputs
// Display the prediction and accuracy on the webpage
```

Polynomial Regression

Since it is observed that the wind speed has a very strong correlation with the predicted wind system power, the polynomial regression is an appropriate technique that can be investigated and employed with the dataset. The appropriate degree of the polynomial is dependent on the Mean Absolute Percentage Error (MAPE) of the model.

CHAPTER 2   UTILIZING MACHINE LEARNING ALGORITHMS FOR POWER GENERATION
PREDICTION AND CLASSIFICATION IN WIND FARMS

The flowchart in Figure 2-6 shows the program workflow using this algorithm.

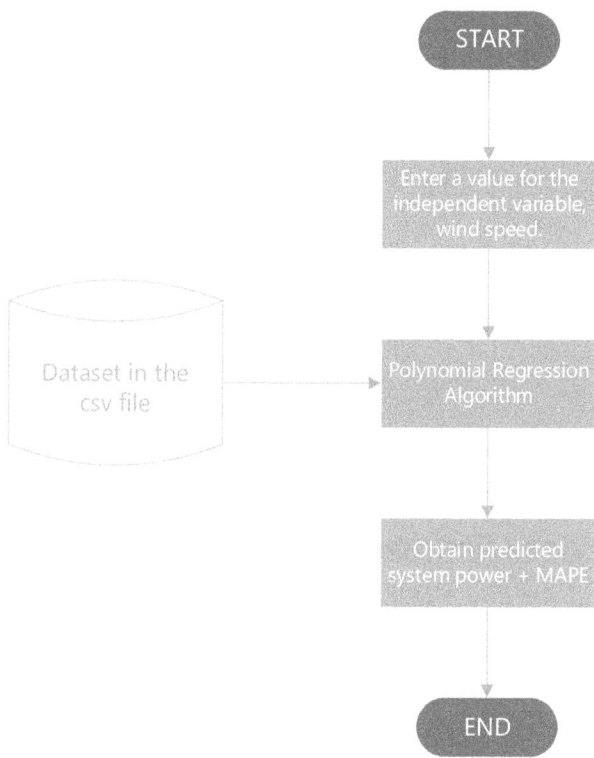

Figure 2-6. *Program workflow, polynomial regression*

The user is allowed to choose the degree of the polynomial so that maximum accuracy of the model is obtained. However, in this case, only a single predictor is taken into consideration. Figure 2-7 illustrates the functions present in the poly.js file.

CHAPTER 2 UTILIZING MACHINE LEARNING ALGORITHMS FOR POWER GENERATION PREDICTION AND CLASSIFICATION IN WIND FARMS

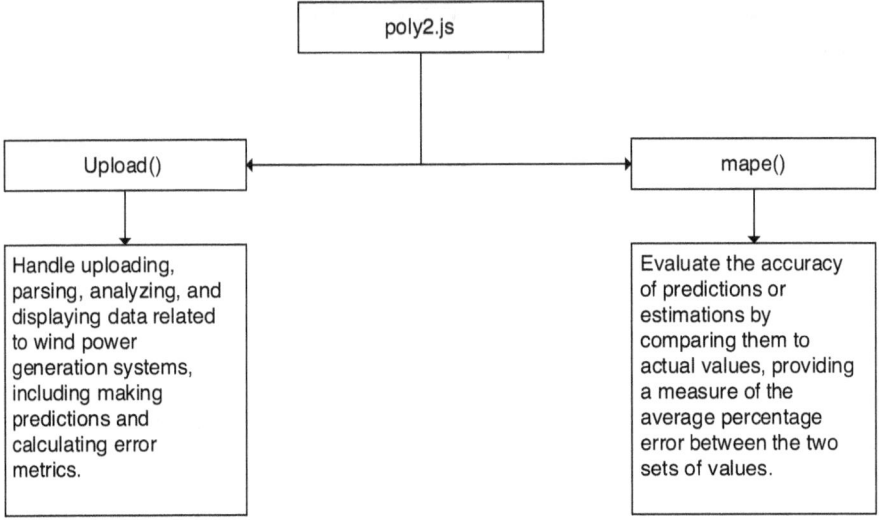

Figure 2-7. poly.js

Multiple Linear Regression

To investigate the relationship of the all the predictors on the dependent variable, the multiple linear regression technique was used, and its corresponding accuracy was assessed. The model takes as input the wind speed, wind direction, pressure, and temperature to predict the system power. Figure 2-8 shows the main steps involved in the training of this model.

CHAPTER 2   UTILIZING MACHINE LEARNING ALGORITHMS FOR POWER GENERATION PREDICTION AND CLASSIFICATION IN WIND FARMS

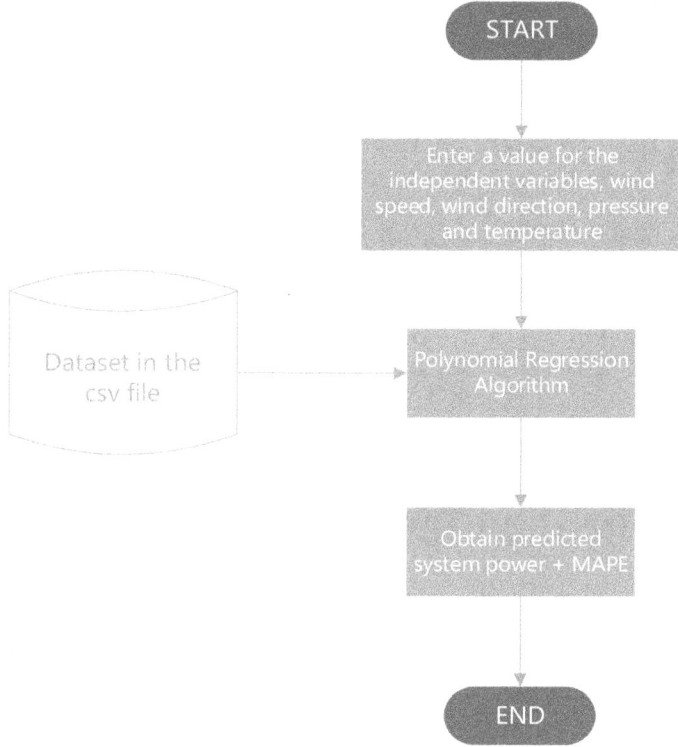

Figure 2-8. *Program workflow, MLR*

The program uses the Multivariate Linear Regression library available in ml.min.js to obtain the necessary coefficients and predictions. Moreover, a function for calculating the MAPE is also introduced in the program to assess the accuracy of the system. The file main3.js shown in Figure 2-9 is used to implement the process of MLR.

CHAPTER 2 UTILIZING MACHINE LEARNING ALGORITHMS FOR POWER GENERATION PREDICTION AND CLASSIFICATION IN WIND FARMS

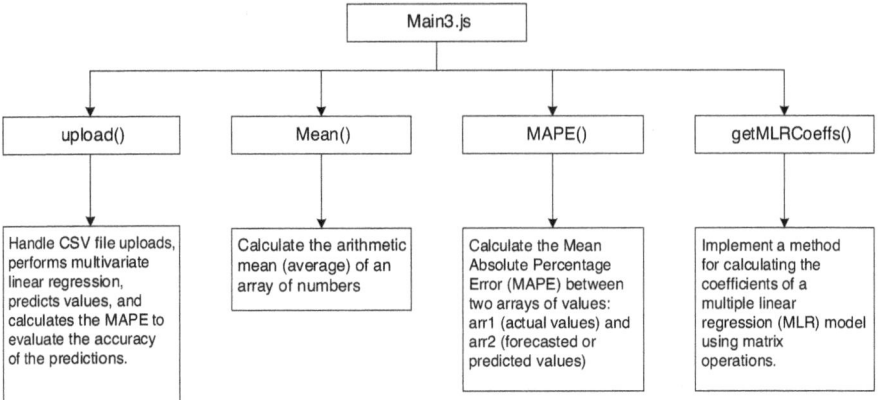

Figure 2-9. *main3.js*

2.4 Application Testing and Analysis

In this series of experiments, three different regression techniques, namely, polynomial regression, k-nearest neighbors (KNN) regression, and multilinear regression, were applied and evaluated to understand their performance in predicting a target variable. The target variable in each experiment is represented by the Mean Absolute Percentage Error (MAPE), which quantifies the accuracy of the predictions made by each regression model.

For experiment 1, polynomial regression models were trained and tested using degrees ranging from 4 to 14. For experiment 2, KNN regression models were built and evaluated using various values of K ranging from 2 to 10. For experiment 3, multilinear regression was applied without specifying the degree or K value.

2.4.1 Application Testing

This section summarizes the set of results obtained while applying the different machine learning algorithms to the dataset. The test values used for the different parameters are as follows:

CHAPTER 2   UTILIZING MACHINE LEARNING ALGORITHMS FOR POWER GENERATION
PREDICTION AND CLASSIFICATION IN WIND FARMS

Wind Speed = 10 ms^{-1}

Wind direction = 120 deg

Pressure = 1 atm

Temperature = 25 ^{0}C

The outputs for the best MAPE obtained with each model are depicted as under:

i. **KNN Classification**

This algorithm aims at classifying the category of power that would be generated under the previously mentioned conditions. The optimum value of k in this case was set to 3, as demonstrated in Figure 2-10.

Figure 2-10. KNN classification

CHAPTER 2   UTILIZING MACHINE LEARNING ALGORITHMS FOR POWER GENERATION
PREDICTION AND CLASSIFICATION IN WIND FARMS

ii. **Multiple Linear Regression**

The dataset was also tested using the Multiple Linear Regression algorithm to predict the system power. A typical output under the chosen weather conditions is shown in Figure 2-11.

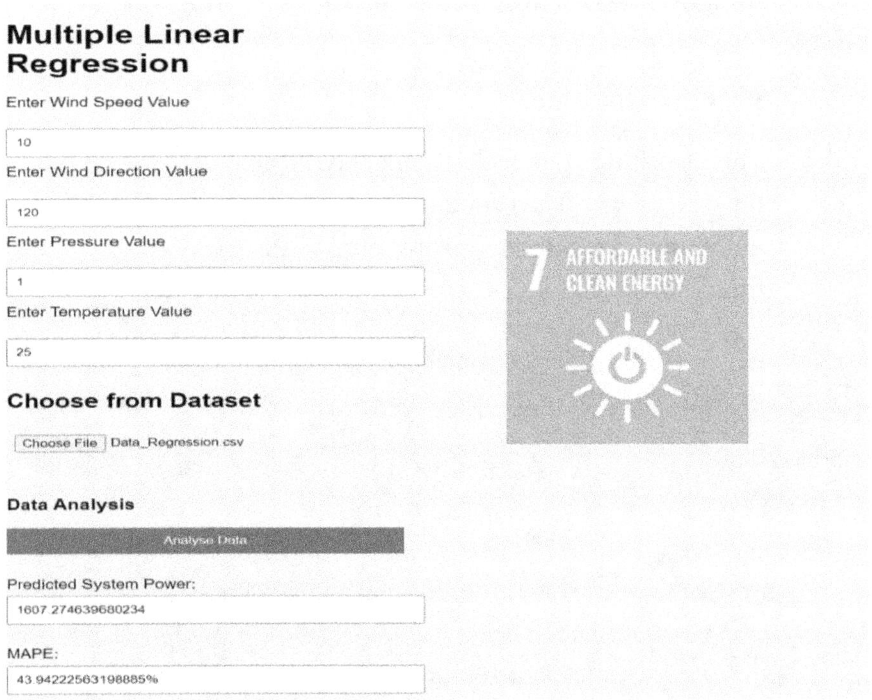

Multiple Linear Regression

Enter Wind Speed Value

| 10 |

Enter Wind Direction Value

| 120 |

Enter Pressure Value

| 1 |

Enter Temperature Value

| 25 |

Choose from Dataset

Choose File | Data_Regression.csv

Data Analysis

| Analyse Data |

Predicted System Power:
| 1607.274639680234 |

MAPE:
| 43.94222563198885% |

Figure 2-11. Multilinear regression

iii. **KNN Regression**

The KNN regression model exploits the distance between the nearest neighbors to obtain the predicted system power. In this case, the four nearest neighbors provided better accuracy than other values of k, as shown in Figure 2-12.

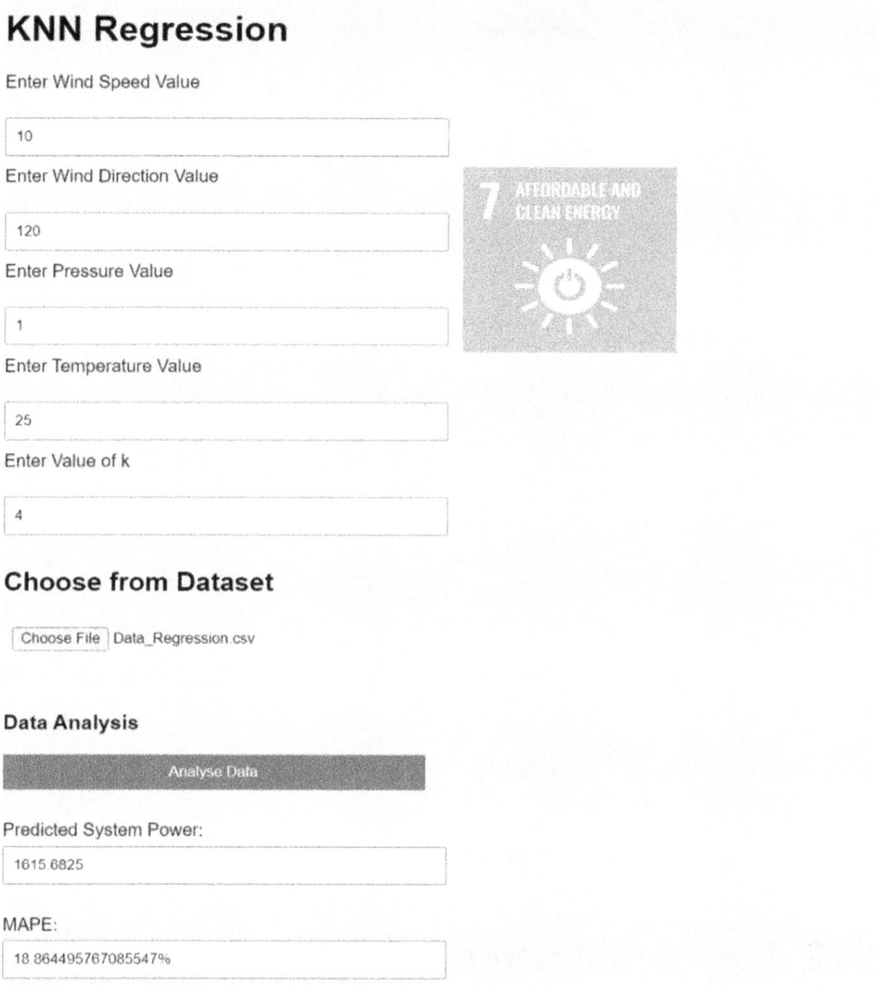

CHAPTER 2   UTILIZING MACHINE LEARNING ALGORITHMS FOR POWER GENERATION PREDICTION AND CLASSIFICATION IN WIND FARMS

KNN Regression

Enter Wind Speed Value

```
10
```

Enter Wind Direction Value

```
120
```

Enter Pressure Value

```
1
```

Enter Temperature Value

```
25
```

Enter Value of k

```
4
```

Choose from Dataset

Choose File | Data_Regression.csv

Data Analysis

[Analyse Data]

Predicted System Power:

```
1615.6825
```

MAPE:

```
18.864495767085547%
```

Figure 2-12. *KNN regression*

iv. **Polynomial Regression**

The polynomial regression algorithm proved to provide the best accuracy by resulting in a MAPE as low as 7.57%, as illustrated in Figure 2-13.

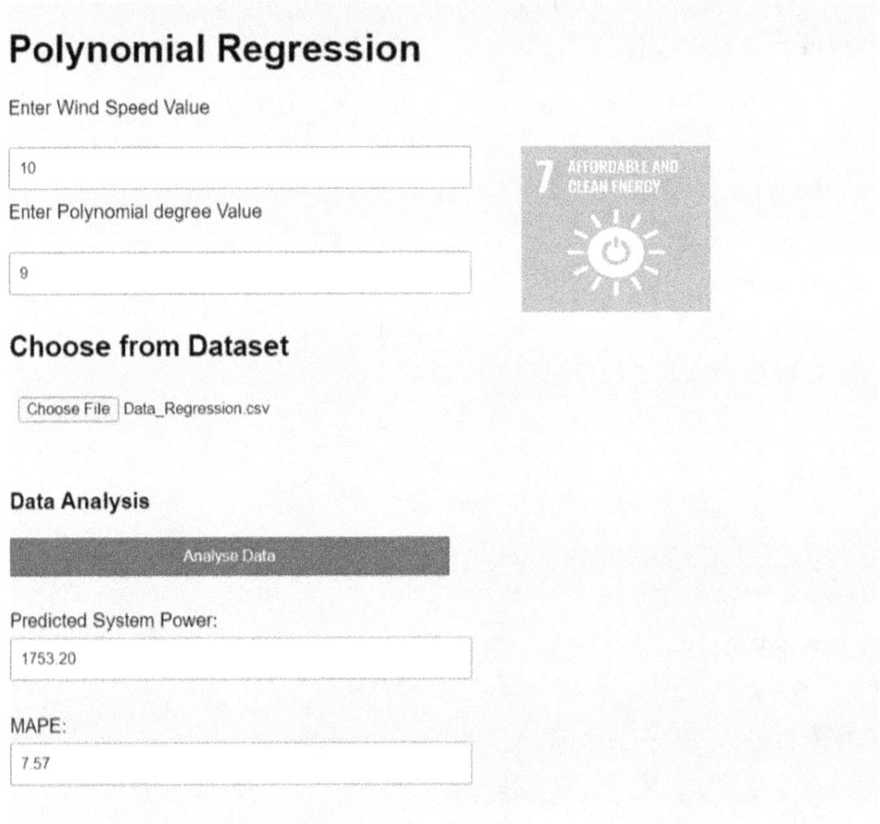

CHAPTER 2 UTILIZING MACHINE LEARNING ALGORITHMS FOR POWER GENERATION PREDICTION AND CLASSIFICATION IN WIND FARMS

Polynomial Regression

Enter Wind Speed Value

`10`

Enter Polynomial degree Value

`9`

Choose from Dataset

Choose File | Data_Regression.csv

Data Analysis

Analyse Data

Predicted System Power:

`1753.20`

MAPE:

`7.57`

Figure 2-13. *Polynomial regression*

2.4.2 Polynomial Regression Results

Figure 2-14 and Table 2-4 illustrates the results obtained when the polynomial degree is increased. The MAPE values ranged from 7.57% to 68.66%, showcasing the variability in model performance. Of particular interest was the observation that the relationship between the degree of the polynomial and MAPE was nonlinear. Instead, it followed a more intricate trajectory. The MAPE values reached their lowest point at degree 9, where the error rate was 7.57%, indicating a high level of accuracy and effectiveness in predicting power system behavior. This result demonstrated that a polynomial of degree 9 provided the most accurate predictions for this dataset. It emphasized the importance of selecting an appropriate polynomial degree to achieve a balance between model complexity and accuracy. Degree 9 emerged as the optimal choice, delivering superior predictions by effectively capturing the underlying patterns in the data.

Table 2-4. Polynomial Regression

Degree	MAPE
2	56.36
3	100.52
4	20.88
5	68.66
6	38.67
7	43.14
8	19.03
9	7.57
10	13.31
11	12.24
12	12.81
13	11.05
14	14.33

CHAPTER 2   UTILIZING MACHINE LEARNING ALGORITHMS FOR POWER GENERATION PREDICTION AND CLASSIFICATION IN WIND FARMS

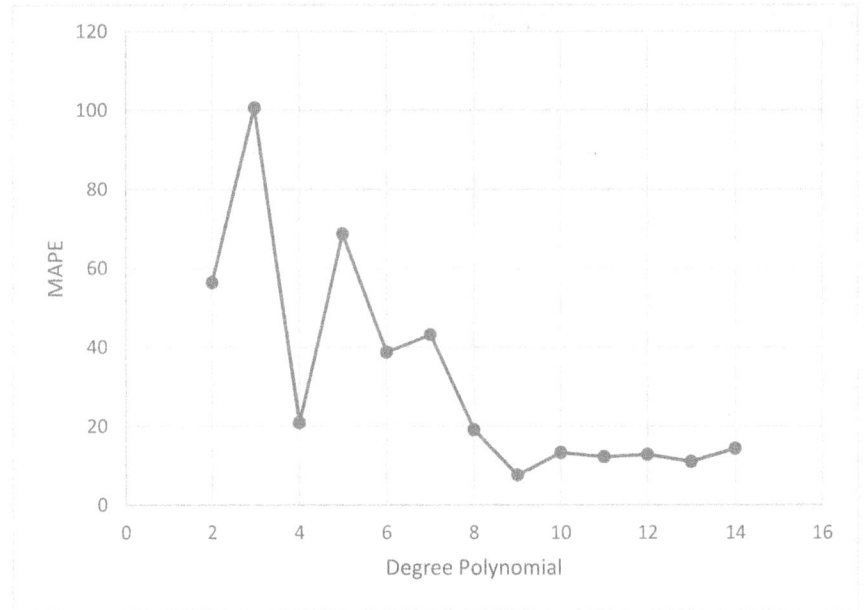

Figure 2-14. *Mape versus degree polynomial*

2.4.3 KNN Regression

The results show MAPE values for different values of K ranging from 1 to 10. As K increases from 1 to 10, the MAPE generally increases, indicating a degradation in model performance as K becomes larger. This behavior is common in KNN regression. A smaller K value means the model relies heavily on a few nearest neighbors, which can lead to overfitting. As K increases, the model considers more neighbors, which can result in a smoother but potentially less accurate prediction. KNN regression doesn't provide explicit coefficients or equations like linear regression. Instead, it relies on the similarity of data points. Looking at our results, K=4 seems to have a relatively low MAPE of 13.288, indicating better predictive performance than K=1 or K=10. See Table 2-5.

Table 2-5. *K-Value vs. MAPE for KNN Regression*

K-Value	MAPE
1	0
2	13.29
3	16.66
4	13.29
5	20.25
6	21.77
7	22.51
8	23.11
9	23.83
10	24.28

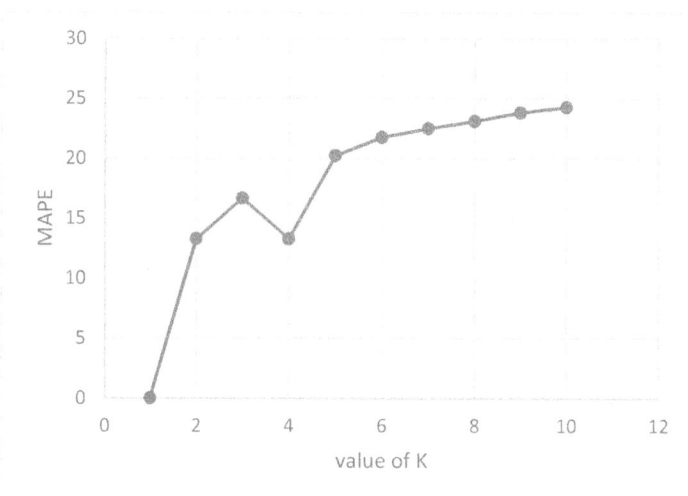

Figure 2-15. *K-Value versus MAPE for KNN regression*

2.4.4 Multilinear Regression

Multilinear regression is a statistical method used to model the relationship between a dependent variable and multiple independent variables. It assumes a linear relationship between the predictors and the target variable. In this case, a MAPE of 42.20 indicates that, on average, the model's predictions have an absolute percentage error of approximately 42.20% compared to the true values. A MAPE of 42.20% suggests that the multilinear regression model, as currently configured, may not be providing highly accurate predictions for the target variable. The relatively high MAPE value indicates that the model's predictions deviate significantly from the actual values, and this level of error may not be acceptable for certain applications.

2.4.5 KNN Classification

Lastly, for experiment 4, we will analyze the results obtained from KNN classification experiments with varying values of K (the number of nearest neighbors) and their implications for wind power prediction accuracy. The classifications "high," "medium," and "low" are used to represent the predicted wind power levels. The results from our KNN classification experiments are presented in Table 2-6, where K ranges from 1 to 10, and the corresponding accuracy percentages are recorded as shown in Table 2-6. When values of K being larger than 10 were used, the classification remains the same as when K=10.

CHAPTER 2   UTILIZING MACHINE LEARNING ALGORITHMS FOR POWER GENERATION
            PREDICTION AND CLASSIFICATION IN WIND FARMS

Table 2-6. *Result-KNN Classification*

K-value	Accuracy (%)	Classification
2	100	Medium
3	96.997	Medium
4	98.19	Medium
5	95.58	Medium
6	96.71	Medium
7	94.77	Medium
8	95.799	Medium
9	93.926	Medium
10	94.63	Medium

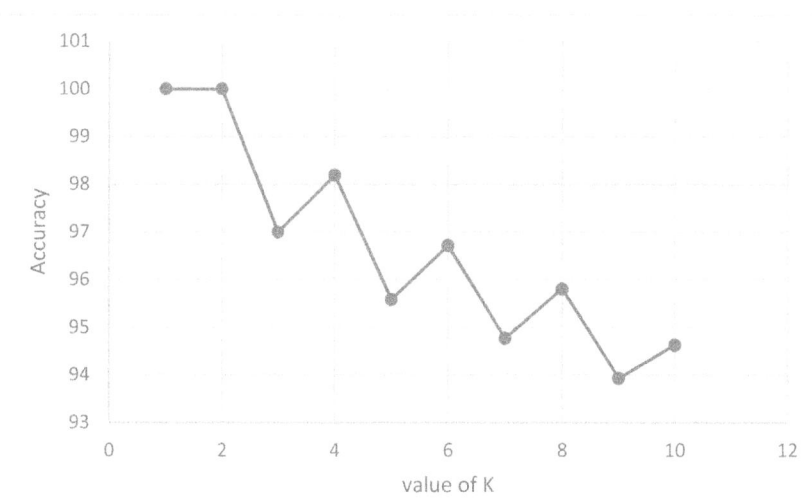

Figure 2-16. *Accuracy versus value of k*

CHAPTER 2   UTILIZING MACHINE LEARNING ALGORITHMS FOR POWER GENERATION
            PREDICTION AND CLASSIFICATION IN WIND FARMS

As the value of K increases, the model's accuracy remains impressively high, with only slight fluctuations. The accuracy percentages associated with various values of K showcase the model's ability to categorize wind power levels effectively. It is evident that the accuracy is exceptionally high when K equals 1 and 2, both achieving a perfect accuracy rate of 100%. This indicates that when the model considers only the closest neighboring data points, it excels in making precise predictions about wind power levels. This level of accuracy is crucial in applications where fine-grained predictions are required for immediate decision-making, such as managing grid loads during fluctuating wind conditions.

For K values ranging from 3 to 10, the model consistently classifies wind power as "medium" and occasionally as "medium." When values of K being larger than 10 were used, the classification remains the same as when K=10. Therefore, it has been concluded that best results are obtained when K=10. This alignment with the high accuracy rates achieved for these K values suggests that the model is confident in categorizing wind power as "medium" but introduces slight variations in classification when considering slightly more distant neighbors.

With an accuracy rate of 96.997%, K=3 strikes a balance between precision and robustness. It is a strong choice for applications where a slightly broader perspective of neighboring data points is acceptable, and a high level of accuracy is still required. This level of precision is particularly valuable in scenarios such as optimizing the integration of renewable energy sources into the power grid. When the goal is to ensure that wind power levels are categorized with the utmost accuracy, this setting delivers exceptional results.

Moving on from K=4 to K=10, these values offer slightly greater adaptability to variations in wind power conditions while maintaining high accuracy. They are suitable for applications that can tolerate a broader consideration of neighboring data points and may encounter more diverse wind power scenarios.

2.4.6 Comparative Analysis of Regression Models: Polynomial Regression vs. KNN Regression vs. Multilinear Regression

In this comprehensive analysis, we delve into the performance of three distinct regression models: polynomial regression, k-nearest neighbors (KNN) regression, and multilinear regression, utilizing their respective Mean Absolute Percentage Error (MAPE) results as the yardstick. MAPE serves as a vital metric, quantifying the accuracy of these regression models in forecasting continuous target variables. In this section, we provide a thorough examination of the merits and demerits of each model, drawing insights from the furnished results. See Figure 2-17.

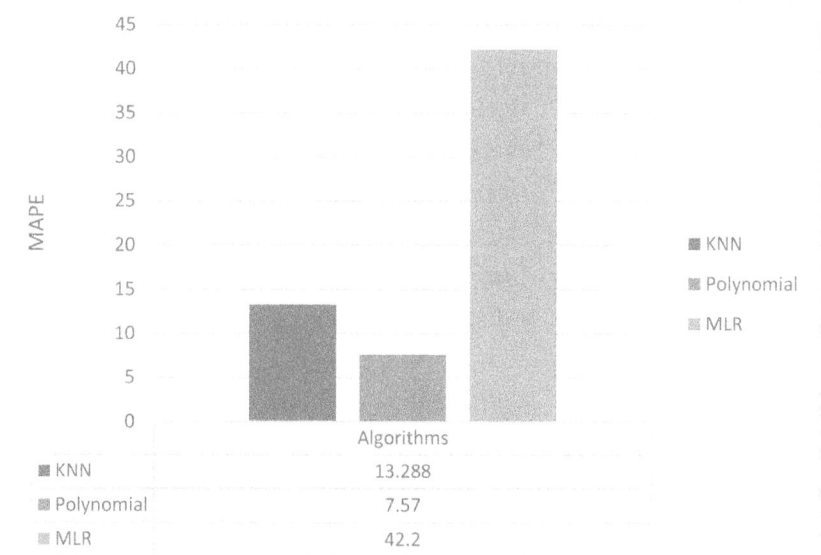

Figure 2-17. Mape for KNN, polynomial regression, and MLR

For polynomial regression, a range of polynomial degrees from 4 to 14 were explored. These degrees were associated with varying Mean Absolute Percentage Error (MAPE) values, with a noteworthy improvement observed at degree 9, where the MAPE dropped to 7.57. polynomial regression's strengths lie in its ability to handle complex, nonlinear relationships between variables. This makes it particularly well-suited for capturing intricate patterns in power system data, which often exhibit nonlinear behavior. Additionally, the model offers a considerable degree of flexibility, accommodating a wide range of data patterns and variations.

However, polynomial regression is not without its weaknesses. One of the primary concerns is its susceptibility to overfitting, especially when the degree is excessively high. Overfitting occurs when the model fits the training data too closely, capturing noise and irrelevant fluctuations. Another challenge with this model is the selection of the optimal polynomial degree. It requires meticulous consideration to strike a balance between model complexity and predictive accuracy. Selecting too high a degree can lead to overfitting, while too low a degree might result in underfitting, where the model oversimplifies the relationship.

The experiment conclusively revealed that, among the explored degrees, degree 9 emerged as the optimal choice. It delivered the lowest MAPE of 7.57%, underscoring the importance of fine-tuning the model's complexity to align with the data's characteristics. This optimal degree struck a balance between capturing the complexity of power system behavior and avoiding the pitfalls of overfitting.

Moving on to KNN regression, our investigation delved into the realm of K values, ranging from 2 to 10. This exploration brought to light an intriguing trend in the model's behavior regarding the choice of K values. Notably, the MAPE exhibited a tendency to increase as K grew larger. However, what stood out was the model's remarkable achievement of a flawless MAPE of 0 when K was set to 1. While this result might appear exceptionally promising, it raised a critical concern—overfitting. Notably, K=4 resulted in the lowest MAPE of 13.288, indicating better predictive performance.

KNN regression boasts its strengths in simplicity and intuitiveness. It is straightforward to understand and implement, making it an attractive choice for various applications. Additionally, KNN operates in a nonparametric manner, meaning it doesn't require assuming a specific functional form for the relationship between variables. This flexibility can be advantageous when dealing with data where the underlying relationship is not well-defined.

Nonetheless, KNN regression has its share of weaknesses. One significant limitation is its sensitivity to the choice of K. The model's performance can vary significantly depending on the selected K value, making it crucial to perform cross-validation to determine the optimal K. Additionally, for larger datasets, KNN can become computationally expensive, as it involves calculating distances between data points.

Lastly, in the domain of multilinear regression, we received a single MAPE value, which stood at 42.20%. This model is characterized by its simplicity and the provision of coefficients for each predictor variable.

Multilinear regression's strengths lie in its simplicity and interpretability. It is a straightforward model that is easy to comprehend, and it provides interpretable coefficients for each predictor variable. This transparency makes it a valuable tool when there is a need to understand the individual contributions of different variables to the target variable.

However, multilinear regression is not exempt from its own set of limitations. One of the fundamental assumptions of this model is a linear relationship between predictors and the target variable. While this assumption can be valid in many cases, it may not accurately capture complex, nonlinear relationships that exist in real-world data. Therefore, its performance may not be optimal when the actual relationship is not genuinely linear.

The reported MAPE of 42.20% suggests that the multilinear regression model may not adequately grasp the intricacies of the dataset, especially if nonlinear relationships are at play. While it may not deliver the same level of predictive accuracy as polynomial regression or KNN regression, it still holds relevance and applicability in scenarios where simplicity and interpretability are valued over sheer predictive power.

Finally, when comparing the three regression techniques, it became evident that polynomial regression, particularly with a degree of 9, achieved the best predictive performance, with the lowest MAPE of 7.57.

2.5 Benefits of Classification in Wind Power Prediction

Classification in wind power prediction, which involves categorizing wind power into low, medium, or high levels, offers a multitude of significant advantages crucial for effective energy management and the pursuit of sustainability.

2.5.1 Accurate Energy Generation Forecasting

One of the primary benefits of classification models in wind power prediction is their ability to provide precise and reliable forecasts of expected wind power output. By categorizing wind power into these three levels, energy providers gain valuable insights into the availability of energy resources. This information is instrumental in scheduling energy production and distribution. For instance, when wind power is predicted to be high, energy providers can allocate resources and plan to harness this clean and renewable energy source optimally (Verhoef et al., 2020).

2.5.2 Optimized Energy Distribution

Predicting wind power levels in low, medium, or high categories empowers energy grid operators to make well-informed decisions regarding the balance of electricity supply and demand. Grid operators can allocate resources more efficiently, adjust energy generation according to forecasted wind power levels, and strategically activate or deactivate power plants to meet consumer needs without overloading or underutilizing the grid. This optimization enhances the overall reliability and efficiency of energy distribution (Brázdil et al., 2019).

2.5.3 Cost Reduction

Classification models play a pivotal role in cost reduction within the energy sector. By accurately predicting wind power levels, energy providers can minimize their reliance on backup power sources, such as fossil fuels, during low wind power generation periods. This reduction not only results in cost savings by reducing fuel expenses but also decreases operational costs associated with conventional power generation. In essence, it fosters a more cost-effective and sustainable energy production process (Gupta et al., 2021).

2.5.4 Grid Stability

Wind power generation is inherently variable due to fluctuations in wind speed and direction. Classification models offer early warnings and insights into potential fluctuations in wind power output. Armed with this information, grid operators can proactively manage the energy grid, ensuring a stable and consistent energy supply. By preemptively addressing variations in wind power, these models help prevent power outages and maintain grid stability, especially during periods of rapidly changing weather conditions (Thomas et al., 2022).

2.5.5 Enhanced Energy Planning

Classification-based wind power predictions significantly benefit energy infrastructure planning. Energy providers and stakeholders can make informed decisions about the construction, expansion, and maintenance of wind farms and related infrastructure. This level of foresight ensures that energy infrastructure aligns with current and future energy demands efficiently. By investing in the right projects at the right time, energy providers can maximize the utilization of wind energy resources and bolster the overall sustainability of their operations (Larson et al., 2023).

2.6 Summary

The aim of this chapter was to use machine learning to predict wind power using data obtained from a dataset from Kaggle while targeting SDG 7, which aims at increasing the use of clean energy by using sustainable approaches globally. Polynomial regression, KNN regression, KNN classification, and multilinear regression were used in the chapter, and the accuracy of the three machine learning algorithms was then compared.

Essentially, a web page was built using HTML and JavaScript that will allow the user to enter the independent variables: wind speed, wind direction, pressure, and air temperature, and the predicted power value and accuracy will be outputted on the web page. A MAPE value of 7.57% was obtained when a degree of 9 for polynomial regression was used indicating the highest accuracy value. For KNN regression, the lowest MAPE which of 13.288% was obtained when a k value of 4 was used. For multiple linear regression, a MAPE of 42.20% was obtained, which demonstrated that the model's predicted value was not highly accurate for KNN classification.

A limitation of the chapter is that no API was used to obtain real-time data to perform a real-time prediction based on timing values. An interesting future work would be to use more machine learning algorithms such as multiple linear perceptron to compare the different accuracies of the models used. The main conclusion of this chapter is that machine learning algorithms can be used to increase the use of green technologies

CHAPTER 2   UTILIZING MACHINE LEARNING ALGORITHMS FOR POWER GENERATION
PREDICTION AND CLASSIFICATION IN WIND FARMS

to produce energy efficiently. Machine learning algorithms can be used in energy industries to help improve the efficiency of sustainable energy systems. While doing so, it can also be concluded that machine learning algorithms can be used to achieve SGD target goals and help improve the condition of the environment and the welfare of the community.

CHAPTER 3

A Crop Recommendation System Using Machine Learning Algorithms for Achieving SDGs 2, 9, and 12

Chapter authors:
Domah Avishaye, avishaye.domah@umail.uom.ac.mu
Hanumunthadu Vandana, vandana.hanumunthadu@umail.uom.ac.mu
Radjoo Dheeraj, dheeraj.radjoo@umail.uom.ac.mu

CHAPTER 3   A CROP RECOMMENDATION SYSTEM USING MACHINE LEARNING ALGORITHMS FOR ACHIEVING SDGS 2, 9, AND 12

The 17 UN SDGs play a pivotal role in providing standards to address global pressing challenges. This includes related issues such as poverty, hunger, and more. Machine learning is essential for accomplishing the SDGs because of its ability to analyze large amounts of data and predict their outcomes. This study focuses on applying machine learning to achieve SDGs 2, 9, and 12.

The algorithms chosen are k-nearest neighbor, decision tree, random forest, and multilayer perceptron. The system predicts 22 crop yields based on input parameters of nitrogen, phosphorus, potassium, temperature, humidity, pH value of the soil, and rainfall. The web application was designed in JavaScript and HTML utilizing a crop recommendation dataset from the Kaggle platform. All four models achieved high accuracy, with the random forest model at 100% likely due to overfitting. This aligns with the targeted SDGs. An increase in the accuracy of the crop recommendation leads to better agricultural practices and better food security. Furthermore, the models foster innovation and allocate resources more efficiently in the agricultural field. In comparison with traditional systems in which historical data comparisons and estimations were made, machine learning manages extensive datasets and adapts to the scalability of the increasing number of farms. Diverse algorithms improve crop yield prediction.

3.1 Introduction

This chapter introduces the application of machine learning algorithms on a crop dataset to target SDGs 2, 9, and 12. The main goal behind SDG 2 is to eradicate hunger, ameliorate nutrition, enable access to nutritious and sufficiently safe food, and promote sustainable farming practices. SDG 9 aims to develop robust infrastructure, foster inclusive and sustainable industrial growth, and encourage innovation. Due to global population growth, the demand for natural resources such as land and freshwater is increasing at an alarming rate. SDG 12 ensures sustainable patterns of

CHAPTER 3 A CROP RECOMMENDATION SYSTEM USING MACHINE LEARNING ALGORITHMS FOR ACHIEVING SDGS 2, 9, AND 12

consumption and production. Since agriculture is globally considered to be one of the most water-dependent activities, significant changes are necessary to fulfill this SDG [1]. Machine learning helps farmers to plant the best profitable crops considering environmental factors and also the market demand. This helps farmers to increase their profit and also reduce the possibility of crop failure [2].

In [3] five machine learning models predicted the crop yield of mustard based on soil analysis. It fulfills SDGs 2, 9, and 12 through the application of machine learning for crop prediction and sustainable agricultural practices. [4] uses machine learning algorithms to predict soil types and recommend suitable crops in the Khulna region of Bangladesh. This aligns with the previously mentioned three SDGs. [5] focuses on using machine learning to predict soil qualities. It actively contributes to SDG 2 through improved soil fertility and so ensures greater crop production, which results in an increase in food security. Also, it achieves the other two specified SDGs.

In this work, a web application is designed that makes use of classification algorithms, including KNN, decision tree, random forest, and multilayer perceptron. Our objective is to contribute to the achievement of SDGs 2, 9, and 12 focusing on enhancing crop yield prediction.
The main focus of this work is the performance of these classification algorithms on the selected dataset aimed at achieving food security, advancing agricultural innovation, and promoting sustainable patterns of consumption and production. By utilizing a crop dataset, the main findings of this study demonstrate the accuracy of these algorithms. The main novelty, in contrast to previous studies, lies in the examination of several machine learning algorithms applied to the crop dataset for the prediction of optimal crop yields.

3.2 AI Use Cases for SDGs 2, 9, and 12

In [6], the study offered a neural network design that can significantly affect and support the UN Sustainable Development Goal of zero hunger, such as convolutional long short-term memory. The authors sought to increase water use efficiency, lessen reliance on irrigation, and lessen the risk of crop loss due to drought and extreme weather. They used sensor data and ground data in real time to apply machine learning to crop segmentation, soil classification, NDVI, and soil moisture prediction. The experiment demonstrated that improving agricultural productivity and decreasing the waste of natural resources like water might result in favorable economic outcomes for the farmer. It was also demonstrated that using ML with earth observation data for analytics and forecasting might be useful for predicting agricultural productivity and alleviating poverty.

The sustainable development concept and its objectives were reviewed in [7], along with earth observation methods that are pertinent to this area. Special emphasis was placed on the contribution of machine learning methods and algorithms, as well as their potential and capabilities to aid in the achievement of sustainable development goals. Performance is seen to be strongly influenced by the capacity to extract and synthesize qualities from data. This in-depth analysis examined various ML categories for handling earth observation data to address various SDGs. All types of machine learning encompass a wide range of SDGs and disciplines, whereby classification, clustering, regression, and dimension reduction techniques are suitable for SDGs 2, 9, 11, 14, and 15. The paper supported the importance of EO and ML in achieving the sustainable development goals and provided a summary of the strategies and tactics that support the attainment of SDGs.

In [8], sustainable transport planning was performed to contribute to the achievement of SDGs 9, 11. and 12 related to transport. A machine-learning-based predictive modeling approach was proposed for metro ridership prediction, taking the built environment around the stations. Consequently, the creation and testing of the model used a time-series database. Ridge regression, lasso regression, elastic net, k-nearest neighbor, support vector regression, decision tree, random forest, extremely randomized trees, adaptive boosting, gradient boosting, extreme gradient boosting, and stacking ensemble learner were among the machine learning (ML) models that had their predictive performance assessed. According to the findings, the decision tree performed the best among the base learners, with an R2 of 87.4% on the test dataset. The second and third-best models among the base learners were KNN and SVR. The feature relevance investigation also demonstrated how each sort of land use density contributes differently to the forecasting of metro ridership.

The authors in [9] investigated the possibility of aiding SDGs 2 and 12 by implementing a combination of nanotechnology and ML to decrease food wastage and increase responsible consumption by determining potential presence of contaminants in food. The paper made use of a small sensor system (S3), a device comprising primarily a gas sensor, along with temperature, humidity. and flow sensors, that will be used to efficiently measure food contamination, i.e., to determine the contamination rate (bacteria, yeasts) of the food sample being analyzed. Several food samples were measured with different contamination levels using the S3 device and data was collected and fed to ML algorithms like k-NN, random forest, and SVM. Results demonstrated that amount of food contaminants on test samples were correctly identified, and the microbiological compositions of the contaminants were also accurately predicted.

An innovative and novel approach was proposed in [10] in which SDGs 7 and 9 were considered. The authors put forward the integration of photovoltaic (PV) in the agriculture industry, a solution that will massively help promote clean energy along with industry innovation. A deep Q-network (DQN) is used, which is a reinforcement learning technique utilized as an AI assistance to investors on implementation of PV panels, which makes decision based on various parameters like budget, costs, and energy requirements. DQN aids in determining the optimal type of PV required for different farms in the agricultural sector, enabling the investors to efficiently deploy PV systems within a region. This RL method helped in boosting sustainable energy uses with an innovative combination of PV systems and agriculture while also yielding increased profits.

In [11], the authors reviewed the research studies on the importance of machine learning techniques in production of agricultural crops. They stated that accurate and timely forecast for crop production is significant for important policy choices like import-export and pricing marketing distribution. Various techniques such as artificial neural network, information fuzzy network, decision tree, regression, clustering, Bayesian belief network, time-series analysis, and Markov chain model were outlined. The research results demonstrated that computer science in agriculture aids in crop forecasting. Building on an objective methodology was necessary for pre-harvest crop forecasts. A good model would offer advantages above the conventional forecasting approach.

In [12], the paper proposed a system that would help apprentice farmers by guiding them for planting and harvesting the most appropriate crops by deploying machine learning for crop prediction. The system proposed use naïve Bayes classifier to calculate and predict the crop for the current climate. The implementation of the system was done using an Arduino UNO with moisture sensor for data collection and also a mobile application that would be used to predict the crop depending on the user's input such as temperature. The output obtained by the supervised machine learning algorithm, naïve Bayes classifier, proved to be accurate and would help farmers in developing sustainable crops.

The authors in [13] proposed a novel machine learning algorithm called *crop selection method* (CSM) that performs crop classification based on the type of crop and weather conditions throughout the year. Crop yield rate was optimized efficiently by using a crop dataset comprising sowing, plantation, and harvesting time durations from previous years for each crop class to establish the best possible sequences of crops that can be grown throughout the season. Multiple sequences were determined whereby the CSM algorithm outputs the sequence with highest yield rate. Results illustrated that land use is maximized when CSM is used with higher crop yield rate per day as maximum crop types are planted and yield effectively throughout the year.

Additionally, a crop recommendation method based on soil nutrients was investigated by [14], which used three ML classifications methods: k-NN, SVM, and logistic regression. These algorithms utilized an existing soil dataset consisting the chemical compositions required for each crop, and based on pH value, phosphorus, and soil salinity, the algorithms output the crop suitable for such soil environments. A land database was also used for geographical classification whereby the model predicts the best crop type for the land based on its chemical features. The results demonstrated a significantly high accuracy of 98% in crop classification; with the SVM ML model, 92% model accuracy was achieved with K-NN and LR.

A soil fertility technique was analyzed in [15] in which the crop yield rates were categorized in terms of three classes, Low, Medium, and High, whereby soil categorized as low implies poor crop yielding, while high implies excellent crop adaptability. The goal of this paper was to determine whether the soil (land) tested comprises the entailed chemical compositions for good crop harvesting. The soil fertility categories are determined from predefined conditions that classifies the soil type by L, M, or H. The paper used naïve Bayes and k-NN as classification ML models to predict the soil fertility based on the chemical parameters of the land tested. This method aids farmers in deducing the land's viability for harvesting and the soil's ability for crop yield.

3.3 Data Processing and Application Design

This section provides a thorough description of the implementation of the web application used for crop prediction. The system is built on JavaScript and HTML, using ML.js as a dependency to implement K-NN, decision trees, and random forest classification. The aim of the application is to provide a user-friendly interface for users to perform prediction based on the inputs.

3.3.1 Data Collection Process and Description of the Datasets

The data for this work was collected by conducting a thorough search on Kaggle, a well-known platform for data science and machine learning enthusiasts. The dataset used in this study can be found at [16]. Kaggle is a reputable resource that hosts a vast array of datasets contributed by researchers, data scientists, and organizations from around the world. This particular dataset provides valuable information related to crop recommendation, making it a suitable choice for our analysis and research purposes.

The dataset consists of eight columns as shown in Figure 3-1.

CHAPTER 3 A CROP RECOMMENDATION SYSTEM USING MACHINE LEARNING ALGORITHMS FOR ACHIEVING SDGS 2, 9, AND 12

N	P	K	temperature	humidity	ph	rainfall	label
90	42	43	20.87974371	82.00274423	6.502985292	202.9355362	rice
85	58	41	21.77046169	80.31964408	7.038096361	226.6555374	rice
60	55	44	23.00445915	82.3207629	7.840207144	263.9642476	rice
74	35	40	26.49109635	80.15836264	6.980400905	242.8640342	rice
78	42	42	20.13017482	81.60487287	7.628472891	262.7173405	rice
69	37	42	23.05804872	83.37011772	7.073453503	251.0549998	rice
69	55	38	22.70883798	82.63941394	5.70080568	271.3248604	rice
94	53	40	20.27774362	82.89408619	5.718627178	241.9741949	rice
89	54	38	24.51588066	83.5352163	6.685346424	230.4462359	rice
68	58	38	23.22397386	83.03322691	6.336253525	221.2091958	rice
91	53	40	26.52723513	81.41753846	5.386167788	264.6148697	rice

Figure 3-1. *Crop dataset*

The columns are as follows:

- **N:** The nitrogen content ratio in the soil
- **P:** The phosphorus content ratio in the soil
- **K:** The potassium content ratio in the soil
- **Temperature:** The atmospheric temperature in degree Celsius
- **Humidity:** The relative humidity in %
- **pH:** The pH value of the soil
- **rainfall:** The amount of rainfall in mm
- **label:** The name of the crop

The dataset entails of 2,200 data for 22 crops, with 100 data per crops. The crops involved are coffee, jute, cotton, coconut, papaya, orange, apple, muskmelon, watermelon, grapes, mango, banana, pomegranate, lentil, black gram, mung bean, moth beans, pigeon peas, kidney beans, chickpea, maize, and rice.

3.3.2 Data Preprocessing Steps

To perform decision tree and random forest classification, the labels should be encoded as the string labels would result in errors for the ML.js dependency. Therefore, to preprocess the dataset, a Python library known as Pandas was used to encode the labels. The process of encoding the label is done using an online integrated development environment called Google Colab. Colab is a cloud-based Jupyter Notebook platform that provides an inexpensive, no-setup solution. It is ideal for machine learning modeling, offering access to graphics processing units (GPUs) and tensor processing units (TPUs) [17]. The data can easily be manipulated and displayed.

Figure 3-2 shows the flowchart for the data preprocessing step. First, the dependency for Pandas is imported. Panda is a Python library for data analysis. Since Google Colab is being used, the dataset also needs to be imported. To load the dataset, the drive storage has to be mounted on the Colab application. After loading drive, the dataset. which is in a CSV file format, is read by calling panda's `read_csv()` method.

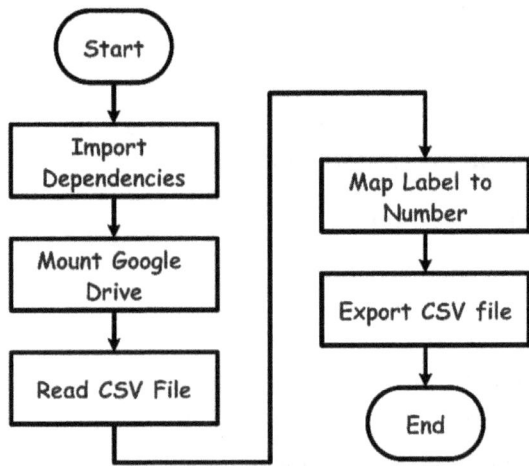

Figure 3-2. *Flowchart for data preprocessing*

CHAPTER 3   A CROP RECOMMENDATION SYSTEM USING MACHINE LEARNING ALGORITHMS FOR ACHIEVING SDGS 2, 9, AND 12

To encode the labels, a dictionary is defined to map the labels to their corresponding values. The map() method is called to add a column to the dataset with the encoded label. Now each label will have a corresponding number to represent them.

3.3.3 Program Structure

Figure 3-3 shows the programming model as block diagrams for the machine learning classifications algorithm implemented. It is to be noted that all the code for this chapter can be found in the folder Chapter 3 – Codes hosted on the GitHub page for this book.

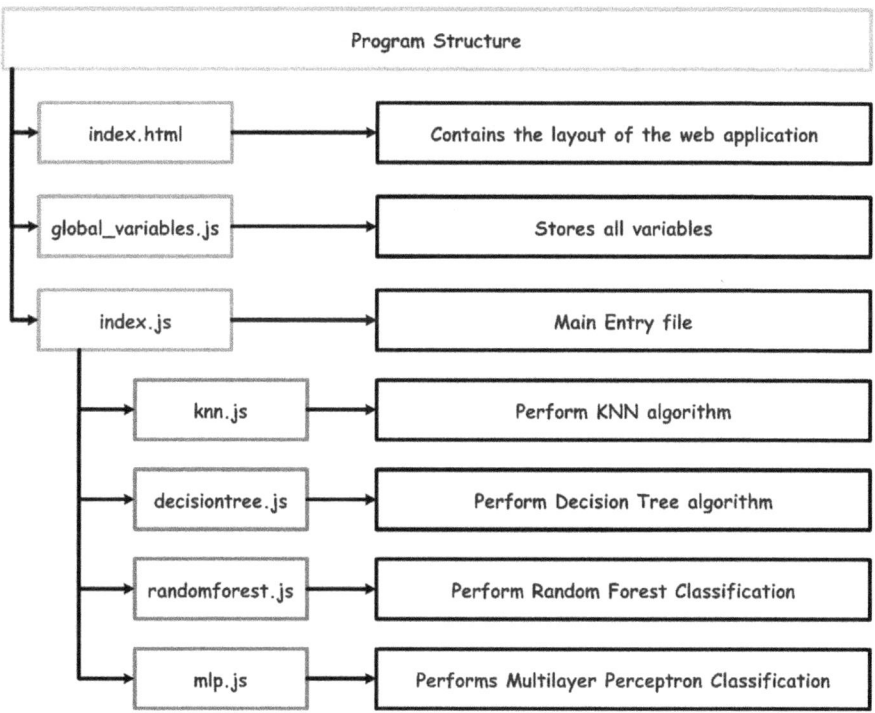

Figure 3-3. *Program structure for web application*

The main file that runs the application is the index.js file. It holds the event listener for a button that would run the algorithms depending on what the user chose. A radio button group is available from which user can pick whether to run the k-NN, decision tree classifier, random forest classifier, or multilayer perceptron. The index file uses an if-else statement to verify which radio button is checked and then call the corresponding method for that algorithm.

The global_variables.js files hold all the variables used throughout the web application including HTML elements, such as containers, radio group, text fields and buttons, and arrays to store the values read from the dataset.

3.3.4 Layout of Web Application

Figure 3-4 shows the web application layout.

CHAPTER 3   A CROP RECOMMENDATION SYSTEM USING MACHINE LEARNING ALGORITHMS
FOR ACHIEVING SDGS 2, 9, AND 12

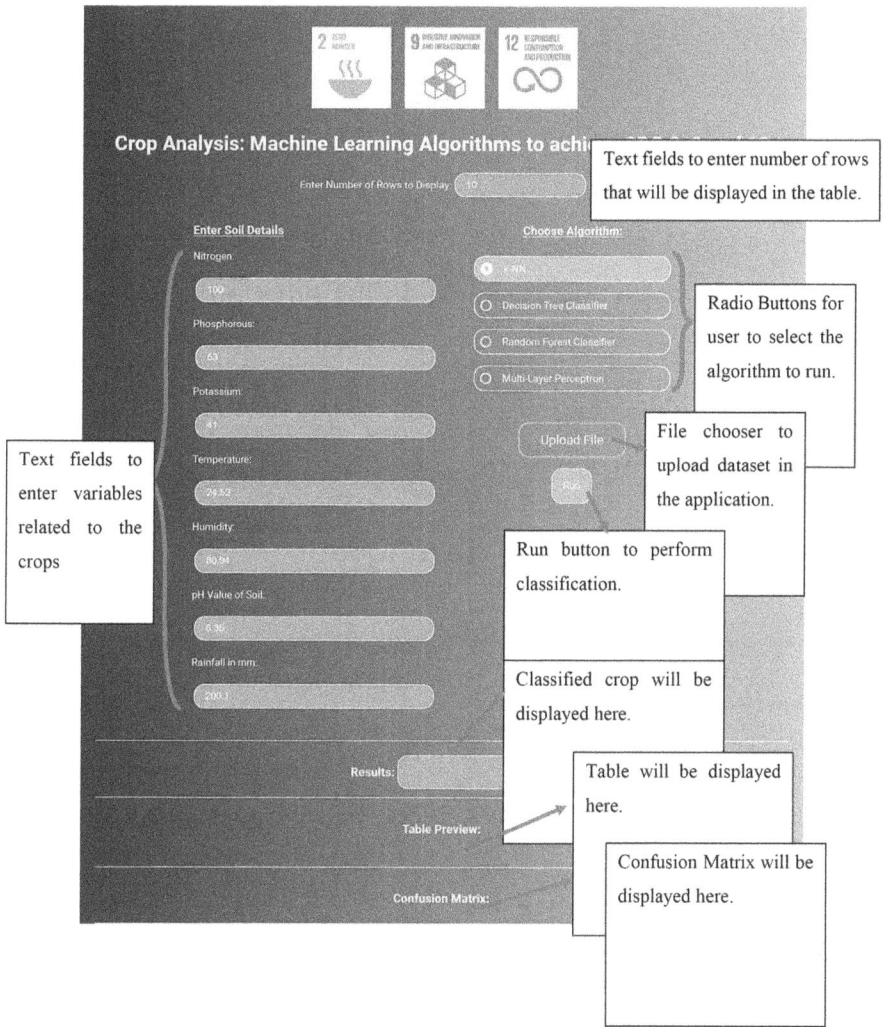

Figure 3-4. Web application layout

Figure 3-5 shows the flowchart for the classification of crops. First, the program will wait for the user to select the dataset, which will be in form of a CSV file. Using the `FileReader` dependency, the CSV file is read, and from this object, each row and column can be extracted. To extract the rows and columns, a library called `PapaParse` [18] is used as it provides easy integration of reading and working with CSV files.

CHAPTER 3 A CROP RECOMMENDATION SYSTEM USING MACHINE LEARNING ALGORITHMS FOR ACHIEVING SDGS 2, 9, AND 12

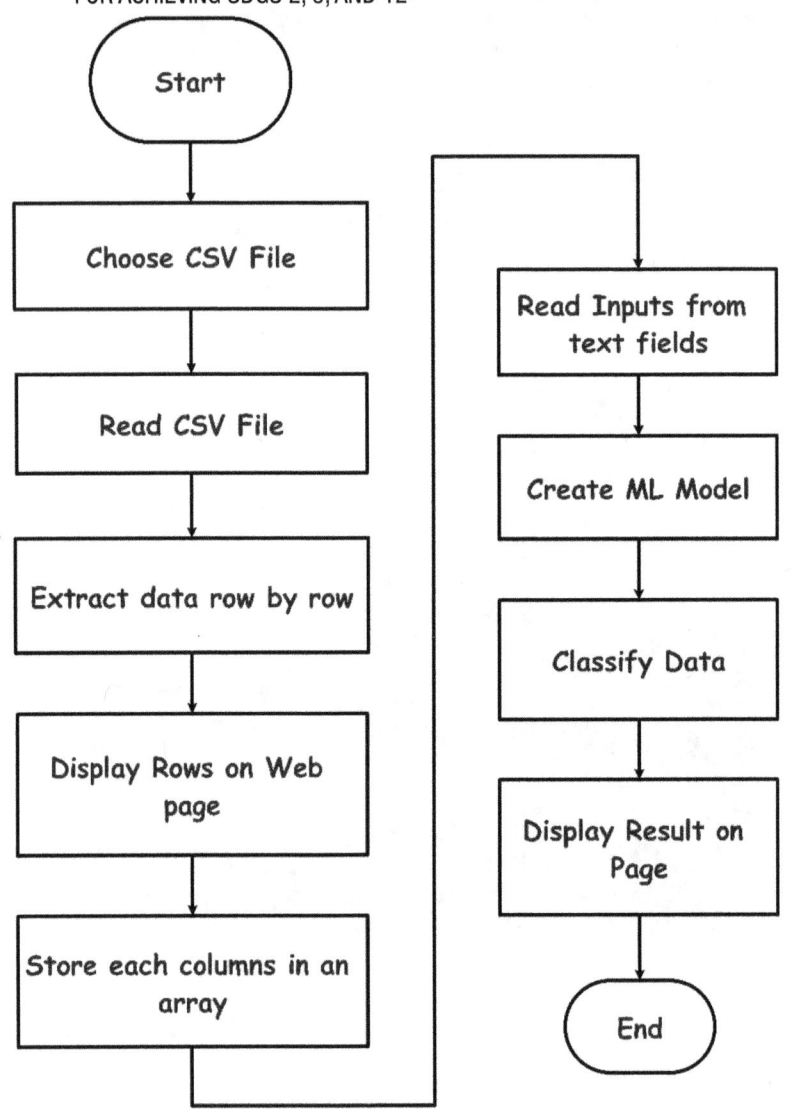

Figure 3-5. *Flowchart for classification*

The data from the file is displayed on the web page for users to analyze. A for loop is used to iterate over the number of rows so that each column can be stored in an array. After iterating over the whole dataset, a new

CHAPTER 3 A CROP RECOMMENDATION SYSTEM USING MACHINE LEARNING ALGORITHMS FOR ACHIEVING SDGS 2, 9, AND 12

array is created to store the data in the same row order as they were in the CSV file. Another array is created to store the labels only, which will be used to check the accuracy of the machine learning model at a later stage.

When all the data are set programmatically, the application will read the user inputs from the text fields. The input consists of the contents of nitrogen, phosphorous, potassium, temperature value, humidity value, pH value, and rainfall value. The machine learning model is created depending on whether the user chooses the knn.js, decisiontree.js, randomforest.js, or mlp.js for the algorithm. The input is passed as an argument to the machine learning object, and the classification of the crop is performed. The obtained result is displayed on the webpage.

The library used for the machine learning model is [19]. Table 3-1 describes the associated functions and methods.

Table 3-1. Summary of Methods for Classification

Methods	Description
runBtn.onclick()	Event listener for user's button click
radioButton.checked	Returns Boolean value whether a specific radio button is selected
FileReader()	Creates an object to read a file
reader.onload(){}	Event listener for successful loading of the file
Papa.parse()	Parse the csv file to obtain the content
array.push()	Adds the data to an array
document.createElement("")	Creates element for the HTML page dynamically
container.appendChild("")	Adds the element to the HTML page
ML.KNN()	Creates a model for KNN

(continued)

Table 3-1. (*continued*)

Methods	Description
`ML.DecisionTreeClassifier()`	Creates a model for decision tree classification
`ML.RandomForestClassifier()`	Creates a model for random forest classification
`model.train()`	Trains the model
`model.predict()`	Uses the model to classify the input data and gives the result
`Brain.NeuralNetwork()`	Creates a neural network for classification
`network.train()`	Trains the neural network
`network.run()`	Passes input in the neural network to obtain a prediction

Figure 3-6 shows the flowchart to analyze the model accuracy.

CHAPTER 3   A CROP RECOMMENDATION SYSTEM USING MACHINE LEARNING ALGORITHMS FOR ACHIEVING SDGS 2, 9, AND 12

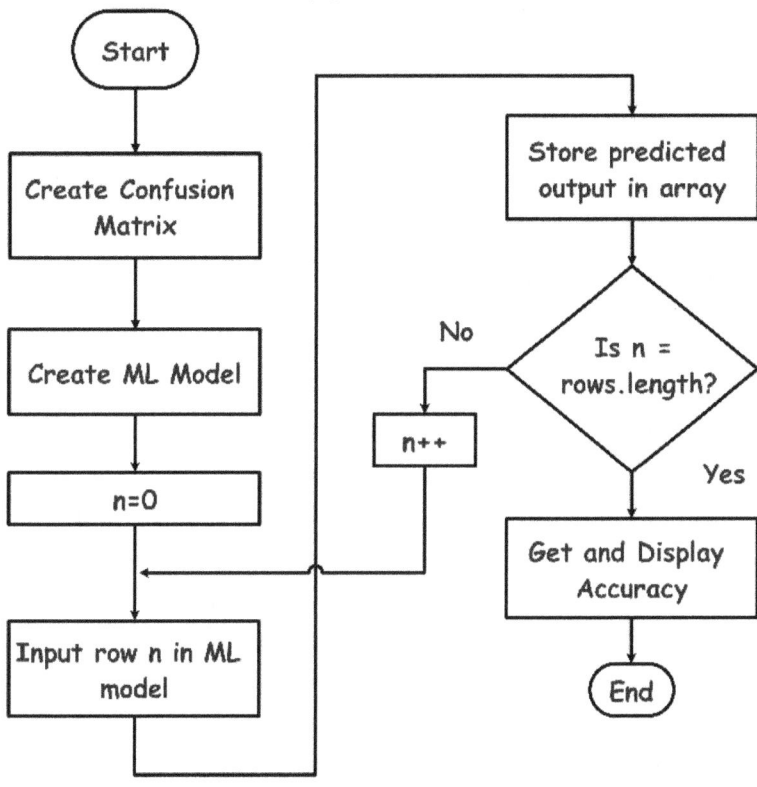

Figure 3-6. *Flowchart for model accuracy*

To test the accuracy of each model, a confusion matrix is implemented using the ML.js dependency itself. To use the confusion matrix, the original set of labels is stored. Depending on the chosen algorithm, a machine learning model is created. The application will loop over each row in the dataset and take the values of the fields as input for the model. The predicted output is stored in a new array. The process is repeated with every row of the dataset. Finally, a new array of labels will be obtained with outputs obtained with the model. A confusion matrix object is created using TensorFlow.js [20] and d3.js [21]. The original and predicted label are passed as arguments. The accuracy is obtained by calling the getAccuracy method. Table 3-2 summarizes the methods for accuracy.

CHAPTER 3   A CROP RECOMMENDATION SYSTEM USING MACHINE LEARNING ALGORITHMS FOR ACHIEVING SDGS 2, 9, AND 12

Table 3-2. *Summary of Methods for Accuracy*

Methods	Description
`ML.confusionMatrix.fromLabels()`	Creates a confusion matrix that will use the labels
`confusionMatrix.getAccuracy()`	Returns a double value which represent the percentage accuracy of the model

3.4 Application Testing and Analysis

This section illustrates in detail the different algorithms used and their outcomes. A critical analysis is also performed to analyze their impact on the SDGs 2, 9. and 12. The four algorithms implemented, k-NN, decision trees, random forest, and MLP, are built within a single HTML page, whereby the user can select one of each algorithm and perform crop classification. The subsections describe the experiments for each algorithm, with their model parameters and hyperparameters and different functions used. Since we are dealing with a classification problem, we evaluated the ML model by using a confusion matrix. It is simply a table comparing the similarity level between the predicted and true outcomes. The confusion matrix gives a clear indication of what percentage accuracy the model predicts the actual outcome for a specified crop. As we have 22 crops to classify, a 22 x 22 matrix table was built to determine the performance of the ML technique. We calculated the model's accuracy by computing the number of true predictions over the total number of predictions.

CHAPTER 3   A CROP RECOMMENDATION SYSTEM USING MACHINE LEARNING ALGORITHMS FOR ACHIEVING SDGS 2, 9, AND 12

3.4.1 Application Testing

Figure 3-7a and Figure 3-7b shows the user's input about the soil details in the text fields. Each field is filled, and the number of rows to display in the table is also selected. The user selects the desired algorithm to run and chooses the option from the radio buttons. The dataset is uploaded via the file chooser upon clicking the Upload File button. After running the algorithm, the first 10 rows of the dataset are displayed in the container for Table Preview. Similarly, the confusion matrix obtained is displayed in the container for the Confusion Matrix. The final classification result in shown in the text field for Results.

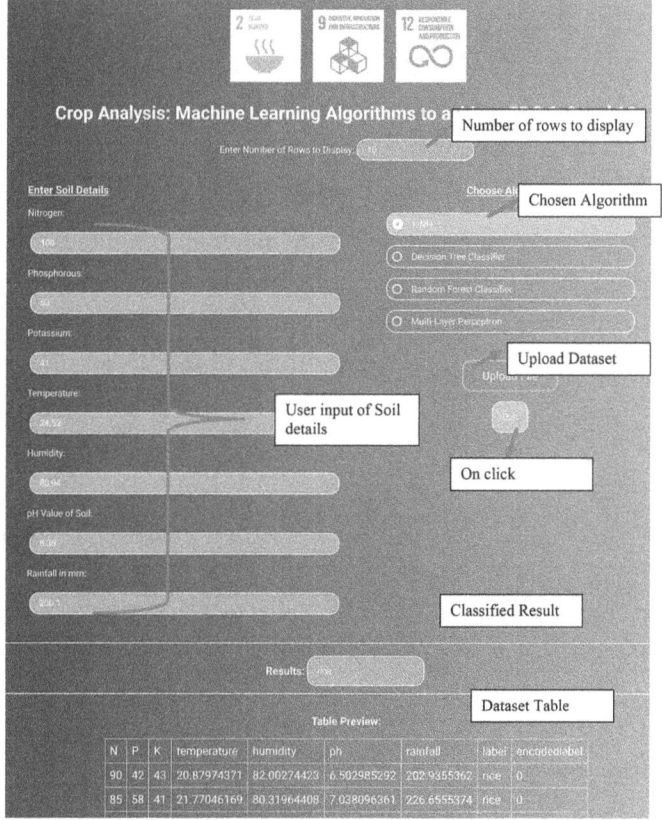

Figure 3-7a. *Application Layout*

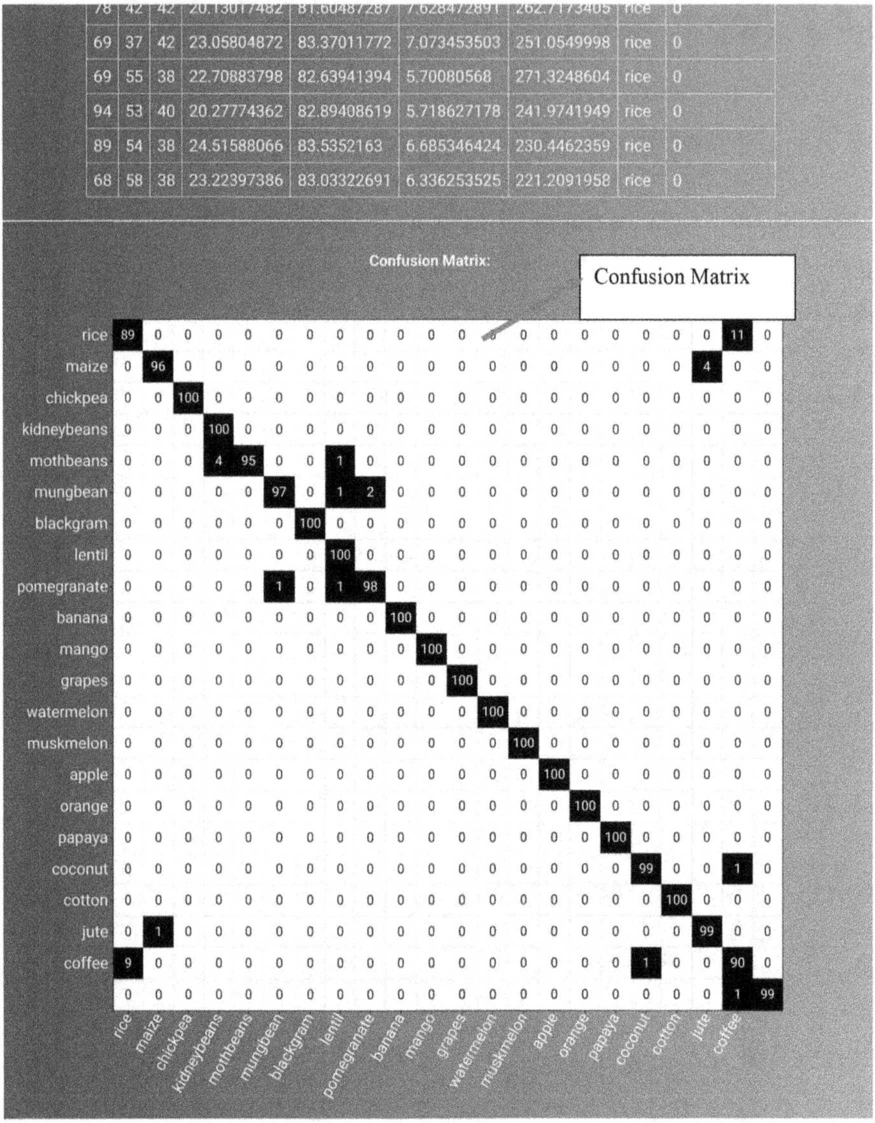

Figure 3-7b. Application layout continued

CHAPTER 3 A CROP RECOMMENDATION SYSTEM USING MACHINE LEARNING ALGORITHMS FOR ACHIEVING SDGS 2, 9, AND 12

3.4.2 K-NN Classification Results

The effectiveness of the k-NN classifier for making precise crop recommendations based on multiple input parameters is studied as illustrated in Table 3-3, 3-4, and 3-5.

The value of k is set to 3, 4, and 5.

(i) **For K = 3,**

Table 3-3. $k = 3$

N	P	K	temperature	humidity	pH	rainfall	Results obtained	encodedlabel
100	53	41	24.52	80.94	6.35	200.1	rice	0
50	42	20	23.44	60.54	6.89	72.44	maize	1
41	60	75	25.56	20.22	9.0	78.55	chickpea	2
5	10	3	9.55	100.50	8.55	120.33	orange	16
95	30	22	26.91	50.74	7.42	140.48	coffee	21
Accuracy = 0.9890909090909091								

(ii) **For K = 4,**

CHAPTER 3   A CROP RECOMMENDATION SYSTEM USING MACHINE LEARNING ALGORITHMS
          FOR ACHIEVING SDGS 2, 9, AND 12

Table 3-4. $k = 4$

N	P	K	temperature	humidity	pH	rainfall	Results obtained	encodedlabel
100	53	41	24.52	80.94	6.35	200.1	rice	0
50	42	20	23.44	60.54	6.89	72.44	maize	1
41	60	75	25.56	20.22	9.0	78.55	chickpea	2
5	10	3	9.55	100.50	8.55	120.33	orange	16
95	30	22	26.91	50.74	7.42	140.48	coffee	21

Accuracy = 0.9827272727272728

  (iii)   **For K = 5,**

Table 3-5. $k = 5$

N	P	K	temperature	humidity	pH	rainfall	Results obtained	encodedlabel
100	53	41	24.52	80.94	6.35	200.1	rice	0
50	42	20	23.44	60.54	6.89	72.44	maize	1
41	60	75	25.56	20.22	9.0	78.55	chickpea	2
5	10	3	9.55	100.50	8.55	120.33	orange	16
95	30	22	26.91	50.74	7.42	140.48	coffee	21

Accuracy = 0.9881818181818182

When k is set to 3, the model achieved an accuracy of around 98.90%. This indicates that the model can make accurate crop predictions from the input data. Next, when k is set to 4, the model maintains a high accuracy of approximately 98.27%. This confirms the robustness and reliability of the model. At k = 5, a high accuracy of approximately 98.82% is obtained. The algorithm's consistency across the different values of k is observed. This result has a positive impact on addressing SDGs 2, 9, and 12. Accurate crop recommendations lead to better agricultural practices, which in turn leads to increased crop yields and, eventually, improved food security (SDG 2). This model brings an innovative approach to farming. Additionally, by choosing an appropriate k value and fine-tuning the model, farmers can optimize their use of resources such as water and fertilizers. This optimization leads to better sustainable agricultural practices (SDG 9). Moreover, by recommending the appropriate crop types, resources are more efficiently used and so this encourages sustainable consumption and production patterns (SDG 12).

Figure 3-8 indicates the confusion matrix for the K-NN model. This model correctly predicts crops such as chickpea, kidney beans, and others with 100% true positives (TP). For class rice, it is correctly classified as 92 true positives but incorrectly classified as coffee with 8 false negatives. Class coffee is correctly classified 94 times but misclassified as rice six times. It is observed that other classes such as maize, mothbeans, mungbean, pomegranate, jute, and coffee are also incorrectly classified. Since most classes have zero false positives and false negatives, this demonstrates that k-NN with a k value of 3 performs with high precision.

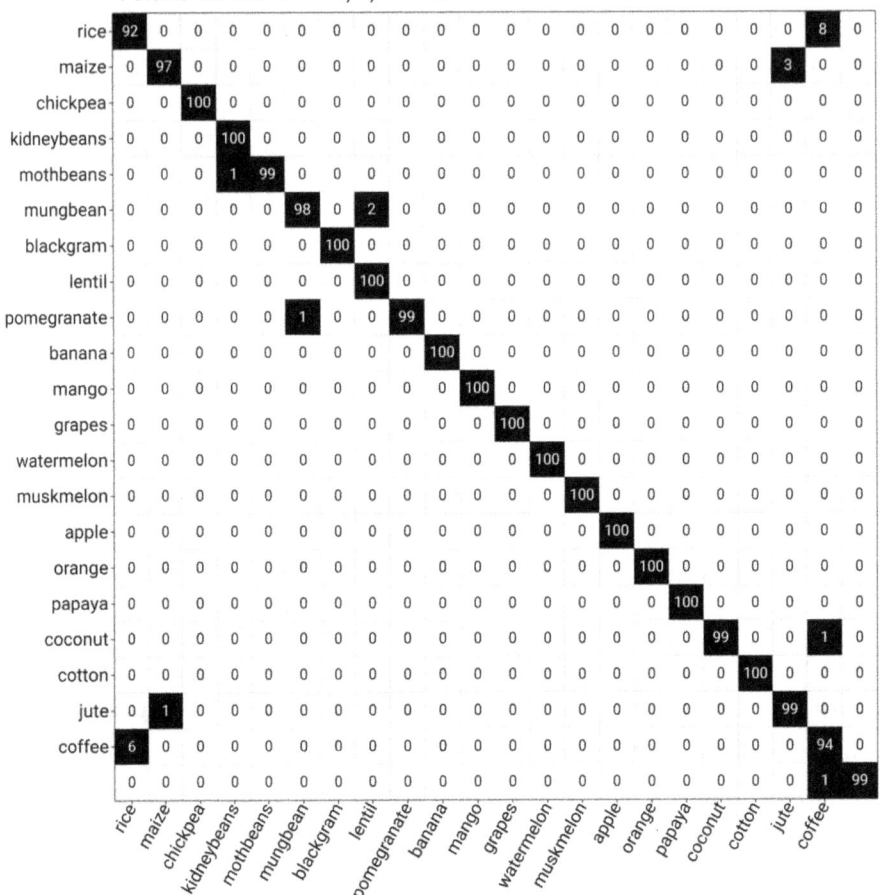

Figure 3-8. *Confusion matrix for k-NN with k = 3*

For k = 4,

Figure 3-9 displays the confusion matrix for the K-NN model with a k value of 4. In this case, class rice is classified correctly 89 times but is confused with coffee 11 times. Class coffee is classified correctly 90 times but is confused with rice 9 times and coconut 1 times. The model demonstrates high precision for 13 crops out of 22. In addition to that, instances of false positives and false negatives are also present in the matrix. Overall, the model has some difficulty in distinguishing between crops.

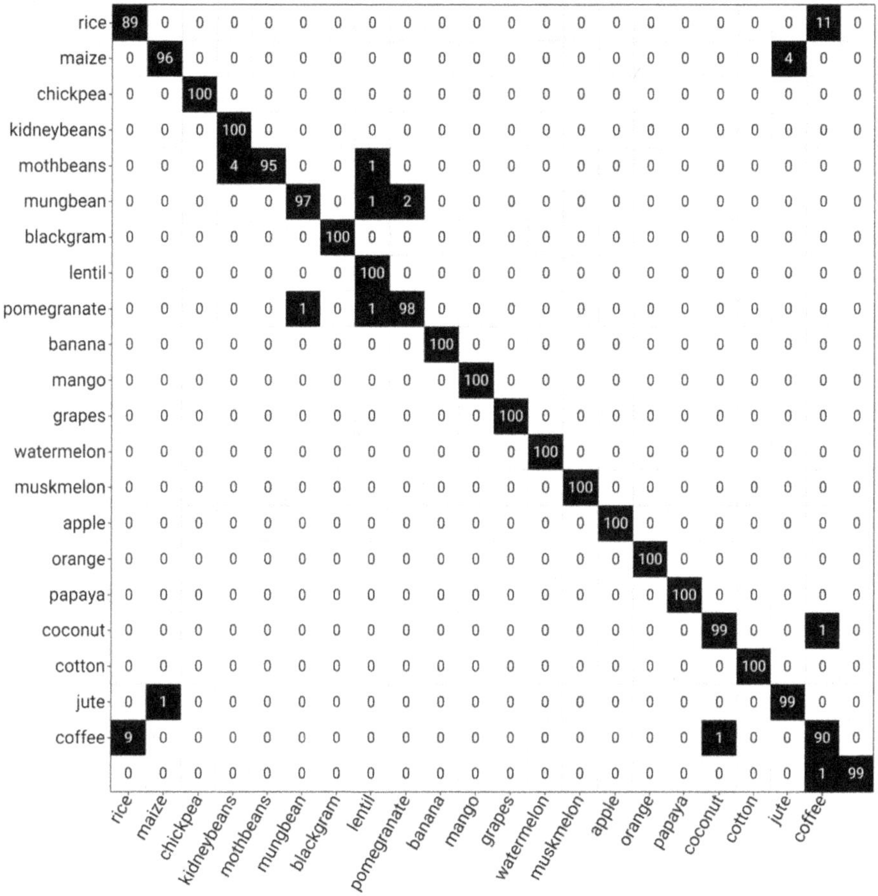

CHAPTER 3   A CROP RECOMMENDATION SYSTEM USING MACHINE LEARNING ALGORITHMS FOR ACHIEVING SDGS 2, 9, AND 12

Figure 3-9. *Confusion matrix for k -NN with k = 4*

For k =5,

Figure 3-10 illustrates the confusion matrix for the K-NN model with a k value of 5. Here class rice is classified correctly 92 times but is confused with coffee 8 times. Class coffee is classified correctly 94 times but is confused with rice 6 times. The model correctly identifies 14 crops out of 22. Some instances of false positives and false negatives are also present in the matrix. After selecting the different values of k, it is noted that with a k value of 5, the model is capable of classifying the crops most precisely.

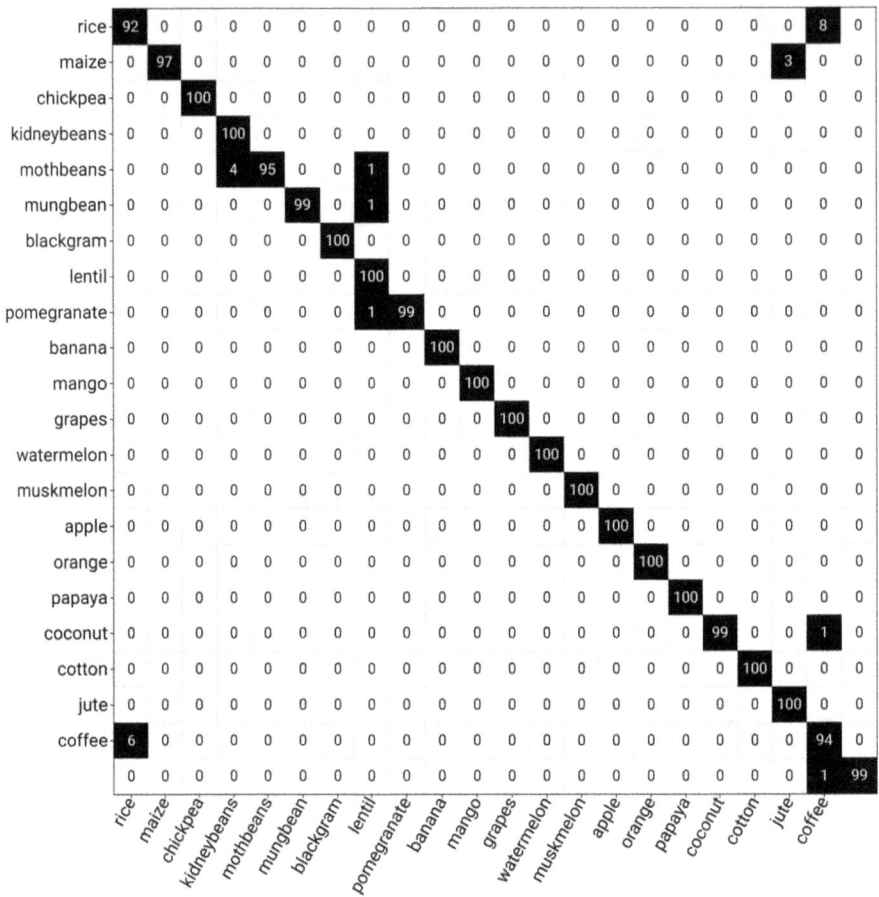

Figure 3-10. *Confusion matrix for k-NN with k = 5*

3.4.3 Decision Trees Classification Results

For this experiment, the CART algorithm was used as the `gainFunction` to identify the root node and construct the decision tree. Likewise, for the k-NN algorithm, the values for the different parameters are inputted to the text fields, and the outcomes are tabulated. Table 3-6 illustrates the results when the decision tree option is selected.

Table 3-6. Decision Trees Results Using CART Algorithm

N	P	K	Temperature	Humidity	Ph	Rainfall	Results Obtained
100	53	41	24.52	80.94	6.35	200.1	Jute
50	42	20	23.44	60.54	6.89	72.44	Mothbeans
41	60	75	25.56	20.22	9.0	78.55	Chickpea
5	10	3	9.55	100.50	8.55	120.33	Orange
95	30	22	26.91	50.74	7.42	140.48	Coffee

The accuracy obtained after running the decision tree model is 0.981.

Figure 3-11 illustrates the output of the decision trees algorithm with the same inputs applied to the previous ML method. It can be observed that, compared to k-NN, the first two outputs are different. k-NN predicted rice and maize for the first two input values. while decision trees with CART predicted Jute and Mothbeans, respectively. Figure 3-11 illustrates the confusion matrix for the decision trees, and it can be observed that the model may confuse outputs for rice and maize, providing a similarity value of 80 % for rice and 79 % for maize. This may be attributed to the decision tree algorithm's inability to detect small variations in datasets for rice, maize, and coffee. However, the other outcomes were correctly predicted, similar to the k-NN outputs. A significantly high accuracy of 98% was obtained for decision trees with the CART algorithm.

CHAPTER 3   A CROP RECOMMENDATION SYSTEM USING MACHINE LEARNING ALGORITHMS FOR ACHIEVING SDGS 2, 9, AND 12

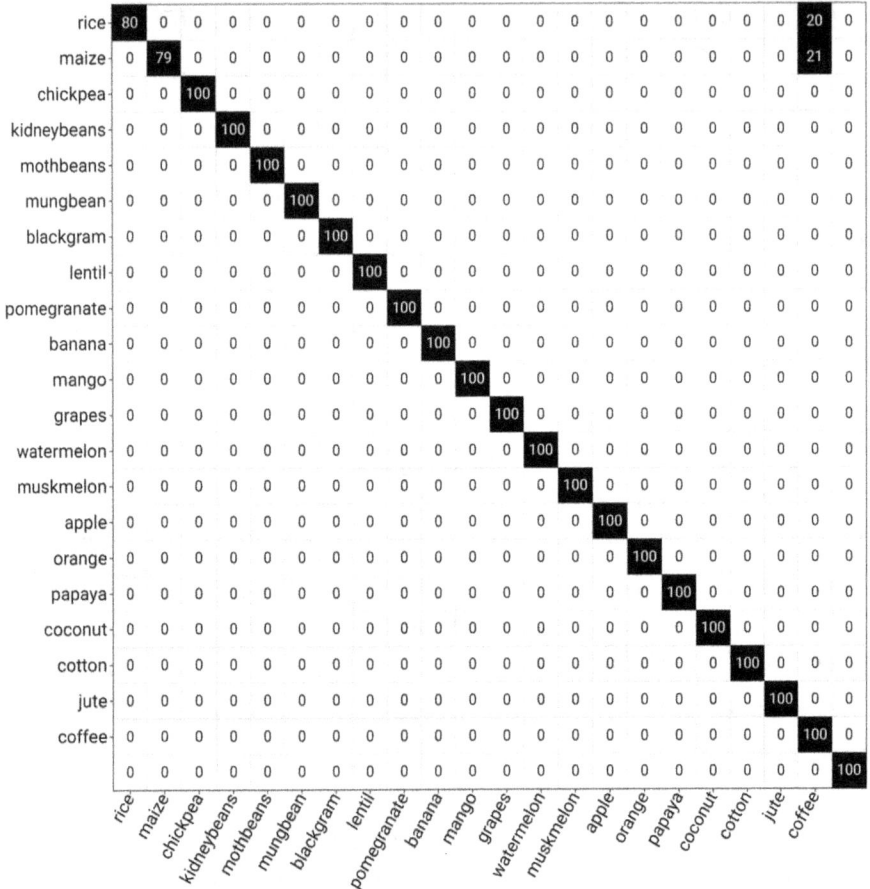

Figure 3-11. Confusion matrix for decision trees

3.4.4 Random Forest

Similar to previous two classification algorithm, the same inputs are applied to the random forest algorithm, and the outputs are tabulated as in Table 3-7. Six different test data with their known output are applied, and the results are compared to the true class.

CHAPTER 3   A CROP RECOMMENDATION SYSTEM USING MACHINE LEARNING ALGORITHMS
            FOR ACHIEVING SDGS 2, 9, AND 12

Table 3-7. Random Forest Algorithm

N	P	K	Temperature	Humidity	Ph	Rainfall	Results Obtained
100	53	41	24.52	80.94	6.35	200.1	Rice
50	42	20	23.44	60.54	6.89	72.44	Maize
41	60	75	25.56	20.22	9.0	78.55	Chickpea
5	10	3	9.55	100.50	8.55	120.33	Orange
95	30	22	26.91	50.74	7.42	140.48	Coffee

The accuracy obtained after running the decision tree model is 0.981.

It can be seen that when the input values for the different crops' requirements are fed to the model, the recommended crop is accurately proposed by the RF algorithm. The crop classification are also in conformity with the k-NN outcomes and highlight RF's accuracy. Additionally, the confusion matrix in Figure 3-12 signifies the accuracy and performance of the model, whereby the RF algorithm correctly recommends the best possible crop for every input, achieving 100% for every class. The random forest algorithm is very accurate since it comprises a collection of decision trees, allowing the model to generalize over the dataset better and provide an average of the results. RF is also efficient for this dataset since there are seven features, which allow an ensemble of the decisions, resulting in a not too deep tree solution, compared to decision trees, which considers all features at once. RF's ability to generalize over data without overfitting, yielding highly accurate results, makes it an excellent candidate for crop recommendation problems.

CHAPTER 3   A CROP RECOMMENDATION SYSTEM USING MACHINE LEARNING ALGORITHMS FOR ACHIEVING SDGS 2, 9, AND 12

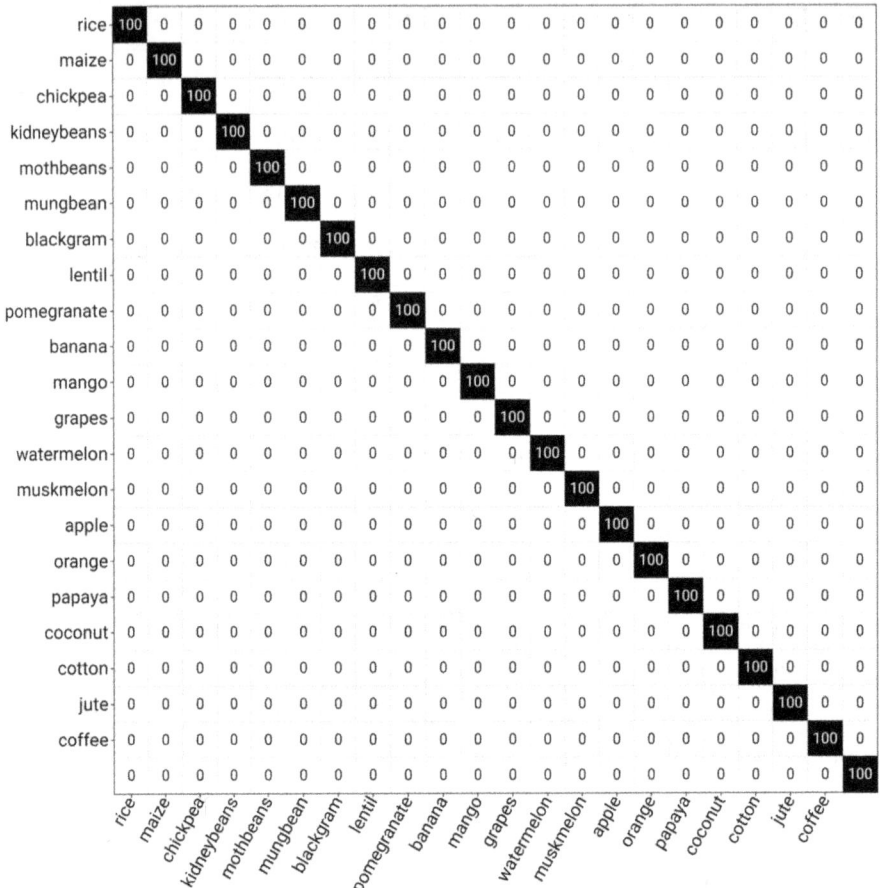

Figure 3-12. Confusion matrix for random forest algorithm

3.4.5 Multilayer Perceptron

For this experiment, the multilayer perceptron algorithm is tested with the number of input features being 7, for the amount of phosphorus, potassium and nitrogen, temperature, humidity, pH value, and rainfall. The number of hidden layers was set to 44, learning rate at 0.01 and error threshold at 0.005. The results obtained have been tabulated in Table 3-8.

Table 3-8. *Number of Epochs = 25 000*

_	_	_	Number of Epochs: 25 000				
N	P	K	Temperature	Humidity	pH	Rainfall	Result Obtained
100	53	41	24.52	80.94	6.35	200.1	Chickpea
50	42	20	23.44	60.54	6.89	72.44	Jute
41	60	75	25.56	20.22	9.0	78.55	Chickpea
5	10	3	9.55	100.50	8.55	120.33	Orange
95	30	22	26.91	50.74	7.42	140.48	Chickpea
			Model Accuracy: 77.2 %				

The number of epochs was increased to 50 000 and the results have been tabulated as shown in Table 3-9.

Table 3-9. *Number of Epochs = 50 000*

_	_	_	Number of Epochs: 50 000				
N	P	K	Temperature	Humidity	pH	Rainfall	Result Obtained
100	53	41	24.52	80.94	6.35	200.1	Jute
50	42	20	23.44	60.54	6.89	72.44	Maize
41	60	75	25.56	20.22	9.0	78.55	Chickpea
5	10	3	9.55	100.50	8.55	120.33	Orange
95	30	22	26.91	50.74	7.42	140.48	Coffee
			Model Accuracy: 89.3 %				

The number of epochs has been increased to 100 000. Table 3-10 shows the results obtained.

CHAPTER 3   A CROP RECOMMENDATION SYSTEM USING MACHINE LEARNING ALGORITHMS FOR ACHIEVING SDGS 2, 9, AND 12

Table 3-10. *Number of Epochs = 100 000*

\multicolumn{8}{c}{Number of Epochs: 100 000}
N	P	K	Temperature	Humidity	pH	Rainfall	Result Obtained
100	53	41	24.52	80.94	6.35	200.1	Jute
50	42	20	23.44	60.54	6.89	72.44	Blackgram
41	60	75	25.56	20.22	9.0	78.55	Chickpea
5	10	3	9.55	100.50	8.55	120.33	Orange
95	30	22	26.91	50.74	7.42	140.48	Coffee
			Model Accuracy: 90%				

It is observed that when increasing the number of iterations, the model accuracy increases. For 25,000 iterations, the accuracy of the model was equal to 77.2%. The output obtained based on the values of the inputs was highly inaccurate, as for multiple different values, the model was classifying them as chickpea. When increasing the number of epochs to 50,000, a higher accuracy of 89.3% was obtained. The predicted labels were more accurate than the previous results obtained. Setting the number of iterations at 100,000, showed a slightly improvement in the model's accuracy. However, further testing was performed with the number of epochs equal to 150,000. The results obtained showed that the model accuracy dropped below 90%, possibly caused due to overfitting. The model begins to memorize the training data if it is trained for an excessively long period of time rather than learning to generalize to new, untried data. Monitoring the model's performance on validation data and applying strategies like early halting or regularization are crucial for reducing overfitting.

Figure 3-13 shows the confusion matrix obtained for MLP. It can be observed that for rice, there is 42% confusion with coffee. Coconut also gives a probability of 24% while being confused with coffee data. The

CHAPTER 3   A CROP RECOMMENDATION SYSTEM USING MACHINE LEARNING ALGORITHMS
              FOR ACHIEVING SDGS 2, 9, AND 12

ambiguity of some data values may make it difficult for any model to anticipate them with accuracy. In this circumstance, the model generated both false positives and false negatives.

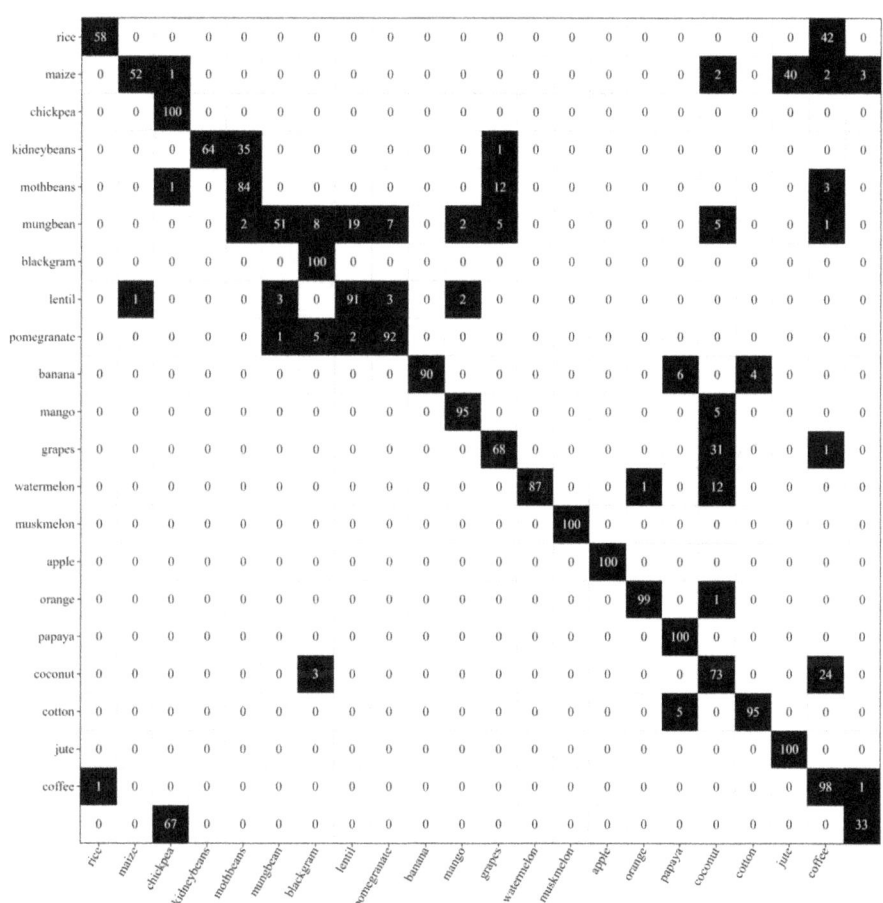

Figure 3-13. Confusion matrix for MLP

3.4.6 Discussion

All four algorithms demonstrated very high accuracy in crop classification methods. Each ML method accurately recommends the best adaptable crop, based on the soil composition and the amount of rainfall a land is normally subjected to. Each algorithm employed is distinct, and each exhibits different working strategies leading to the classification results. Table 3-11 summarizes the accuracy obtained for each algorithm implemented.

Table 3-11. Accuracy of ML Algorithms Used

Algorithm	Accuracy (%)
k-NN	99
Decision Trees	98
Random Forest	100
Multilayer Perceptron	90

Table 3-11 indicates that random forest algorithm showcased the highest accuracy in crop classification. RF stands out as the best model that can be used in helping toward the SDG goals targeted. The four ML models used would help farmers and cultivators as well as the agriculture industry to innovatively identify what crop is viable and cultivable on the type of soil compositions the land has, which will lead to effective and productive crop yield after harvesting. An advantage of the dataset is that it encompasses an extended number of features, NPK variants, pH Value, and rainfall entailed by the crop type for harvest.

The results allow the users to plan their crop harvesting throughout the year, maximizing crop yield through every season, by knowing the best cultivable crop through the ML model. The web application enables industries having expansive lands for agriculture over different regions, which are subjected to different environmental conditions, to efficiently grow the required crop, pertaining to the specific soil nutrients and rainfall, aiding extensively to SDG 9.

Furthermore, effective, and maximized crop yield contributes massively to responsible production and decreases to a large extent the scarcity of food supply throughout the market, thus contributing to SDGs 2 and 12. Use of ML for crop recommendation diminishes manual computations, inaccuracies, and estimations. Traditional method for crop selection involves soil testing, used for historical data for comparison and the need for agricultural experts to estimate the crop with highest yield rate. These methods have already proven to be inaccurate and are merely estimations, due to the decrease in crop yield. The ML algorithms make use of rainfall factor, which helps as an adaptation to climate change. Industries and farmers would learn which crop adapts efficiently to their climate. Each algorithms has its benefits and disadvantages.

RF's ensemble learning with high accuracy and good generalization over data highlights its effectiveness for the crop recommendation system. However, trade-offs for such accuracy are extended storage requirements and increased prediction time. Use of larger dataset will enhance the model's performance, with lesser overfitting and increased accuracy of predictions.

One of the major benefits of using the k-NN model is its ease of implementation. It is also flexible allowing the possibility to fine-tune the model for different values of k. However, when dealing with large datasets, k-NN can become computationally expensive. This is because of the calculation of the Euclidean distance. And so, this model is inappropriate for real-time applications. With the distance functions, k-NN can be easily influenced by the presence of noisy data points and outliers in the dataset.

MLPs are well suited for a wide range of tasks because they can model complicated, nonlinear relationships in data. Increasing the number of hidden layers and neurons, MLPs can be scaled up making them adaptable for simple and complex datasets. When the model learns to memorize the training data instead of generalizing from it, MLPs, especially deep networks with many parameters, are vulnerable to overfitting. To counteract this phenomenon, careful regularization approaches are required. An MLP's architecture, including its number of layers, neurons, and activation functions, needs to be carefully tuned, which can take some time. When applying a different learning rate when training model with this dataset, the application would freeze and take a lot of time to output the model.

3.5 Summary

The aim of this chapter was to show how machine learning algorithms could be used to achieve SDGs 2, 9, and 12. The dataset obtained through research consisted of data related to 22 different crops. Essentially, a web application was developed that would read the dataset and apply different machine learning algorithms. A dependency called ml.js was used to implement algorithms such as k-NN, decision tree, random forest classifier, and multilayer perceptron. Each algorithm was tested using different hyperparameters respective to the algorithm.

The results obtained showed that the random forest classifier gave the highest accurate model compared to the other algorithms. The different machine learning algorithms applied to the crop dataset helps to reduce manual computations and inaccuracies in choosing which crop to plant depending on the different variables. This would help in increasing the percentage of crop yield, helping to accomplish the sustainable development goals. A typical limitation of this report is the use of only one dataset to test the different ML algorithms. More research could be performed to find more datasets that can be used to test how the ML algorithms perform. Moreover, additional classification algorithms such as K-Means, hierarchical clustering, and others can be implemented in the application. The main conclusion is that ML can help achieve SDGs by performing predictions and classifications with higher accuracy than traditional methods of data analysis. An interesting future work would be to use more datasets related to crops and analyze how each machine-learning algorithm would perform.

CHAPTER 4

Aligning Manufacturing Emissions with SDGs 9 and 13 Using Machine Learning Algorithms

Chapter authors:
Mohadeb Sai Maadhavee, sai.mohadeb@umail.uom.ac.mu
Radhakeesoon Aishani, aishani.radhakeesoon@umail.uom.ac.mu
Seeballack Oushna, oushna.seeballack@umail.uom.ac.mu

The UN Sustainable Development Goals (SDGs) are a global blueprint for addressing social, economic, and environmental challenges. The emergent tool of machine learning (ML) provides an innovative approach for sustainable development. This chapter focuses on SDG 9 (Industry, Innovation, and Infrastructure) and SDG 13 (Climate Action) by employing ML algorithms using regression techniques to predict and quantify the

CHAPTER 4 ALIGNING MANUFACTURING EMISSIONS WITH SDGS 9 AND 13 USING MACHINE LEARNING ALGORITHMS

impact on the targeted SDGs. The methodology involves the selection of diverse datasets encompassing carbon dioxide (CO_2), greenhouse gas (GHG) emissions, gross domestic product (GDP) annual growth, and population count of the manufacturing industry in Mauritius.

Simple linear regression (SLR), multiple linear regression (MLR), and k-nearest neighbors (k-NN) algorithms were used to determine the relationships between economic factors, demographics, and environmental impact. The application of ML algorithms provides predictions and insights for sustainability by shedding light on how GDP and population influence CO_2 and GHG emissions in the manufacturing sector. Moreover, the difference between predicted GHG and CO_2 emissions was further computed to obtain a numerical value pertaining to other gases contributing to the greenhouse effect and by using the threshold value of 25,000 metric tons set by the U.S. Environmental Protection Agency (EPA), and necessary measures were highlighted on whether the predicted value of GHG emissions exceeds or falls below the threshold. Based on the results obtained, for the SLR algorithm the accuracy for CO_2 emission was 82.704% and for GHG emission was 84.117%.

For the MLR algorithm the accuracy for CO_2 emission was 88.818%, and for GHG emission was 89.215%. It was noted that the accuracy for MLR was higher than SLR, thus indicating better model accuracy for prediction. The main novelty is the use of regression techniques to forecast GHG emissions in manufacturing industry with its related impacts and sustainable solutions. Thus, the adopted ML integration with industry and climate action emphasizes the possibility of catalyzing transformative change in achieving the SDGs.

CHAPTER 4 ALIGNING MANUFACTURING EMISSIONS WITH SDGS 9 AND 13 USING MACHINE LEARNING ALGORITHMS

4.1 Introduction

The SDGs, also known as global goals, represent a worldwide initiative urging collective efforts to alleviate poverty, safeguard the planet, and guarantee that every individual lives in peace, justice, and prosperity by 2030 [1]. They were embraced by all countries in the United Nations, as an integral component of the 2030 Agenda for Sustainable Development. There are 17 SDGs with 169 targets, each with distinct objectives and indicators [2].

This assignment targets two of these SDGs: SDGs 9 and 13. SDG 9 centers around industry, innovation, and infrastructure, and SDG 13 focuses on climate action [3]. Machine learning (ML) algorithms play a crucial role in advancing these goals by offering innovative solutions for sustainable development. Integrating ML into SDGs highlights its transformative potential to accelerate progress toward a more sustainable and equitable world. For instance, it can be applied to forecast the energy efficiency of residential areas using classifiers like decision trees (DT).

Furthermore, neural and Bayesian network models can be used to create models that optimize environmental protection for industrial facilities and goods. It has become possible to understand the priorities of sustainable development using various ML algorithms such as K-nearest neighbors (k-NN), naïve Bayes (NB), decision trees (DT), and support vector machine (SVM) [4].

Another example of ML used in the context of UN SDGs can be found in in [5], where the long short-term memory (LSTM) deep learning algorithm predicted energy demand in a smart power grid, in line with SDG 13 on climate action. There was a comparative results analysis with other forecasting algorithms: Facebook Prophet, random forest (RF), and support vector regression (SVR). The ability of the ML algorithm to contribute to achieving SDG 9, 13, and, additionally, SDG 7 was assessed[5]. Moreover in [6], 17 SDG datasets (including SDG 9 and 13) from five states of South India (Andhra Pradesh, Karnataka, Kerala, Tamil

Nadu and Telangana) were considered. The ML techniques employed to obtain numerical results included Gaussian process, linear regression, RF, and REP tree with specific accuracy parameters set [6].

The primary focus of this chapter is to analyze the relationship between SDG 9 and SDG 13 by predicting carbon dioxide (CO_2) and greenhouse gas (GHG) emissions in the manufacturing industry, considering gross domestic product (GDP) annual growth and population as contributing factors. A methodology that combined data-driven analysis and regression techniques was employed.

For the prediction of CO_2 and GHG emissions, the principles of regression techniques established a mathematical relationship between the independent variables (GDP and population) and the dependent variables (CO_2 and GHG emissions). The regression models such as simple linear regression (SLR), multiple linear regression (MLR), and k-nearest neighbors (k-NN) provided valuable insights regarding the extent to which changes in GDP and population impact the variations in emissions while analyzing the correlation between contributing factors and prediction of CO_2 and GHG.

The main findings revealed significant linkages between GDP, population, and emissions in the manufacturing industry whereby as GDP and population grew, there was a corresponding increase in CO_2 and GHG emissions. These findings highlighted the intricate connection between economic development and the environmental impact of the manufacturing industry, emphasizing the importance of aligning SDG 9's goals to foster sustainable industrialization with SDG 13's priority to mitigate climate change.

CHAPTER 4 ALIGNING MANUFACTURING EMISSIONS WITH SDGS 9 AND 13 USING MACHINE LEARNING ALGORITHMS

The main research questions addressed in this chapter are as follows:

i To what extent do GDP and population contribute to CO_2 and GHG emissions in the manufacturing industry?

ii How accurately do linear regression models such as SLR and MLR predict emissions based on GDP and population data?

iii How accurately does the k-NN algorithm predict the emissions values?

iv How can the predicted data be further analyzed?

The main novelty proposed in this chapter is the use of regression techniques using SLR, MLR, and k-NN to derive multifaceted perspective on the forecast of GHG emissions pertaining to the manufacturing industry, which paves the way for more data-driven and sustainable solutions to mitigate the impacts of greenhouse effect on climate.

4.2 Use Cases for SDGs 9 and 13

This section will review the analysis conducted by other researchers that are related to the application of ML algorithms to achieve UN SDGs.

A "ML-driven decision support model for implementing greenhouse gas reduction" was introduced in [7]. Lee and Tae proposed the use of ML techniques to assess greenhouse gas (GHG) reduction, aiming to determine the economic and environmental benefits of GHG reduction technologies. They analyzed 1,199 GHG reduction projects in Korea by developing the simple assessment method (SAM) database for assessing GHG technologies. Subsequently, ML models such as gradient boosted regression trees (GBRTs), SVM, and deep neural networks (DNNs) were employed to create the GHG reduction technology assessment model (GRTM) decision-support tool. Among the three ML models, DNN demonstrated a better predictive accuracy. A practical case study confirmed the potential to reduce 111 tons of CO_2-equivalent emissions through optimal GHG reduction technologies like high-efficiency lighting, solar power, and geothermal energy, correcting an initial overestimation of 358 tons. The study shows the application of ML in assessing GHG reduction technologies while considering real-world building conditions and data.

A study was conducted by authors[8] where they developed a machine-learning model using regression-kriging to categorize the radiative energy flux at the earth's surface. The objective was to promote environmental sustainability by using solar panels. The study used multiple input factors and data modeling to assess environmental sustainability and involved conducting several simulations to evaluate the model's effectiveness. The results demonstrated a significant improvement in sustainability when compared to other approaches. The study shows how ML models can be employed to promote sustainable practices and reduce environmental impact.

A study was proposed by Piryonesi and El-Diraby [9] on the impact of climate change on infrastructures by employing ML to predict pavement condition index. Various machine algorithms including DT, k-NN, NB classifier, RF, and gradient-boosted trees were tested on a vast dataset extracted from the Long-Term Pavement Performance (LTPP) database. Subsequently, the last three algorithms achieved the highest accuracy of at least 90%. The attributes for the model were deliberately selected, to associate them with the climate stressors including temperature ranges, perspiration, and freeze-thaw cycle to allow the models to quantify the impact of climate change.

The proposed tool enables the examination of the impacts of different climate scenarios by inputting attributes specific to each scenario. To illustrate its utility, the tool was used to assess the deterioration of two sets of roads, one in Ontario and another in Texas, under two different climate scenarios. The analysis revealed that the Ontario roads exhibited lower levels of deterioration, while the roads in Texas experienced an exacerbation of deterioration. This suggests that the effects of climate change on road deterioration vary by location.

In [10] Asadikia et al. the authors showcased a technique using an ML algorithm to prioritize SDGs based on their synergetic properties. The primary goal of this paper was to discover synergies among SDGs through the use of the Boosted Regression Trees model, which is an ML and data mining technique. Their study illustrates how each SDG contributed to the formation of the SDG index, and a "what-if" analysis was performed to understand the importance of these goal scores. The results demonstrated that their scores were greater than 60%, and SDGs 3, 4, and 7 exhibited the highest synergies. These research findings can guide decision-makers in implementing effective strategies and resource allocation, by prioritizing goals that have high synergy.

The authors in [11] proposed and evaluated several ML models for their predictive performance considered as DT, RF, k-NN, and Support Vector Regression (SVR) to predict metro ridership in line to achieve sustainable transportation and environment while contributing to the SDGs 9, 11, 12, and 13. The transportation sector faces prolonged and intense congestion, and vehicles contribute to 25% of CO_2 emissions, which are dependent on non-renewable energy. Innovative solutions for sustainable transport necessitated the use of computational technology to evaluate a metro transport system for sustainable development in line to reduce CO_2 emissions. The analysis of the prediction's accuracy on the test data with the ML used are as follows: 87.4% with DT using the CART algorithm, 84.4% with k-NN, and 69.7% using SVR.

In [12], the use of ML algorithm ANN by Rao et al., consisting of 2 layers of neurons, promoted the usage of renewable energy sources while mitigating the impact of CO_2 emissions to achieve SDGs 7 and 13. From the ML results, the error of the model was measured using evaluation metrics Root Mean Squared Error (RMSE) and Mean Absolute Percentage

Error (MAPE). The MAPE value was 0.3, which is 30% as a percentage representation. Thus, the accuracy of the artificial neural network (ANN) model, which predicted the amount of CO_2 generated by the use of clean and renewable energy sources, is 70%.

The study by Sami et al. [13] meticulously compared the accuracy of machine and deep learning algorithms such as convolutional neural network (CNN), support vector machine (SVM), RF, and DT to automate waste classification, which can be categorized in SDGs 9 and 12 with industrial waste management. The models' results are as follows; CNN provided a high accuracy value of 90%, SVM had an accuracy value of 85%, DT had 65% accuracy, and RF was 55% accurate.

The work of Liu et al. in [14] analyzed the interconnections of SDG 8 and SDG 13 whereby climate actions can have both synergies and trade-offs for economic growth and social employment. ML algorithms such as RF and extreme gradient boosting (XGB) were used to capture the impacts of climate change on the economy. The overall accuracies were determined as 78% and 72% for XGB and RF models, respectively.

The enthusiasm of the Asian youth for achieving SDGs was evaluated Gaur et al. [15] . Evidence of the successful use of ML algorithms to highlight their viewpoints about a sustainable future was provided. In the study, building blocks from previous research were used, and a comparative analysis of the prediction accuracy of Adaptive Neuro-Fuzzy Inference System (ANFIS) and RF models for three categories of SDGs was made. Possible differences in viewpoints on the importance of the categories among both Asian and Serbian youth were considered. Data collection was from 425 youth respondents. ANFIS better predicted SDGs than the RF model. The Asian and Serbian youth had the greatest SDG preference for the environment, followed by the society and, lastly, the economy.

Conventional and intelligent control methods were studied by Parvin et al. in [16] with emphasis on their classification, configuration, features, pros and cons. Different optimization objectives and constraints as

CHAPTER 4 ALIGNING MANUFACTURING EMISSIONS WITH SDGS 9 AND 13 USING MACHINE LEARNING ALGORITHMS

applicable to energy consumption, comfort management, and scheduling were investigated. Different methodological approaches to optimization algorithms used in building energy management were outlined, and the contributions of controller and optimization in relation to SDGs were critically explained. Building Energy Management System (BEMS) can represent a sustainable model to improve economic growth, linked to SDG 9.1. Additionally, BEMS contribute to addressing environmental impacts, related to SDG 13. In BEMS, the control methods can be classified into conventional and intelligent. However, the intelligent approach is preferred due to their design based self-learning skills. In the intelligent approach, either learning methods are used or model-based predictive control methods are used. The learning methods include hybrid methods, ANN, and fuzzy system.

In a study by Ghaffarian and Emtehani in [17], the monitoring of deprived urban areas over a 4-year period, following the impact of super Typhoon Haiyan, in the Philippines, in 2013, has been considered using both satellite imagery and ML methods. The severity and impact of natural disasters in such areas has significantly increased, requiring effective disaster risk reduction strategies as catered for in SDG 13. A SVM classification method supported by a local binary pattern feature extraction model initially detected slum areas in pre and post disaster imageries. Afterward, a dense conditional random fields model produced final slum areas maps. The developed method detected slum areas with high accuracy. The results revealed that the city returned to the pre-existing vulnerability level.

The research by [15] the predictive accuracy of the adaptive neuro-fuzzy inference system (ANFIS) and RF ML models were compared for three categories of SDGs (environmental, social, and economic). ANFIS better predicted SDGs than the RF model. The SDG preference among Asian and Serbian youth was found to be highest for the environmental pillar.

4.3 Data Processing and Application Design

4.3.1 Data Collection Process and Description of Datasets

We gathered data from multiple sources to create a diverse dataset that would be used to predict the amount of CO_2 emissions and GHG emissions caused by the manufacturing sector in Mauritius.

- We gathered data on CO_2 emissions by sector and GHG emissions by sector from the Our World in Data website. The dataset includes information for multiple countries, sectors such as manufacturing, transportation and others, and years from 1990 to 2019 [18] [19].

- Furthermore, we have integrated population numbers and annual GDP growth data in Mauritius from "The World Bank" website from 1990 to 2019. This step enabled us to understand the correlation between GDP and CO_2 emissions, as well as greenhouse gas emissions originating from the manufacturing sector in Mauritius [20] [21].

After gathering these datasets, we extracted information specific to Mauritius while eliminating the missing values and duplicates. Subsequently, we merged and standardized the data into a unified dataset. Our final dataset consists of 31 records, including population numbers, annual GDP growth, CO_2 emissions, and greenhouse gas emissions for the manufacturing industries, ranging from 1990 to 2019. The target is to predict the emissions of CO_2 and greenhouse gas by manufacturing industries in Mauritius depending on factors like the annual GDP growth and the population number.

Figure 4-1 illustrates a snapshot of our dataset consisting of a few data points;

Country	Year	population	gdp_annual_growth	co2_emissionbpt	ghg_emissionbpt
Mauritius	1990	1058775	7.186736771	170000	180000
Mauritius	1991	1070266	4.435446262	190000	210000
Mauritius	1992	1084441	6.512698583	200000	210000
Mauritius	1993	1097374	5.082062956	270000	280000
Mauritius	1994	1112846	4.136142861	240000	250000
Mauritius	1995	1122457	4.287736571	240000	260000
Mauritius	1996	1133996	5.587843927	250000	260000
Mauritius	1997	1148284	5.687477419	250000	260000
Mauritius	1998	1160421	6.071940178	270000	290000

Figure 4-1. *A few data points from our dataset*

4.3.2 Data Preprocessing Steps

In the data preprocessing stage, the raw data is prepared and converted to a suitable format before sending the data to the ML model. In the data that we considered, there were some outliers that were manually removed. Through data preprocessing, specific tasks such as data cleaning and manually removing some outliers to increase the efficiency of the ML model. Additionally, only a specific year range (1990 to 2019) has been considered since the parameters seemed to have more coherent values for analysis.

The data preprocessing stage has been split into the following stages.

Stages of Data Preprocessing

- **Data cleaning:** In the combined CSV file, information about country, year, population, annual GDP growth, amount of CO_2 emitted, and amount of GHG emitted is available. Inaccurate, duplicated, or null values were detected a second time to improve the quality of our work.

CHAPTER 4   ALIGNING MANUFACTURING EMISSIONS WITH SDGS 9 AND 13 USING MACHINE LEARNING ALGORITHMS

- **Noisy data:** Noisy data refers to unwanted data that in our case is information pertaining to other sectors (other than the manufacturing sector). An outlier can also be a source of noisy data and consequently has been removed.

- **Missing data:** For some parameters, data was missing. However, most ML algorithms do not handle missing values. Among the several approaches available to deal with mission data from the dataset, we visually identified the missing data due to the large attribute numerical values. The removal of missing values will not largely impact the distribution of the dataset. Some attributes had null values. However, we chose not to fill missing values since filling missing values affects outliers' analysis.

There were no structural errors in our dataset, including typos. The reason may have been the numerical nature of the data. The data cleaning stage has been successfully done manually since the disparities were clearly visible.

Feature Selection and Removal of Attributes

Selection of the most important variables (features/attributes) with respect to the prediction variable has been made at this stage.

The selected independent variables were population size (million) and annual GDP growth (%), while the dependent variables were CO_2 and GHG emissions (billion per tons) pertaining to manufacturing sector.

CHAPTER 4 ALIGNING MANUFACTURING EMISSIONS WITH SDGS 9 AND 13 USING MACHINE LEARNING ALGORITHMS

4.4 Program Structure for Analysis

The program structure of the ML models used in this assignment provides a comprehensive exploration of regression techniques to understand and predict CO_2 and GHG emissions. In our pursuit of sustainable industrialization and climate mitigation concerning SDGs 9 and 13, we deployed three distinct methodologies: SLR, MLR, and k-NN. Using HTML, websites were displayed that performed tasks such as CSV file uploading, data parsing, regression analysis, and data visualization using the following libraries:

- ml.js [22]

    ml.js is a ML library used for ML tasks in JavaScript, providing various ML algorithms and tools for data analysis.

- Papaparse.js [23]

    PapaParse is a powerful multithreaded CSV parsing library that runs on web pages that parse files on the local system. It converts it into structured data that can be easily used for analysis.

- Plotly.js [24]

    Plotly.js is a high-level, declarative charting library used for creating interactive and visually appealing data visualizations such as plots and 2D and 3D charts.

- Math.js [25]

    math.js is an extensive mathematics library for JavaScript that allows you to perform various mathematical operations, including algebra, calculus, linear algebra, and matrices.

CHAPTER 4   ALIGNING MANUFACTURING EMISSIONS WITH SDGS 9 AND 13 USING MACHINE LEARNING ALGORITHMS

Note that all the code of this chapter is found in the folder Chapter 4 - Codes hosted on the GitHub page of this book. Figure 4-2 shows the program structure of the HTML files with each ML algorithms functions' and interconnections.

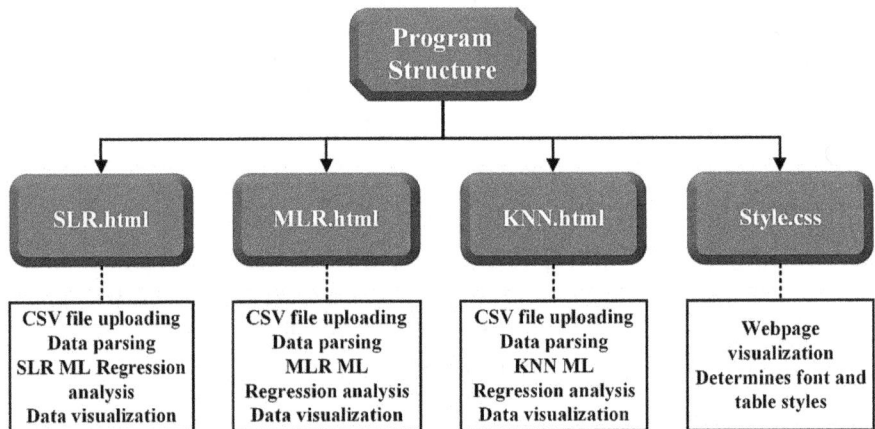

Figure 4-2. *Program structure*

Figure 4-3 illustrates the general layout of the MLR website. The ML algorithms, namely, SLR and k-NN, adhere to the same general layout showcased in Figure 4-2.

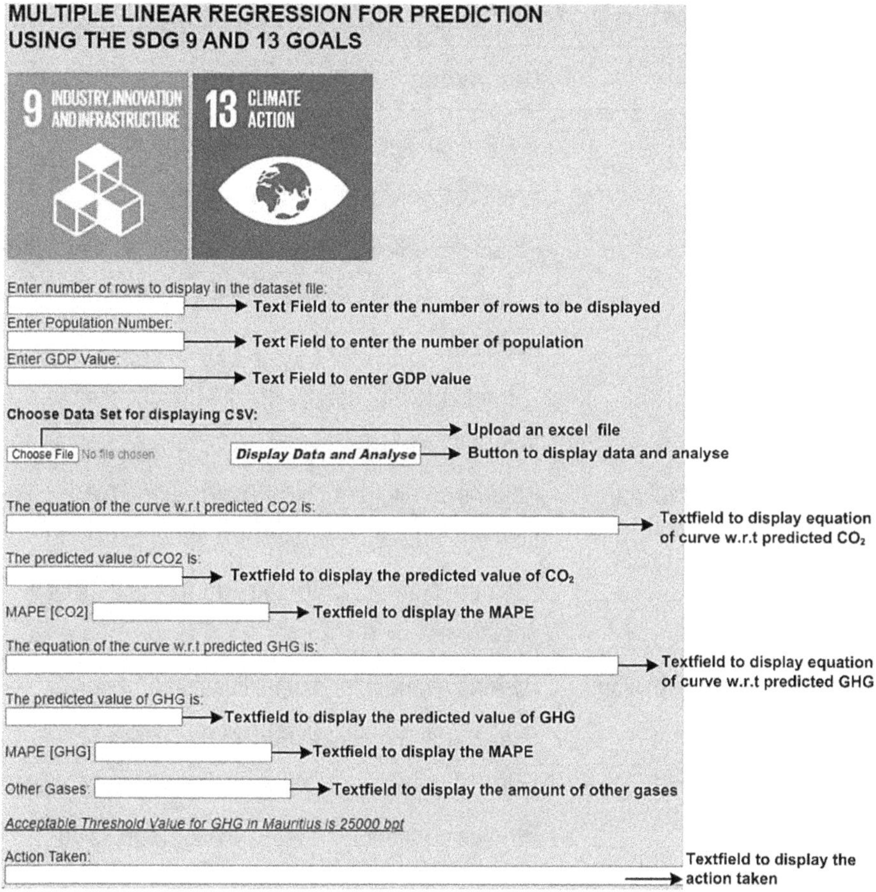

CHAPTER 4   ALIGNING MANUFACTURING EMISSIONS WITH SDGS 9 AND 13 USING MACHINE LEARNING ALGORITHMS

Figure 4-3. General layout of web application

Table 4-1 describes all the functions and methods for each SLR, MLR, and k-NN regression algorithm.

CHAPTER 4 ALIGNING MANUFACTURING EMISSIONS WITH SDGS 9 AND 13 USING MACHINE LEARNING ALGORITHMS

Table 4-1. *Functions and Methods: SLR, MLR, and k-NN Algorithm*

Methods	Description
FileReader()	Creates an object to read the content of a file
reader.onload(){}	Event listener for successful loading of file
Papa.parse()	Reads the CSV file chosen from the local directory
parseFloat()	Converts the value in the CSV file in floating point numbers
array.push()	Extracts the raw data values and populates them in arrays
document.getElementById()	Returns an element object representing the element whose ID matches the specified string
Math.sqrt()	Uses the Math.js library to perform square root operation
ML.SimpleLinearRegression()	Creates a model for simple linear regression
regression.predict()	Uses the SLR model to predict the values of CO_2/GHG based on the user's provided input values
ML.MultivariateLinearRegression()	Creates a model for multiple linear regression
mlr.predict()	Uses the MLR model to predict the values of CO_2/GHG based on the user's provided input values
ML.KNN()	Creates a model for k-NN
knn.predict()	Uses the k-NN model to predict the values of CO_2/GHG based on the user's provided input values

(*continued*)

CHAPTER 4 ALIGNING MANUFACTURING EMISSIONS WITH SDGS 9 AND 13 USING MACHINE LEARNING ALGORITHMS

Table 4-1. (*continued*)

Methods	Description
Math.abs()	Returns the absolute value of the MAPE
Plotly.newPlot ()	Generates 3D scatter plots for the original dataset and predicted CO_2 and GHG emissions

4.4.1 Simple Linear Regression (SLR)

Simple linear regression (SLR) was used as a web-based analysis tool for CO_2 and GHG emissions prediction based on the GDP annual growth using ML.SimpleLinearRegression from the ml.js library.

The prediction process is performed when the Upload () function is called upon clicking the Display Data and Analyse button.

The dataset of CO_2 emissions against GDP and GHG emissions against GDP are plotted. The regression line and predicted values of CO_2 and GHG are plotted using the Plotly.js library. Furthermore, MAPE is also calculated, and an Other Gases value is computed as the difference between the GHG and CO_2 emissions. Lastly, a text field was added to indicate the necessary actions to be taken whether the predicted value of GHG emissions exceeds the threshold of 25,000 or not.

Figure 4-4 shows the flowchart of the SLR algorithm.

CHAPTER 4   ALIGNING MANUFACTURING EMISSIONS WITH SDGS 9 AND 13 USING MACHINE LEARNING ALGORITHMS

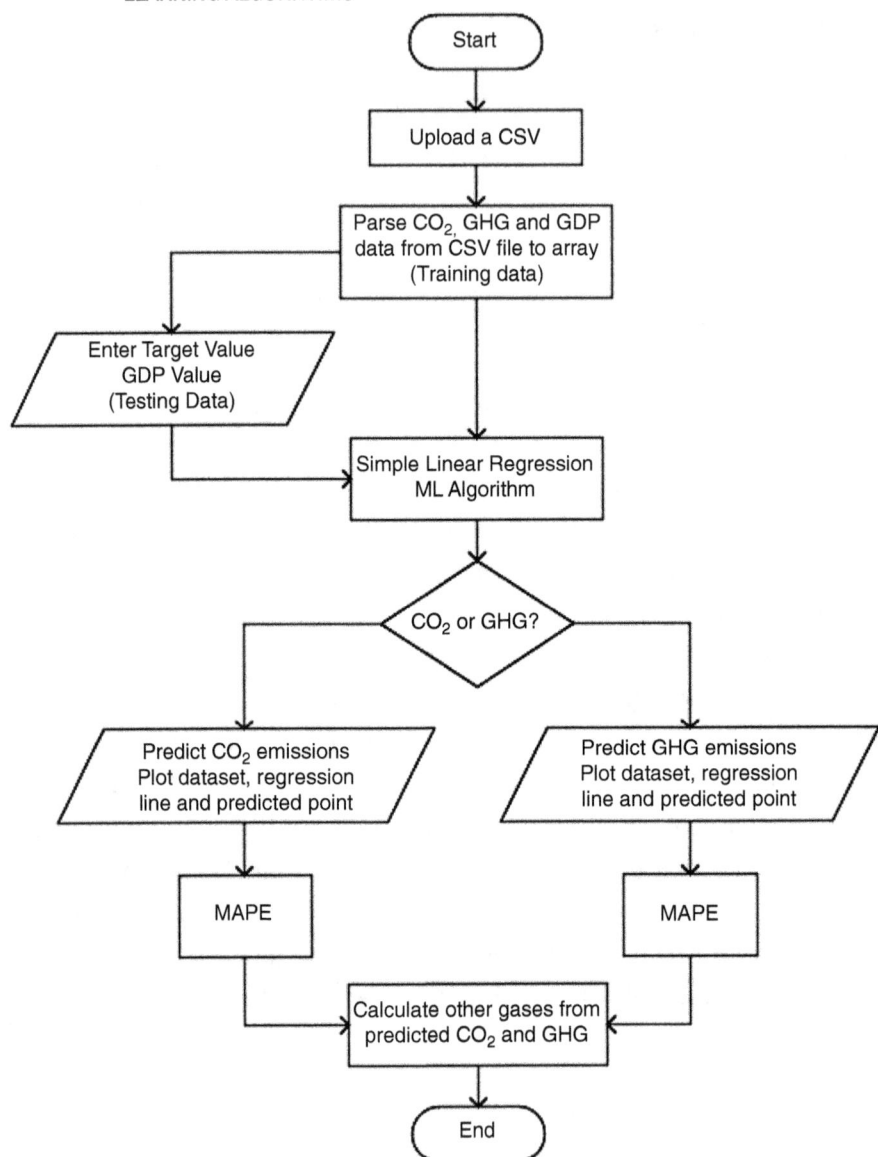

Figure 4-4. *Flowchart, SLR*

Listing 4-1 shows the pseudocode `Upload()` function of the SLR algorithm.

CHAPTER 4   ALIGNING MANUFACTURING EMISSIONS WITH SDGS 9 AND 13 USING MACHINE LEARNING ALGORITHMS

Listing 4-1. Pseudocode Upload() Function: SLR

```
If (valid CSV file uploaded):
   1. Upload and read csv file using PapaParse library.
   2. Specify the number of rows to be read from the csv file.
   3. Specify a target value i.e., GDP value.
   4. Input CO₂, GHG and GDP data to arrays read from the
      csv file.
   5. Perform regression from basic equations.
   6. Calculate the reflection coefficient r of CO₂ and GHG
      using math.js.
   7. Calculate slope, y-intercept and predicted value of CO₂
      and GHG using ML.SimpleLinearRegression library.
   8. Calculate MAPE for CO₂ and GHG.
   9. Generate plots; dataset, regression line and predicted
      points using Plotly.js.
   10. Compute other gases from predicted GHG and CO₂ values.
else:
Specify unsupported CSV file
```

4.4.2 Multiple Linear Regression (MLR)

MLR was used as a predictive model to predict two environmental factors, specifically CO_2 and GHG emissions, based on Mauritius's population size and annual GDP growth using `ML.MultivariateLinearRegression` from the `ml.js` library.

The `Upload()` function is triggered when the Display Data and Analyse button is clicked.

Subsequently, it calculates the MAPE for CO_2 and GHG predictions. Furthermore, it calculates the Other Gases value as the difference between GHG and CO_2 predictions. It also generates 3D scatter plots for the original

CHAPTER 4   ALIGNING MANUFACTURING EMISSIONS WITH SDGS 9 AND 13 USING MACHINE LEARNING ALGORITHMS

dataset and predicted CO_2 and GHG emissions using the `Plotly.js` library. Lastly, a text field was added to indicate the necessary actions to be taken whether the predicted value of GHG emissions exceeds the threshold of 25,000 or not.

Figure 4-5 shows the flowchart of the MLR algorithm.

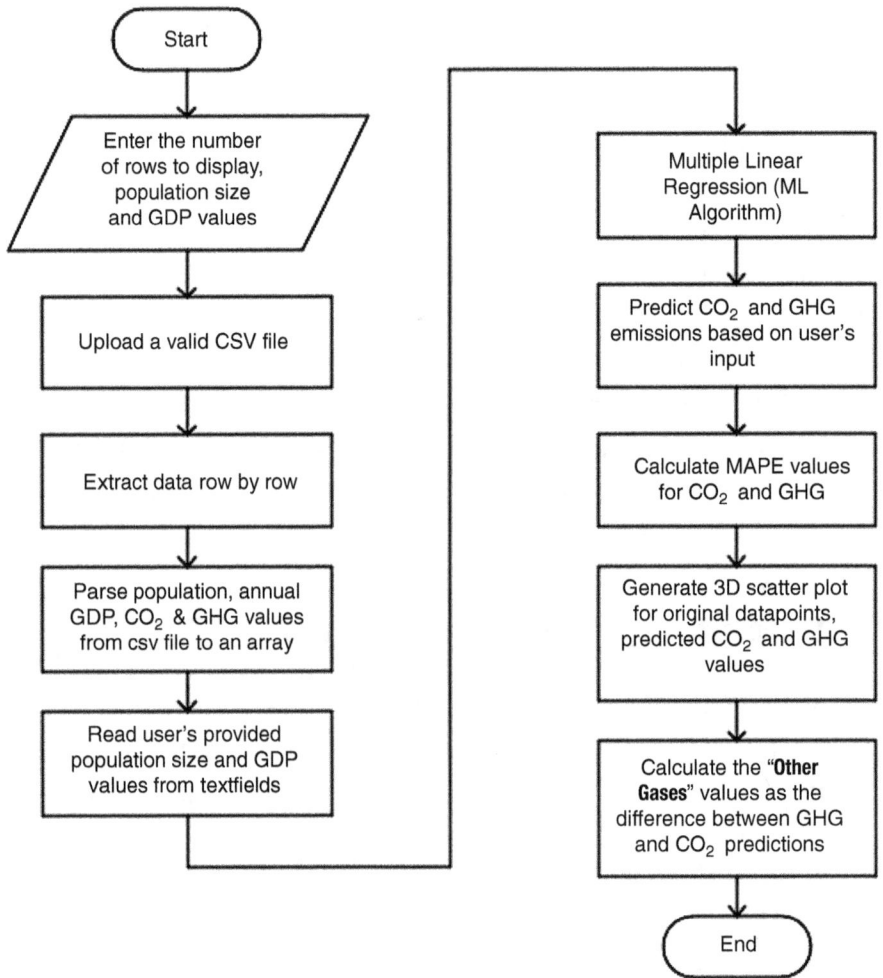

Figure 4-5. Flowchart: MLR

Listing 4-2 shows the pseudocode of the MLR algorithm.

Listing 4-2. Pseudocode Upload() Function: MLR

```
If (valid CSV file uploaded):
  1. Read and parse the uploaded CSV file using the papaparse.js
     library.
  2. Extract data from the CSV file depending on the
     user's input.
  3. Perform MLR for CO₂ and GHG emissions using
     ML.MultivariateLinearRegression.js
  4. Predict CO₂ emissions and GHG emissions based on the
     user's provided population size and GDP values.
  5. Compute the MAPE for CO₂ and GHG using Math.js
  6. Calculate Other Gases as the difference between GHG and
     CO₂ predictions
  7. Generate 3D scatter plots to plot the original data
     points, and predicted CO₂ and GHG emissions using
     plotly.js.
else:
Specify unsupported CSV file
```

4.4.3 k-Nearest Neighbor (k-NN)

The user accesses a web page and can upload a CSV file that consists of information related to the GDP and amount of CO_2 and GHG emissions. ML.KNN from the ml.js library performs k-NN regression to predict the amount of gaseous emissions with respect to population and GDP. 3-D scatter plots then ease data and prediction visualization.

The defined Upload() function will be executed once the user clicks the Display Data and Analyse button on the user interface.

Finally, using the `Plotly.js` library, two 3D scatter plots consisting of predicted and original values were illustrated for the following variables:

- CO_2 emissions against population size and annual GDP growth
- GHG emissions against population size and annual GDP growth

Lastly, a text field was added to indicate the necessary actions to be taken whether the predicted value of GHG emissions exceeds the threshold of 25,000.

Figure 4-6 shows the flowchart of the k-NN algorithm.

CHAPTER 4   ALIGNING MANUFACTURING EMISSIONS WITH SDGS 9 AND 13 USING MACHINE LEARNING ALGORITHMS

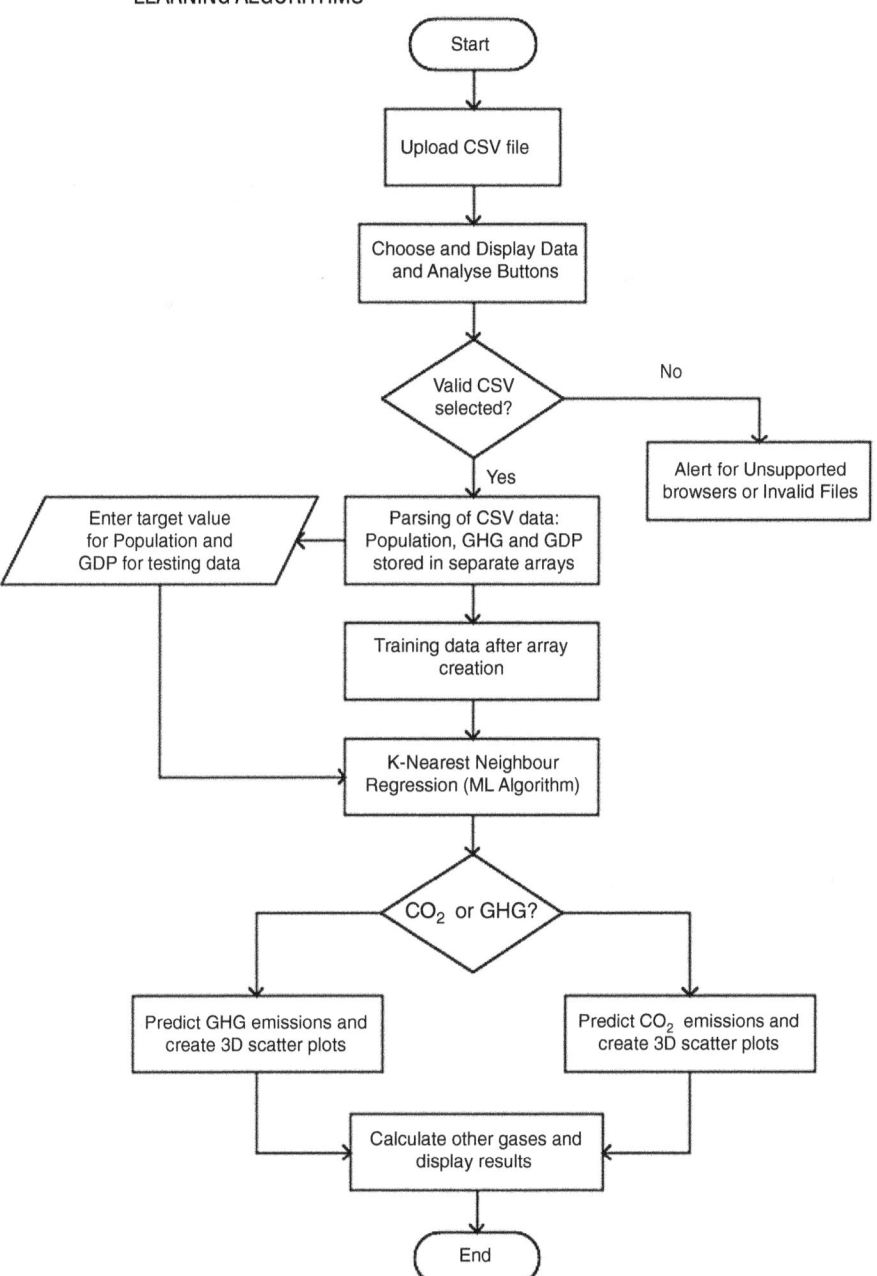

Figure 4-6. *Flowchart: k-NN*

Listing 4-3 shows the pseudocode of the k-NN algorithm.

Listing 4-3. Pseudocode Upload() Function: k-NN

If (valid CSV file uploaded):
  1. Upload and read csv file using PapaParse library.
  2. Specify the number of rows to be read from the csv file.
  3. Enter GDP and population target value for testing dataset.
  4. Apply k-NN regression algorithm using training dataset.
  5. Generate 3-D scatter plots and display predicted values for CO_2 and GHG.
  6. Compute other gases from predicted GHG and CO_2 values.

else:
Specify unsupported CSV file

4.5 Application Testing and Analysis

4.5.1 Simple Linear Regression (SLR)

When the SLR.html program is executed, it prompts the user to enter the number of rows to be displayed from the dataset, enter a value of GDP to be predicted from, and upload a CSV file. Figures 4-7 and 4-8 show the working principle of the program.

CHAPTER 4   ALIGNING MANUFACTURING EMISSIONS WITH SDGS 9 AND 13 USING MACHINE LEARNING ALGORITHMS

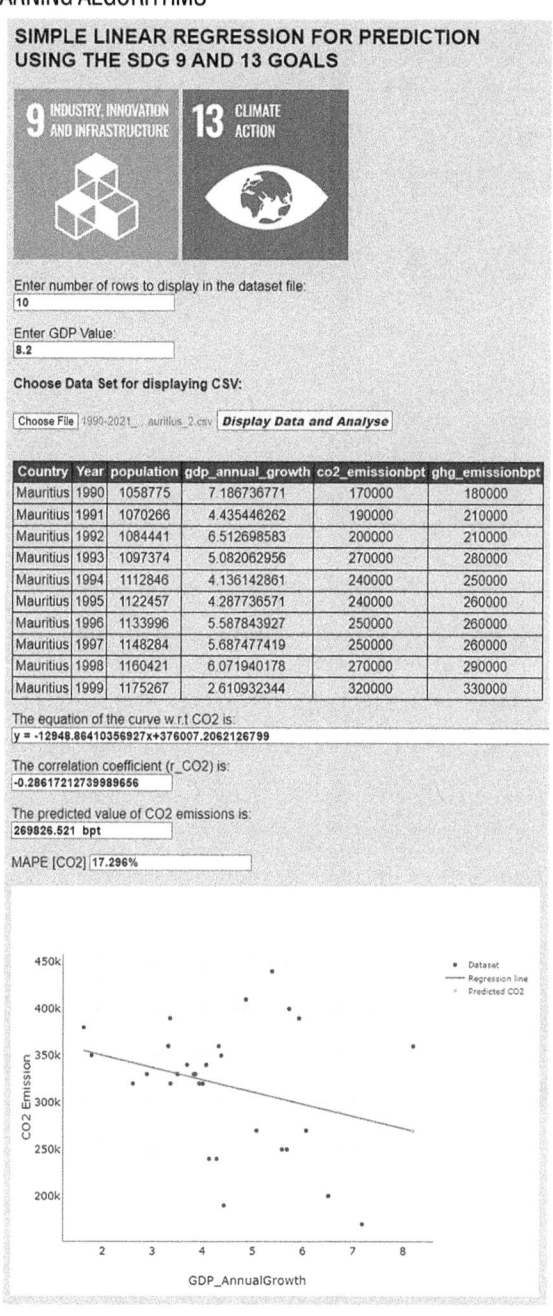

Figure 4-7.   *SLR: Prediction and plot of CO_2 emissions*

CHAPTER 4   ALIGNING MANUFACTURING EMISSIONS WITH SDGS 9 AND 13 USING MACHINE LEARNING ALGORITHMS

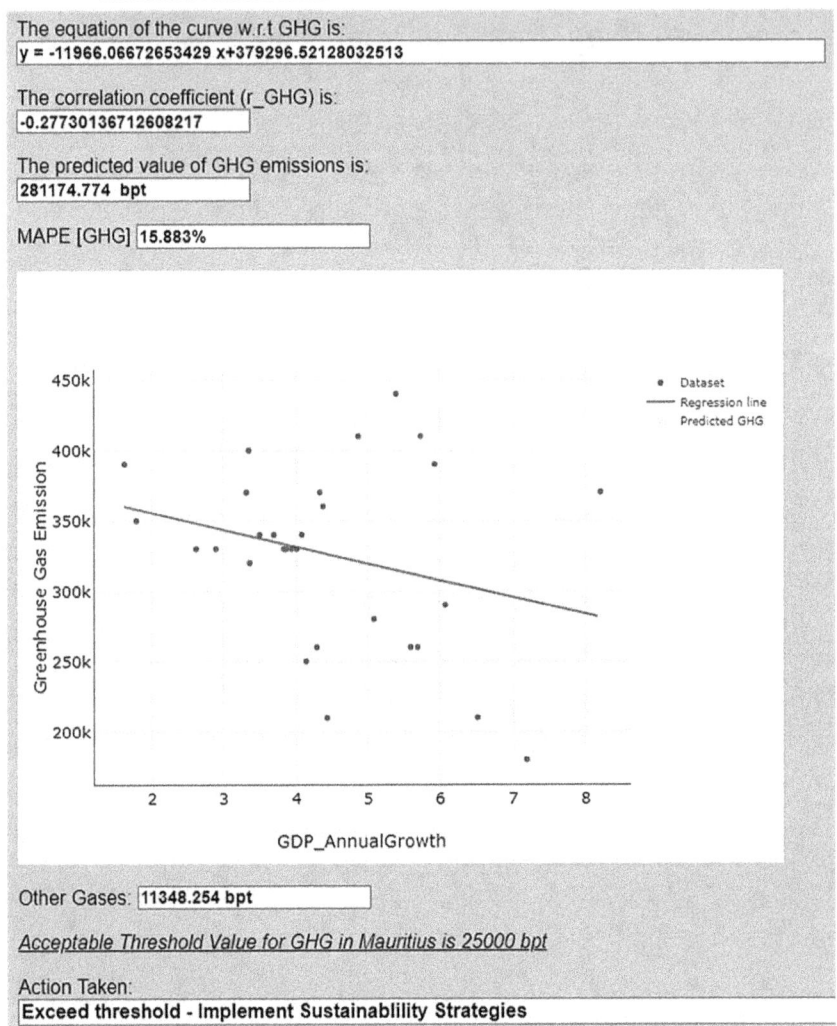

Figure 4-8. SLR: Prediction and Plot of GHG emissions

The results shown in Figure 4-7 illustrate that 10 rows from the CSV dataset were displayed, and the target value for GDP is specified as 8.2. Regression analysis was performed whereby the equation of the line and correlation coefficient was obtained with respect to CO_2, which determined the value of the predicted CO_2 emissions as 269,826.521 bpt.

Likewise, the MAPE for CO_2 is 17.296%, which indicates an accuracy of 82.704% of the SLR model. Moreover, the dataset, regression line, and predicted CO_2 point were plotted on a 2D scatter plot.

Regression analysis was performed whereby the equation of the line and correlation coefficient were obtained with respect to GHG, which determined the value of the predicted GHG emissions as 281,174.774 bpt, as shown in Figure 4-8. Likewise, the MAPE for GHG is 15.883%, which indicates an accuracy of 84.117 % of the model. Moreover, the dataset, regression line and predicted GHG point were plotted on a 2D scatter plot. The value of **Other Gases**, which is the difference between the predicted value of GHG and CO_2, is 11,348.254 bpt. Since the predicted value of GHG emissions exceeded the threshold of 25000 bpt, the actions taken was specified as implementing sustainability strategies.

4.5.2 Multiple Linear Regression (MLR)

When the MLR.html program is executed, it initiates a user prompt where the user specifies the number of rows to display, selects a valid CSV file, and inputs parameters such as population size and GDP value.

The user requested to view 10 rows from the chosen CSV file and specified a population size of 1,300,000 and a GDP value of 8.2. Figure 4-9 illustrates that the program successfully displayed the requested 10 rows based on the user's input. The program also performed a regression analysis and generated the following equation to predict the value of CO_2 depending on the provided population and GDP values. Using the equation with the provided user input (population: 1,300,000 and GDP: 8.2), the program estimated CO_2 emissions at approximately 417,243.689 bpt and calculated a MAPE of 11.182%. This MAPE value indicates a reasonably accurate fit of the model to the data. In addition, we generated a 3D scatter plot that illustrates CO_2 emissions against population and GDP values, displaying the original data points, the predicted CO_2 emissions, and the regression line representing the model's relationship.

CHAPTER 4   ALIGNING MANUFACTURING EMISSIONS WITH SDGS 9 AND 13 USING MACHINE LEARNING ALGORITHMS

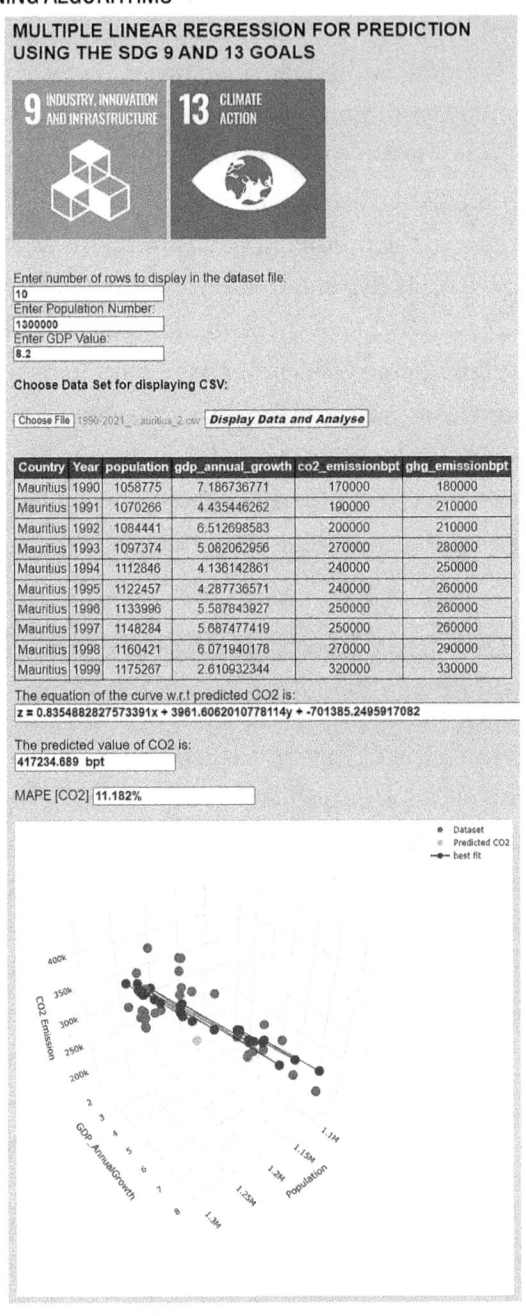

Figure 4-9. *MLR: Prediction and Plot of CO_2 emissions*

CHAPTER 4   ALIGNING MANUFACTURING EMISSIONS WITH SDGS 9 AND 13 USING MACHINE LEARNING ALGORITHMS

Similarly, the program conducted another regression analysis and formulated another equation to predict GHG emissions based on the provided population and GDP values as displayed in Figure 4-10. Based on the user's input (population: 1,300,000 and GDP: 8.2), the program estimated GHG emissions to be approximately 418,083.717 bpt using the equation and obtained a MAPE of 10.785 %. Furthermore, we created a 3D scatter plot depicting GHG emissions against population and GDP values. It displays the original data points, the predicted GHG emissions, and the regression line illustrating the model's relationship. The program also calculates the Other Gases value as the difference between the GHG and CO_2 predictions, yielding a value of 849.028 bpt. Since the predicted value of GHG emissions exceeded the threshold of 25000 bpt, the actions taken were specified as implementing sustainability strategies.

CHAPTER 4 ALIGNING MANUFACTURING EMISSIONS WITH SDGS 9 AND 13 USING MACHINE LEARNING ALGORITHMS

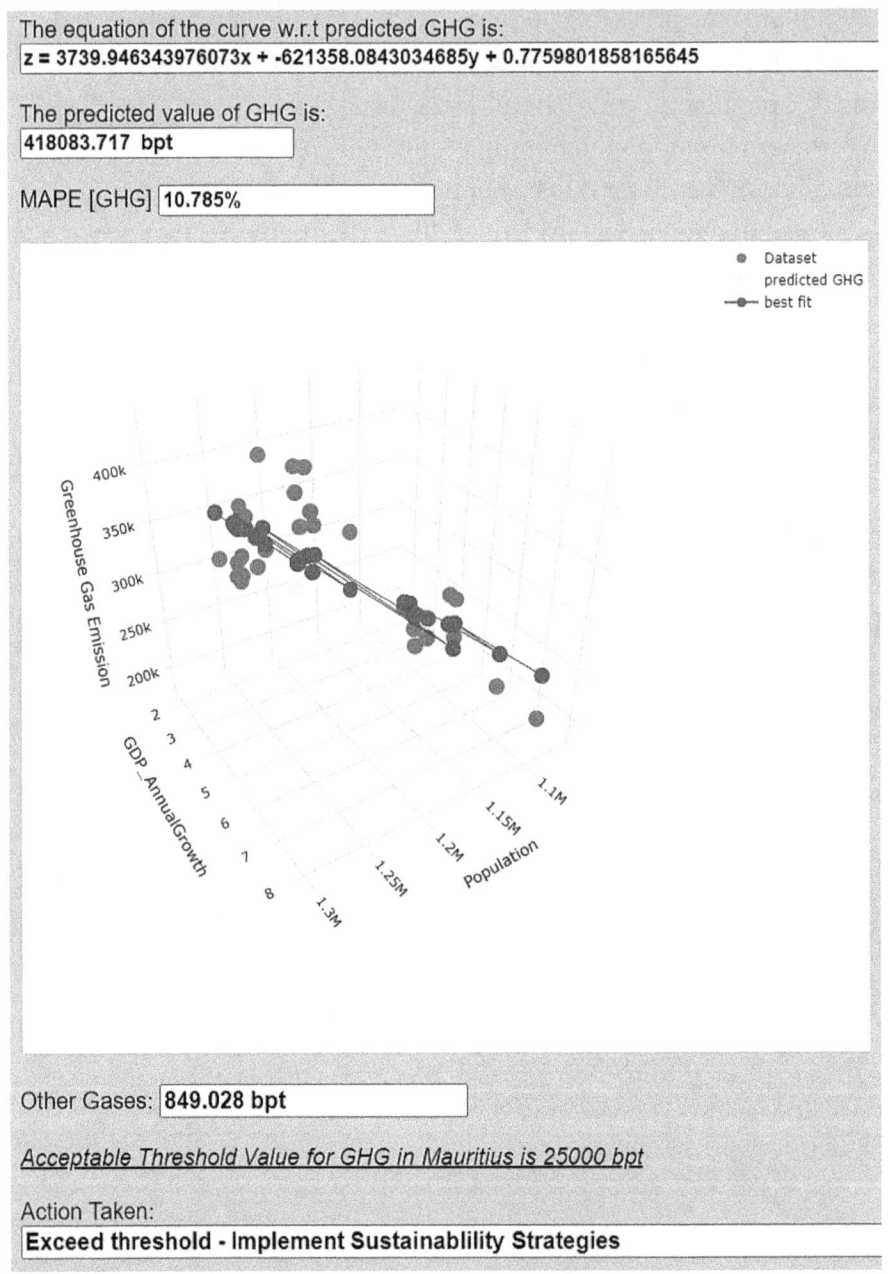

Figure 4-10. MLR: prediction and plot of GHG emissions

4.5.3 k-Nearest Neighbors (k-NN)

When the KNN.html program is executed, it initiates a user prompt to allow the user to specify the number of rows to be displayed and to select a valid CSV file. The selected CSV file consists of data pertaining to the population and GDP parameters.

The user enters a row size of 10 from the selected CSV file, a population size of 1,300,000, and a GDP value of 8.2. The selected row size of 10 is as displayed in the plot. The predicted amount CO_2 emitted is displayed, based on the population and GDP values entered. The predicted value is of 320000 bpt. Furthermore, a 3D scatter plot has been generated to illustrate CO_2 emissions against population, and GDP values. Both the original data points and the predicted CO_2 emissions are as displayed in Figure 4-11.

CHAPTER 4   ALIGNING MANUFACTURING EMISSIONS WITH SDGS 9 AND 13 USING MACHINE LEARNING ALGORITHMS

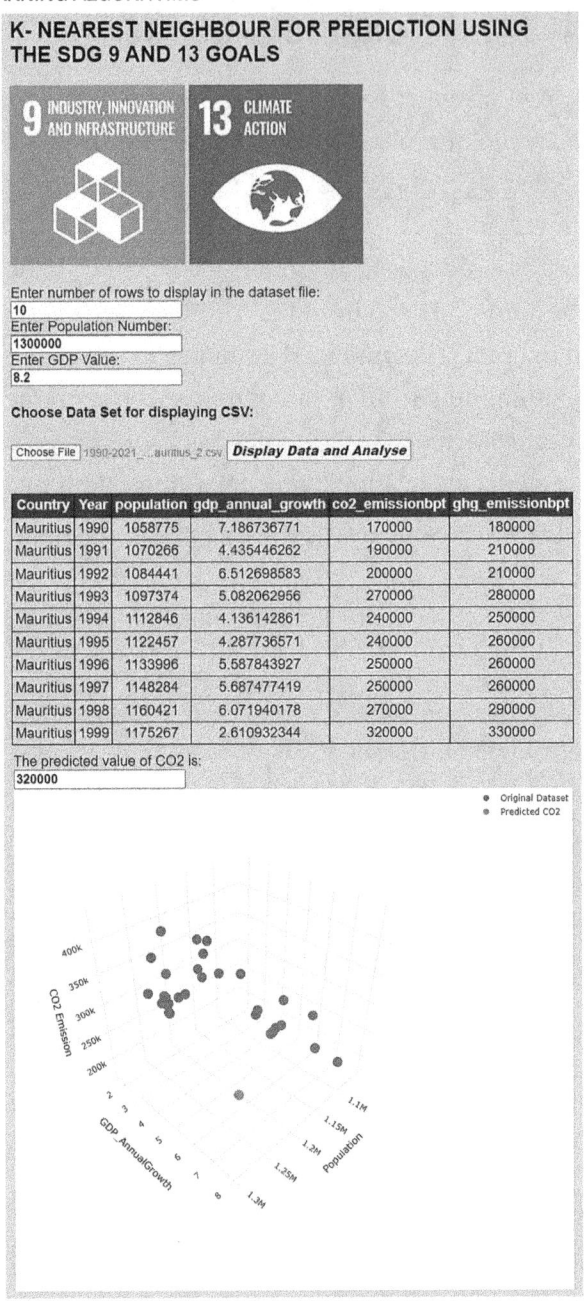

Figure 4-11. k-NN: prediction and plot of CO_2 emissions

Similarly, GHG emissions have been predicted based on the provided population and GDP values, as displayed in Figure 4-12. Based on the user's input of population value of 1,300,000 and GDP value of 8.2, the program estimated GHG emissions to be approximately 330000 bpt. Then, a 3D scatter plot illustrated the relationship between GHG emissions, population values, and GDP values. The program also calculates the Other Gases value as the difference between the GHG and CO_2 predictions, yielding a value of 10,000 bpt. Since the predicted value of GHG emissions exceeded the threshold of 25000 bpt, the actions taken were specified as implementing sustainability strategies.

CHAPTER 4   ALIGNING MANUFACTURING EMISSIONS WITH SDGS 9 AND 13 USING MACHINE LEARNING ALGORITHMS

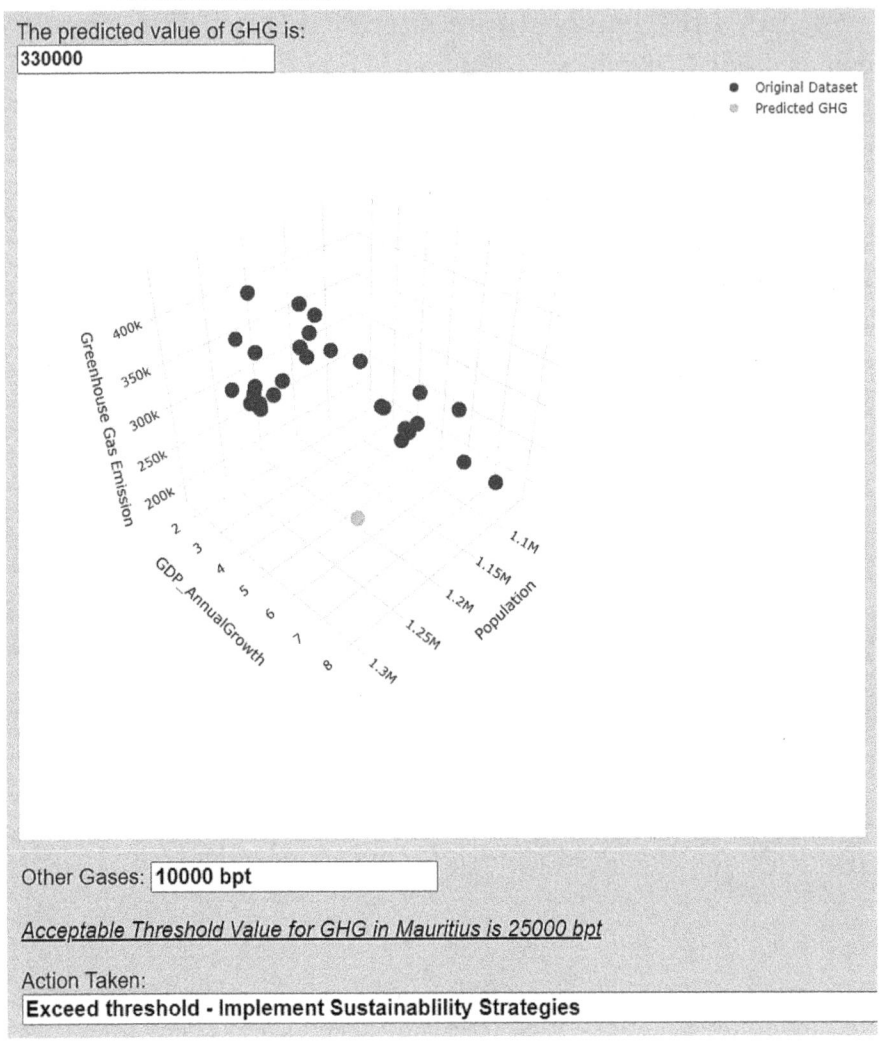

Figure 4-12. k-NN: prediction and plot of GHG emissions

4.5.4 Discussion

Our study aimed to assess whether GHG emissions from the manufacturing sector in Mauritius exceed the threshold value set by the U.S Environmental Protection Agency (EPA), whereby the guideline states,

CHAPTER 4   ALIGNING MANUFACTURING EMISSIONS WITH SDGS 9 AND 13 USING MACHINE LEARNING ALGORITHMS

"Most small businesses would fall below the 25,000 metric ton threshold and are not required to report GHG emissions to EPA" [26]. If our predicted GHG values exceed the EPA's established threshold of 25,000 metric tons, then it implies that Mauritius needs to intensify its climate action efforts, particularly within the manufacturing sector. This evaluation aligns with SDG 13, which focuses on climate action. GHGs contribute to ozone depletion, allowing cancer-causing UV rays to enter the atmosphere.

By assessing Mauritius's compliance with the EPA threshold, we are investigating the extent to which manufacturing industries contribute to elevated CO_2 and GHG emissions, thereby supporting the objectives of SDG 13. Additionally, SDG 9, which aims to promote sustainable industrialization and innovation, is relevant. Manufacturing industries play a pivotal role in achieving SDG 9 as one of the drivers of economic growth and employment. However, the energy consumption and production processes significantly contribute to global CO_2 and GHG emissions, impacting climate change. Quantifying CO_2 and GHG emissions with the help of ML algorithms provides insights into the environmental impact of Mauritius's manufacturing industries, aligning with SDG 9's goal of fostering sustainable industrialization.

Moreover, our analysis of Other Gases reveals that manufacturing industries emit gases like methane, chlorofluorocarbons, nitrous gases, and other toxic gases. These gases contribute significantly to GHG emissions other than CO_2, with equally significant environmental consequences. Taking action to mitigate these emissions aligns with the objectives of SDG 13, which aims to combat climate change. We observed that the MAPE obtained for MLR was lower than for SLR, indicating better model accuracy for prediction. Table 4-2 shows an accuracy measure of the ML algorithms used for prediction.

Table 4-2. Accuracy of ML Algorithms

ML Algorithm	% Accuracy CO_2 Emissions	GHG Emissions
SLR	82.704	84.117
MLR	88.818	89.215

It can be noted that MLR has a higher accuracy value for both CO_2 and GHG emissions predictions compared to SLR. The 3D scatter plots illustrate the relationship between emissions and economic factors, further comprehending the impact of industrial activities on emissions.

In conclusion, our study can serve as a crucial resource for policymakers and stakeholders, enabling them to gain insights into emissions generated by the manufacturing industries. This information empowers them to take action to mitigate these emissions continually. The implemented system will ensure the ongoing monitoring of yearly GHG emissions from Mauritius' manufacturing sector and aligning with environmental protection agencies' predictions. This approach contributes to SDG 9 and SDG 13 by addressing the impact of manufacturing industries and their role in climate action, ultimately advancing sustainable development in Mauritius.

4.6 Recommendations

Since our whole analysis is solely based on SDG 9 and SDG 13, other SDGs relating to other sectors, including agriculture, education, health, among others, could have also been studied for better comparative analysis. Additionally, the extent to which specific SDGs can be achieved varies from continent to continent. ML algorithms can be used to identify SDGs distinct to a specific geographical or topological area. For example, United States is the greatest contributor to GHG emissions (SDG 13) [27], and there are striking poverty issues in Africa (SDG 1) [28].

CHAPTER 4 ALIGNING MANUFACTURING EMISSIONS WITH SDGS 9 AND 13 USING MACHINE LEARNING ALGORITHMS

4.7 Improvements

- For data preprocessing, a better approach would have been to opt for the binning approach whereby the values are first sorted, before being divided into "bins," or rather buckets of the same size. Then, a mean or median is applied to each bin for smoothing.

- When it comes to SLR, the regression analysis could have been used to make informed policy recommendations aiming at promoting SDG 9 and SDG 13. The implemented model could have been extrapolated to meet other projections.

- For MLR, the model could have been used to make more distinct policy recommendations that account for the several factors leading to SDG 9 and to SDG 13. As such, the impact of policy changes on both goals could have been assessed.

- The k-NN model could have been used with other machine learning models for more accurate predictions. Furthermore, the k-NN model lacks interpretable coefficients such as linear regression. Consequently, focus can be shifted on prediction accuracy and on the use of visualization tools to grasp how the k-NN algorithm makes predictions.

Finally, since there are ethical implications associated with the use of machine learning models in decision-making, it is of paramount importance to involve experts and policy makers, if there is room for system commercialization. A confirmation is required as to whether the formerly used regression techniques align with the SDGs considered for the highest good of the public, of a country/continent, and of the environment.

4.8 Summary

On a concluding note, all three ML algorithms were considered in this chapter: MLR, SLR, and k-NN-regression. For either of the algorithms, historical data related to SDG 9 and SDG 13 had to be gathered, with special consideration to the quality, consistency, and accuracy of the data. The most relevant predictor variables were considered related to the SDGs being analyzed. Through SLR, a correlation has been established between CO_2 and GHG as predictor variables and the GDP as a target variable.

Furthermore, for MLR and k-NN, a relationship has been established between CO_2 and GHG as predictor variables with population and GDP as a target variable. To ease data visualization, scatterplots and regression lines were displayed for effective communication of relevant findings. The difference between the predicted value of GHG and CO_2 emissions were used to calculate the amount of other gases. The Other Gases calculation has been included in the program based on the understanding that not only CO_2 contributes to GHG emissions but also gases such as methane, chlorofluorocarbons, nitrous gases, and other toxic gases. Lastly, the MAPE calculation has been performed only in SLR and MLR to obtain an accuracy of the algorithms used.

4.9 Appendix

4.9.1 Dataset

country	year	population	gdp_annual_growth	co2_emissionbpt	ghg_emissionbpt
Mauritius	1990	1058775	7.186736771	170000	180000
Mauritius	1991	1070266	4.435446262	190000	210000
Mauritius	1992	1084441	6.512698583	200000	210000

(*continued*)

CHAPTER 4 ALIGNING MANUFACTURING EMISSIONS WITH SDGS 9 AND 13 USING MACHINE LEARNING ALGORITHMS

country	year	population	gdp_annual_growth	co2_emissionbpt	ghg_emissionbpt
Mauritius	1993	1097374	5.082062956	270000	280000
Mauritius	1994	1112846	4.136142861	240000	250000
Mauritius	1995	1122457	4.287736571	240000	260000
Mauritius	1996	1133996	5.587843927	250000	260000
Mauritius	1997	1148284	5.687477419	250000	260000
Mauritius	1998	1160421	6.071940178	270000	290000
Mauritius	1999	1175267	2.610932344	320000	330000
Mauritius	2000	1186873	8.202791749	360000	370000
Mauritius	2001	1196287	3.347540727	390000	400000
Mauritius	2002	1204621	1.614918659	380000	390000
Mauritius	2003	1213370	5.925445489	390000	390000
Mauritius	2004	1221003	4.330019855	360000	370000
Mauritius	2005	1228254	1.77754302	350000	350000
Mauritius	2006	1233996	4.865544608	410000	410000
Mauritius	2007	1239630	5.72701616	400000	410000
Mauritius	2008	1244121	5.386962542	440000	440000
Mauritius	2009	1247429	3.315076998	360000	370000
Mauritius	2010	1250400	4.377203223	350000	360000
Mauritius	2011	1252404	4.077538066	340000	340000
Mauritius	2012	1255882	3.496118365	330000	340000
Mauritius	2013	1258927	3.3604061	320000	320000
Mauritius	2014	1261208	3.82696982	330000	330000

(*continued*)

CHAPTER 4 ALIGNING MANUFACTURING EMISSIONS WITH SDGS 9 AND 13 USING MACHINE LEARNING ALGORITHMS

country	year	population	gdp_annual_growth	co2_emissionbpt	ghg_emissionbpt
Mauritius	2015	1262879	3.690556904	340000	340000
Mauritius	2016	1263747	3.862468263	330000	330000
Mauritius	2017	1264887	3.937983806	320000	330000
Mauritius	2018	1265577	4.006740572	320000	330000
Mauritius	2019	1265985	2.891284993	330000	330000

CHAPTER 5

Potability Analysis of Water Using Machine Learning

Chapter authors:
Ramdin Diteesha, diteesharamdin01@gmail.com
Ramjansing Roshwar, yanishramjansing@gmail.com
Soodhoo Leena, leenasoodhoo@gmail.com

The United Nations Sustainable Development Goals (SDGs) stand as a pivotal framework in addressing global challenges and enhancing the well-being of both people and the planet. In this chapter, the focus is on SDGs 3 (Good Health and Well-being), 6 (Clean Water and Sanitation), and 12 (Responsible Consumption and Production). Utilizing machine learning algorithms including k-nearest neighbors (K-NN), decision trees, random forests, and naïve Bayes, we aimed to predict water potability. Access to clean drinking water is imperative for ensuring good health, as contaminated sources can lead to waterborne diseases. Accurate prediction of water quality significantly contributes to achieving SDG 3. Moreover, the chapter directly tackled SDG 6 by evaluating water potability. Machine learning played a vital role in identifying and monitoring water quality, ensuring the availability of clean and safe drinking water, a fundamental requirement for achieving this goal. Additionally, under SDG 12, the

CHAPTER 5   POTABILITY ANALYSIS OF WATER USING MACHINE LEARNING

chapter utilized machine learning to optimize resource utilization, specifically by efficiently predicting water potability. This approach fosters responsible water consumption and minimizes wastage, aligning seamlessly with SDG 12's objectives. The chapter utilized a dataset sourced from Kaggle, encompassing parameters such as pH, hardness, solids, chloramines, sulfate, conductivity, organic carbon, trihalomethanes, and turbidity. Rigorous data preprocessing techniques, including handling missing values, feature scaling, and categorical variable encoding, were employed. Machine learning algorithms (KNN, decision trees, random forests, naïve Bayes) were then implemented to achieve accurate predictions of water potability. The application of these machine learning algorithms not only ensured precise assessments of water potability, thereby guaranteeing the availability of clean drinking water (SDG 6), but also contributed significantly to the responsible consumption and production (SDG 12) by optimizing resource allocation.

Machine learning's advantages, including enhanced accuracy, scalability, and automation, were evident in comparison to traditional methods, making it an invaluable tool for addressing SDG-related challenges. A key highlight of this research was its comprehensive comparison of multiple machine learning algorithms for water potability prediction, enhancing transparency and interpretability. Furthermore, the study provides practical guidance for selecting the most suitable model, ensuring accessibility and usability for a wider audience. While other research endeavors have explored machine learning in water quality analysis, this project's multifaceted approach and emphasis on user-friendliness set it apart, making a significant and distinctive contribution to the field of water quality assessment and SDG achievement.

CHAPTER 5 POTABILITY ANALYSIS OF WATER USING MACHINE LEARNING

5.1 Introduction

Generally the UN SDGs promote a world where there is no poverty, no famine issues, basic healthcare facilities, access to education, gender equality, access to drinking water and hygiene, the use of renewable sources of energy, improvement toward economic growth, new innovation and infrastructural development, enhancement toward a sustainable city and economy, wise management about the consumption and production of goods, mediums to cater for the climatic changes, and life below water and on land given the same importance.

This chapter is mainly focused on SDG 3, SDG 6, and SDG 12. This chapter is based on testing the potability of water. It determines whether the water is safe for consumption whereby several parameters such as pH, turbidity, conductivity, and the presence of other chemicals are being analyzed. Testing water quality is crucial to ensure the safety of the public. The principal reason to choose these three SDGs are because they provide a guideline toward a sustainable world whereby the public has access to safe drinking water. Thus, promoting good health is a wise decision to prevent the contamination of water bodies whereby its production and consumption are being assessed.

Machine learning promotes the automation of tasks whereby there is less manual intervention. This technique is more effective and less costly. Machine learning has the ability to analyze large datasets and perform prediction. It has the ability to understand and generate human language by a process known as natural language processing. It is beneficial as it empowers businesses and helps in achieving various goals by extracting important features from data. This promotes the automation of tasks and model prediction and achieves innovation that will shape the future of the world. Several ML algorithms have been employed in different research works to address SDGs 3, 6, and 12.

CHAPTER 5   POTABILITY ANALYSIS OF WATER USING MACHINE LEARNING

To scrutinize water potability issues, in this chapter, four machine learning algorithms have been implemented (naïve Bayes, decision tree, K-nearest neighbor, and random forest) to target the three SDGs mentioned. The `water_potability.csv` file is used as a dataset, and this dataset has been inserted into the four listed machine learning algorithms to check the accuracy obtained. The machine learning algorithm with the highest accuracy level is chosen, and its outcome is used as the final output to determine whether the water is potable. Based on the results obtained, it can be concluded that the naïve Bayes learning algorithm is highly suitable for this context as it obtains the highest accuracy level.

The primary research questions addressed in this report center around the task of predicting water potability through the utilization of four distinct machine learning algorithms: K-nearest neighbors (KNN), decision trees, random forests, and naïve Bayes. These questions encompass the assessment of the predictive accuracy of each of these algorithms in determining whether water is potable. Additionally, it aims to explore the comparative performance of these algorithms in the context of water quality analysis. The research seeks to uncover which algorithms offer the most reliable and accurate predictions for water potability, providing valuable insights into the suitability of various machine learning techniques for this specific domain. The primary novelty in this research lies in its multifaceted approach to water potability prediction. By employing multiple machine learning algorithms and outputting their respective accuracies, it provides a comprehensive comparison, offering a more profound understanding of which algorithms excel in this specific task.

Moreover, the research introduces transparency and interpretability into the analysis, particularly through the application of random forest and decision tree algorithms. This fosters a deeper understanding of the influential factors behind each prediction. Additionally, it extends to the practical guidance it offers for selecting the most appropriate machine learning model for water potability prediction, and it prioritizes user-friendliness, ensuring that the results are accessible and actionable for a broader audience. In summary, this chapter brings together a diverse set of machine learning techniques to tackle a critical real-world problem, enriching the field with comprehensive insights and guidance for future applications.

5.2 AI Use Cases for SDGs 3, 6, and 12

A recognition system has been implemented to determine the quality of water, to monitor water spillage and utilization, and to check the areas where drinking water is available [1]. This system is implemented by using convolutional neural network (CNN) and a Moroccan Automatic Meter Reading (MR-AMR) dataset. In this context, SDG 6 and SDG 12 is being targeted to analyze the range of drinking water and to monitor the consumption of water by analyzing the different usage of water. During the testing process, this system achieved an accuracy level around 98%. SDG 6 has also been assessed in testing water potability whereby adaptive boosting technique has been applied [1]. In this example, a dataset from Kaggle was used whereby the hyperparameters used to determine the potability of water are ammonia, aluminum, arsenic, barium, chloramine, copper, leads, nitrates, and many other chemicals that can affect water quality. SDG 6 has also been targeted for research in Iraq where machine learning has been used to analyze the condition of underground artesian water [2]. In this context the depth of underground water, the density, and the saturation of water are being analyzed in order to drill wells precisely at a lower cost.

AI has also been implemented to achieve sustainable development whereby the system analyzes water infrastructure, forecasts the consumption of water, tests the quality of water in reservoirs and dams, and predicts disasters related to water [3]. This approach targets SDG 3, 6, 11, and 15. It scrutinizes water-related diseases and the number of deaths and infection caused due to water contamination due to hazardous chemicals. Moreover, it analyzes the quality of water and determines whether it is safe for drinking and determines ways to safeguard natural resources. These SDGs aim to reduce its related issues by the end of 2030. In Australia, an AI-based water grid system was implemented to cater for water consumption, for water treatment purposes, and to analyze the water quality index of reservoirs. In Iran, Support Vector Machine (SVM) machine learning has been implemented to check the water quality, and in Shivganga River, multiple linear regression has been used for a similar purpose [3].

SDG 6 is addressed in [4], which focuses on the identification of water quality anomalies (WQAD) in intelligent water distribution systems. They did a thorough analysis of the literature examining the application of machine learning (ML) techniques for WQAD, which is essential for the safety and security of the water supply. While there is rising interest in employing deep learning (DL) models for WQAD, the paper emphasizes that the use of extreme learning machines (ELM) is still being investigated. For the purpose of improving the effectiveness and precision of anomaly detection in water quality, they suggest a unique hybrid DL-ELM framework. According to the research, AI, especially the suggested DL-ELM hybrid technique, has the potential to considerably increase the accuracy and promptness of finding anomalies in water quality. This development is essential for guaranteeing access to safe and clean water, ultimately harmonizing with SDG 6 goals. The study also highlights the significance of real-time data produced by sensors and the requirement for short response times in identifying contaminants, which are crucial components of managing water quality in contemporary smart cities.

SDG 6 is also tackled in [5]. To effectively identify and categorize algae in water, which is a crucial component of determining water quality, the paper proposes the use of machine learning techniques, specifically a modified Faster R-CNN architecture. Based on their small size and diversity, algae are difficult to manually detect and are prone to mistakes.

CHAPTER 5 POTABILITY ANALYSIS OF WATER USING MACHINE LEARNING

A novel multitarget deep learning framework was proposed by the researchers that is capable of handling several tasks at once, such as genus classification, algal detection, and biological class identification. They performed extensive trials on a dataset made up of 27 different algal taxa, and the results were encouraging. The framework was able to identify algal species at the genus level with a mean average precision (mAP) of 74.64% and classify organisms at the biological class level with an even higher mAP of 81.17%.

SDG 12 is addressed in [6]. To maximize resource usage, the paper proposes machine learning approaches for estimating short-term water demand in water supply systems (WSS). Predicting water demand effectively is difficult since it depends on a number of variables, including historical data, weather, and seasonality. To create precise predicting systems, the researchers investigated machine learning approaches, including supervised and unsupervised learning. To make better projections, they took into account elements like past water usage, temperature, and rainfall occurrence. The forecasting technique was informed by the study's examination of the effects of various time periods, such as weekdays and weekends, on demand patterns. A weighted parallel forecasting technique was suggested to further improve accuracy. It integrates various forecasting methods, each with advantages and disadvantages, to create a more accurate and dependable forecast of water demand. This method reduces errors by giving models weights based on how well they function. Overall, the research shows that machine learning-based forecasting works better than conventional time-series analysis techniques, potentially saving up to 18% in operating costs for water supply systems.

SDG 3, 9, and 12 are being targeted. Waste management is a critical global issue, affecting both developed and developing countries. The main problem in waste segregation is the overflowing of open bins long before the cleaning process begins. This cleaning process involves manually sorting waste by unskilled workers, which is inefficient, time-consuming, and often impractical due to the sheer volume of waste generated.

CHAPTER 5 POTABILITY ANALYSIS OF WATER USING MACHINE LEARNING

To address this, the author in [7] proposed an automated waste classification system using machine learning and deep learning algorithms. The objective is to collect a dataset and categorize it into six classes: glass, paper, metal, plastic, cardboard, and general waste. Three machine learning algorithms, namely, support vector machine (SVM), random forest, and decision tree with a deep learning algorithm called convolutional neural network (CNN), were compared. It was revealed that the CNN achieved a high level of accuracy in waste classification, approximately 90%. SVM also showed excellent performance in distinguishing various types of waste, with an 85% classification accuracy, while random forest and decision tree achieved accuracy rates of 55% and 65%, respectively.

In this research, SDG 6 has been mainly addressed. Groundwater (GW) plays a crucial role in providing drinking water and supporting irrigation to address food insecurity and enhance water access in rural sub-Saharan Africa. Recent modeling techniques, specifically machine learning (ML), have proven to be reliable and cost-effective tools for assessing GW recharge. The study in [8] employed ML methods to predict GW recharge in selected areas of Ghana, aiming to evaluate the sustainability of GW resources. Two types of artificial neural network (ANN) models, namely, the Feedforward Neural Network with Multilayer Perceptron (FNN-MLP) and the Extreme Learning Machine (FNN-ELM), were employed to forecast GW recharge using 58 years of GW data spanning from 1960 to 2018. The findings from this study contribute to enhancing current GW assessment and development methods, aligning with the sustainable development goals, particularly those related to water resources and sustainability.

In the sector of freight transportation, there has been a lot of emphasis lately on encouraging sustainable methods. New regulations have been put out by the European Commission and the UN with the intention of promoting sustainability in transportation operations. SDG 9 is mainly being targeted in this context. The aim of the research project in [9] is to develop a model that uses supervised machine learning methods and incorporates key performance metrics and intelligent classification algorithms for various sustainability-related input data. Different classification algorithms were tested and trained in order to do this. The SVM technique, which was used to analyze the dataset in question, was found to have the best accuracy, obtaining a remarkable 98% accuracy rate. This suggests that SVM is the most trustworthy method in this situation for determining sustainability levels. Testing this approach on a European road freight transport firm showed how useful it is in practice. This methodology allowed the business to assess its level of sustainability, allowing it to develop eco-friendly strategies for promoting sustainable growth.

Here are some recent examples of the use of machine learning to promote the following SDGs:

- In 2022, to tackle SDG 6, satellite and drone images have been used to analyze water bodies. Research has been conducted using machine learning to predict the existence of harmful algal blooms and the level of pollution affecting the water bodies. An accuracy of 90% has been obtained, which enables prompt intervention to ensure the safety of drinking water.

- In 2022, India conducted research using machine learning models to tackle the issue of water-borne diseases, whereby contaminants such as bacteria are being detected. This system has been successful in detecting unsafe drinking water. This promotes sustainable development toward SDG 3.

- Additionally, in 2021, Chennai has used machine learning algorithms to forecast water quality.

CHAPTER 5   POTABILITY ANALYSIS OF WATER USING MACHINE LEARNING

5.3 Data Processing and Application Design

In this section, machine learning algorithms are used to classify water quality. We briefly discuss the appropriate methodology to implement this approach.

5.3.1 Data Collection Process and Description of the Datasets

The dataset used in the water_potability.csv file was downloaded from Kaggle. The dataset consists of 3,277 values. The dataset comprises the following parameters:

- pH value

   The pH value determines whether the water is acidic or alkaline. The acceptable range for drinking water is between 6.5 and 9.5.

- Hardness

   Hardness determines the amount of calcium and magnesium dissolved in water.

- Solids

   Total Dissolved Solids (TDS) determines the total concentration of dissolved substances present in water. If the TDS threshold is between 50 and 150, it is considered good for drinking purposes.

- Chloramines

   Chloramines are used in water treatment process, where ammonia is added to chlorine to treat drinking water.

- Sulfate

    The maximum range of sulfate in drinking water is 2250 mg/L. If the concentration exceeds the threshold value, it can lead to health issues.

- Conductivity

    Conductivity determines the ability to conduct electrical current. It determines the amount of minerals dissolved in the water. A higher concentration of dissolved minerals illustrates a better conductivity.

- Organic carbon

    It is the amount of carbon in the organic compound present in water. Organic carbon is generated from the decay of vegetations and the presence of organic matter.

- Trihalomethanes

    It is an organic compound formed when water is infected with chlorine.

- Turbidity

    Turbidity determines whether the water is clear or not. It determines the presence of suspended or colloidal particles in water.

- Potability

    It determines whether the water is safe for drinking by displaying 0 or 1.

The first nine parameters are the inputs of the dataset, and the last one (potability) is the output. 0 illustrates "not potable," and 1 illustrates "potable."

5.3.2 Data Preprocessing Steps

For the preprocessing step, data cleaning has been performed. That is, the dataset has been cleaned by removing rows with empty cells values. Thus, the number of data reduces to 2,012 records. Data cleaning is considered as a crucial step to process the dataset. Its main purpose is to identify and rectify the errors and inaccuracies in the dataset. The following are the key purposes of data preprocessing:

- Improve data quality by eliminating errors and inconsistencies. This helps in obtaining more accurate and reliable results.

- Help to harmonize inconsistencies in dataset in order to create a uniform and stable dataset.

- Handle missing values as missing data can affect the accuracy of the system.

- Detect and manage outliers as they can distort the analysis of the machine learning algorithm,

- Ensure that the dataset is in a consistent format for further processing.

- Improve the performance of the model.

- Enhance the quality and reliability of dataset for analysis and decision making.

5.3.3 General Layout of Web Application

Figure 5-1 illustrates the general layout of the web application. It is to be noted that all the code of this chapter can be found in the folder Chapter 5 - Codes hosted on the GitHub page of this book.

CHAPTER 5   POTABILITY ANALYSIS OF WATER USING MACHINE LEARNING

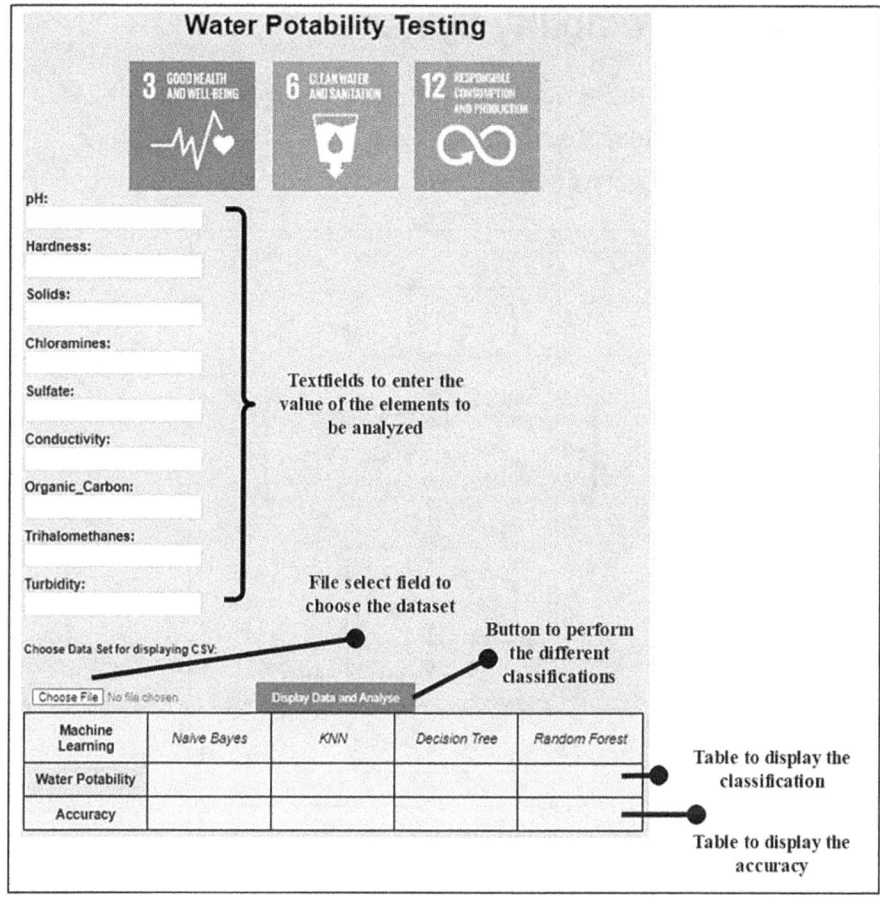

Figure 5-1. *General layout of web application*

These are the links for the libraries used in this web application:

- https://cdnjs.cloudflare.com/ajax/libs/PapaParse/5.4.1/papaparse.min.js
- https://www.lactame.com/lib/ml/6.0.0/ml.min.js
- https://cdn.jsdelivr.net/npm/chart.js
- https://cdn.plot.ly/plotly-latest.min.js

CHAPTER 5   POTABILITY ANALYSIS OF WATER USING MACHINE LEARNING

5.3.4 Water Potability System

Figure 5-2 illustrates the general functioning of the system whereby the accuracy of four machine learning algorithms is being analyze to determine the quality of water.

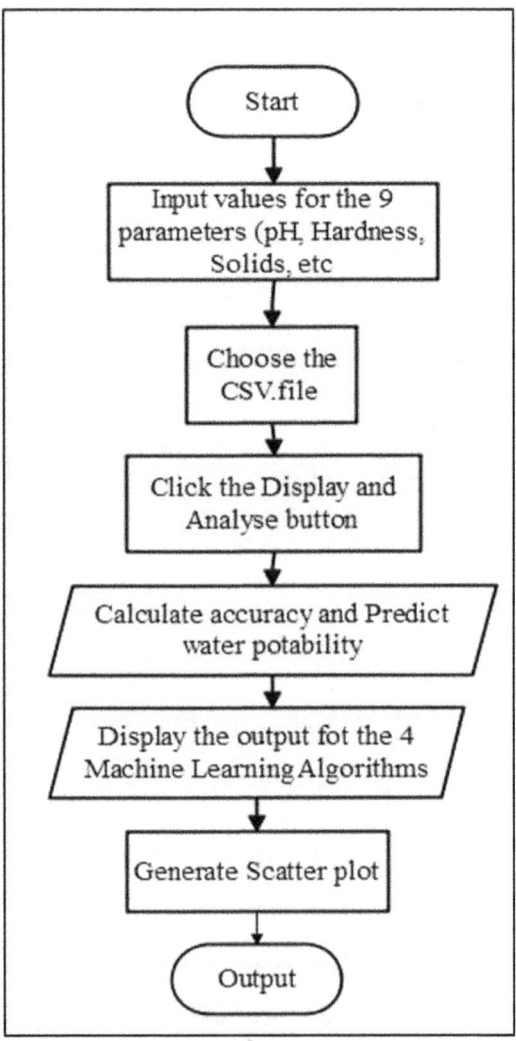

Figure 5-2. *General functioning of the system*

5.3.5 Machine Learning Algorithms
k-NN

Figure 5-3 shows the flowchart of KNN.

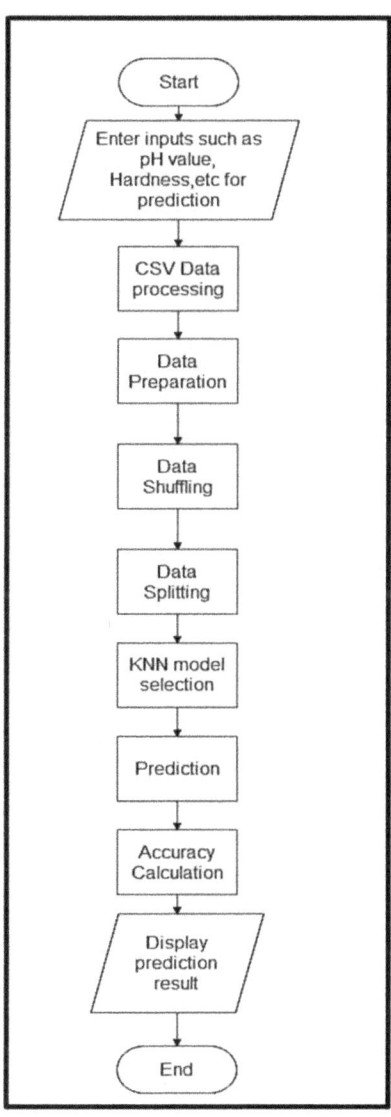

Figure 5-3. *Flowchart of KNN*

JavaScript Libraries:

In the <head> section, several JavaScript libraries are included using <script> tags. These libraries are as follows:

- `ml.min.js`: A machine learning library for k-NN classification
- `papaparse.min.js`: A library for parsing CSV data

User Input Fields:

Within the <body> section, various user input fields are provided. These include the following:

- Input fields for specifying the number of rows to display from a dataset file and values for different water quality parameters like pH, hardness, solids, chloramines, etc.
- A file input field (fileUpload) for selecting a CSV dataset file.
- A button (upload) for triggering data display and analysis.

Display Data:

The user selects a CSV dataset file and clicks the Display Data and Analyze button. The JavaScript function `Upload()` is called in response to this button click.

CSV File Parsing:

The program checks if the selected file is a valid CSV file. If valid, it uses the PapaParse library to parse the CSV data, assuming the first row contains headers. It also extracts the number of rows to display based on the user's input.

Display Data in HTML:

The parsed data is displayed in an HTML table (dvCSV) with the specified number of rows.

Data Preparation for Classification:

The program prepares the dataset and labels for k-NN classification. It extracts values for various water quality parameters and stores them in arrays. It shuffles the dataset to avoid any bias.

Data Splitting:

The dataset is split into training and validation sets based on a specified split ratio (70% training, 30% validation).

k-NN Classification:

The program performs k-NN classification to predict water potability based on user-input parameter values.

It finds the best value of k (number of neighbors) by trying a range of k values and selecting the one with the highest accuracy on the validation set. Using the best k value, it creates a k-NN classifier.

Validation and Accuracy Calculation:

The program uses the trained k-NN classifier to make predictions on the validation set. It calculates the accuracy of the model's predictions by comparing them to the actual labels. The accuracy is displayed in an input field.

Display Classification Result:

The program uses the trained classifier to predict water potability based on user-provided parameter values.

The result (either "potable" or "not potable") is displayed in an input field.

Decision Tree and Random Forest

Figure 5-4 shows the flowchart of random forest and decision tree.

CHAPTER 5   POTABILITY ANALYSIS OF WATER USING MACHINE LEARNING

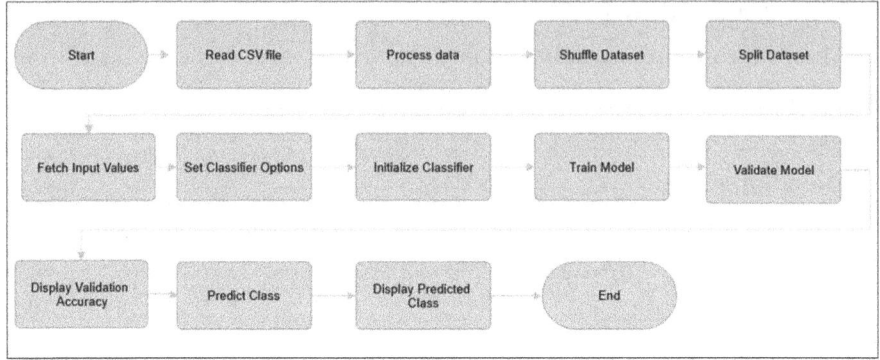

Figure 5-4. Flowchart of random forest and decision tree

Read CSV File:

- FileReader reads the uploaded CSV file. This task is executed using the `reader.readAsText()` function.

Process Data:

- CSV data is split into rows and columns, and features and class labels are extracted. This task is executed within the `reader.onload` event handler function.

Shuffle Dataset:

- The dataset is shuffled randomly to ensure randomness in training. This is done using the `shuffleDataset()` function.

Split Dataset:

- The shuffled dataset is split into training and validation sets. This is achieved using array slicing.

Fetch Input Values:

- Input values for prediction are fetched from HTML input elements. This is done by accessing the values of specific HTML input elements.

Set Classifier Options:

- Options for the decision tree classifier are defined, such as the gain function, maximum depth, and minimum number of samples.

- Options for the random forest classifier are defined, such as seed, maximum features, replacement, and number of estimators.

Initialize Classifier:

For decision tree:

- A new decision tree classifier is instantiated with the provided options. This is done using the new ML.DecisionTreeClassifier(options) constructor.

For Random Forest:

- A new random forest classifier is instantiated with the provided options. This is done using the new **ML.**RandomForestClassifier(options) constructor.

Train Model:

- The classifier is trained using the training dataset. This is done using the classifier1.train() function.

Validate Model:

- Predictions are made on the validation dataset, and accuracy is calculated. This task is executed within the reader.onload event handler function.

Display Validation Accuracy:

- The calculated accuracy is displayed in an HTML input element. This is done by setting the value of a specific HTML input element.

Predict Class:

- The trained model is used to predict the class of a new instance based on the input values. This is done using the `classifier1.predict()` function.

Display Predicted Class:

- The predicted class is displayed in an HTML input element. This is done by setting the value of a specific HTML input element.

Naïve Bayes

Naïve Bayes is a probabilistic machine learning technique that is mostly utilized for classification purposes, and its concept is widely based on probability [10].

Figure 5-5 illustrates the functioning of the naïve Bayes algorithm.

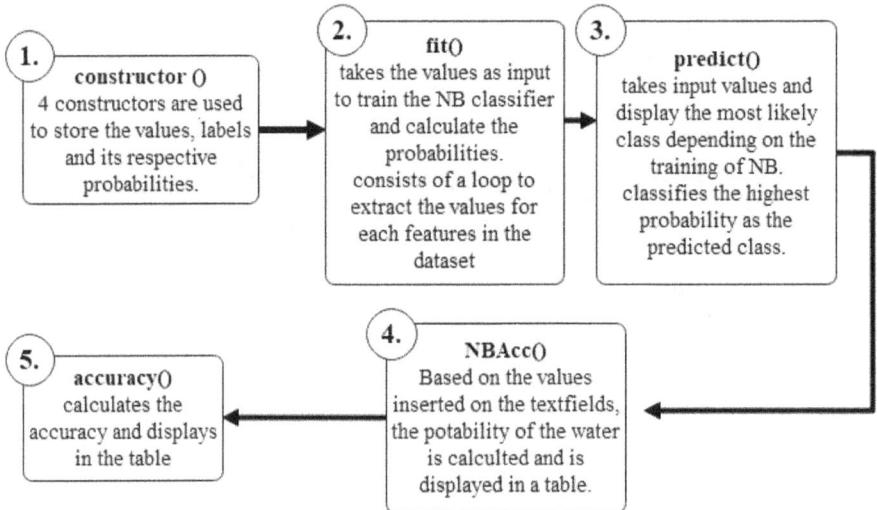

Figure 5-5. Flowchart of naïve Bayes

CHAPTER 5   POTABILITY ANALYSIS OF WATER USING MACHINE LEARNING

For this machine learning algorithm, a naïve Bayes (NB) classifier has been used. The classifier is known as a probabilistic machine learning technique used for classification purposes.

The NB classifier class comprises the four constructors whereby `this.allUniqueAttributes` is used to store the attribute values for each feature. The `this.allAttributesProbabilities` array stores the probabilities associated with each feature, the `this.uniqueClassValues` array stores the labels found in dataset, and the this.classProbabilities array stores the probabilities associated with the label class.

The `fit` method takes the data values, class labels, and the list of variable names as input to train the naïve Bayes classifier to calculate the probabilities of each class and attributes. Inside the `fit` method a `for` loop is used to iterate over each feature in the dataset, and the unique attribute values and unique class values are being extracted. The `count` attribute is initialized to zero to store the count of attribute-value occurrence for each class.

The `predict` method takes input values and displays the most likely class depending on the training of the naïve Bayes model. For each class label, the method calculates the probability of the input, and it classifies the class with the highest probability as the predicted class.

The `NBAcc()` function is used to determine the potability of water, and the `accuracy()` function is used to determine its accuracy. Then its output is displayed in the table of the web application.

CHAPTER 5   POTABILITY ANALYSIS OF WATER USING MACHINE LEARNING

5.4 Application Testing and Analysis

5.4.1 Application Testing

Figure 5-6 shows the testing results.

1. First, we need to insert the different values for each element display in the application.

2. Then, we need to choose the appropriate dataset.

3. On clicking the Display Data and Analyze button, the output is displayed in the form of a table, where the accuracy for each algorithm is being predicted.

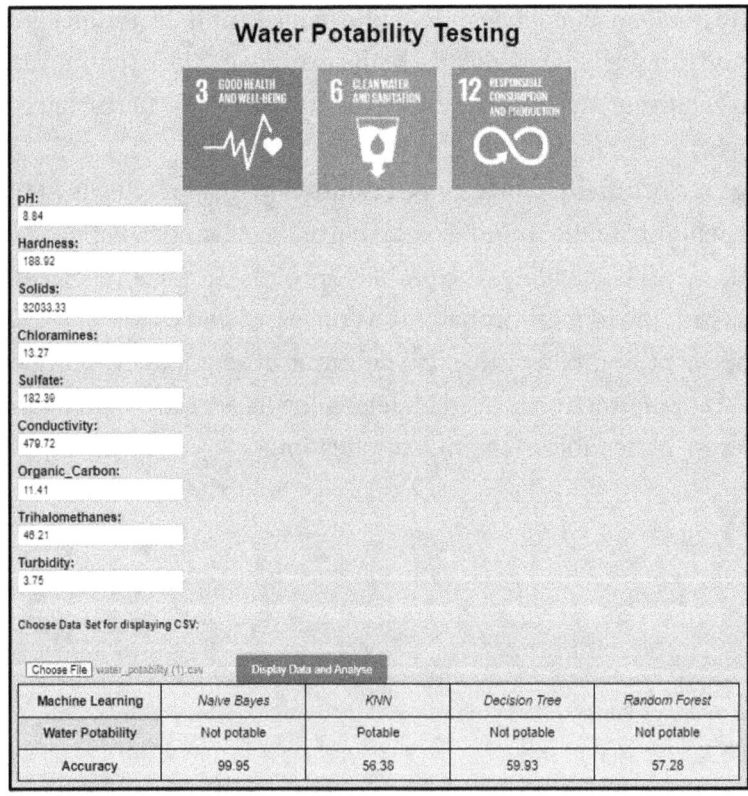

Figure 5-6. *Testing of web application*

200

CHAPTER 5   POTABILITY ANALYSIS OF WATER USING MACHINE LEARNING

4. The algorithm with the highest accuracy is taken into consideration to determine the quality of water.

5. Based on the result obtained, the water is considered to be "Not Potable" according to the naïve Bayes algorithm, which has obtained the highest accuracy.

6. Then a scatter plot is generated, as shown in Figure 5-7.

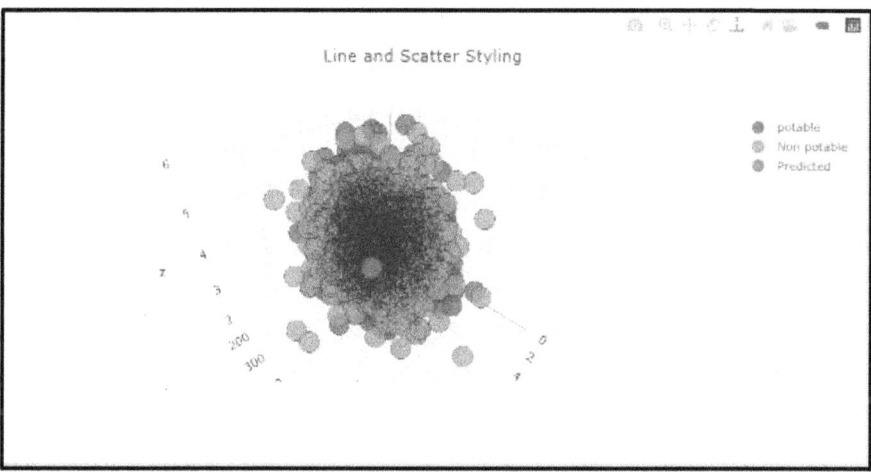

Figure 5-7. Scatter plot

5.4.2 k-NN

The purpose of this section is to analyze and compare the performance of the K-nearest neighbors (K-NN) classification algorithm for various values of K. The K-NN algorithm is widely used for its simplicity and effectiveness in classification tasks. In this analysis, we have experimented with different values of K to understand how it affects the accuracy of our model.

CHAPTER 5 POTABILITY ANALYSIS OF WATER USING MACHINE LEARNING

Experimental Setup

The program was executed using a standardized dataset, and the accuracy of the KNN classifier was recorded for each value of K. The following table summarizes the results:

K-Value	Accuracy
1	54.23%
2	50.08%
3	53.73%
4	53.40%
5	56.55%
6	54.73%
7	56.72%
8	56.88%
9	57.05%
10	58.37%
11	57.55%
12	56.72
13	57.55%

Comparative Analysis

Figure 5-8 visually represents the relationship between the K-value (number of neighbors) and the corresponding accuracy percentage.

CHAPTER 5 POTABILITY ANALYSIS OF WATER USING MACHINE LEARNING

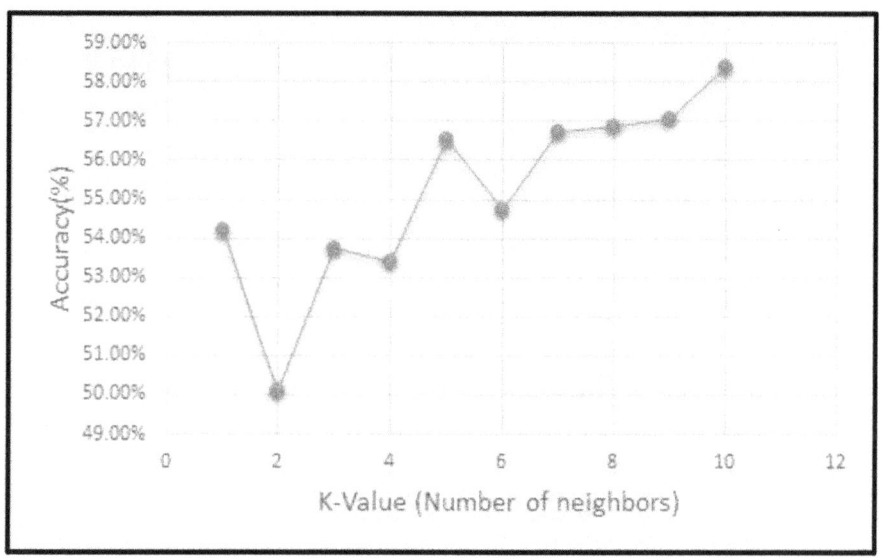

Figure 5-8. Accuracy of K-Values

From the chart, we can make several observations:

1. **Accuracy trend**: The accuracy generally increases as we move from a low K-value (K=1) to a moderate K-value (K=10). This suggests that increasing the number of neighbors considered in the classification process has a positive impact on accuracy.

2. **Optimal K-value**: The highest accuracy of 58.37% is achieved when K is set to 10, indicating that for this specific dataset, considering 10 nearest neighbors leads to the best classification results.

3. **Stability**: After reaching the peak accuracy at K=10, the accuracy remains relatively stable and does not improve significantly as K continues to increase.

Model Selection Considerations

Selecting the appropriate K-value is crucial for achieving the best results with the KNN algorithm. The choice of K depends on the specific characteristics of the dataset and the trade-off between bias and variance. Here are some considerations:

7. **Low K-values (K=1-3)**: These tend to overfit the training data, leading to high variance and sensitivity to noise.

8. **Moderate K-values (K=4-10):** These strike a balance between bias and variance, often resulting in good generalization performance.

9. **High K-values (K>10):** These may lead to over-smoothing of the decision boundary, causing underfitting and reduced accuracy.

5.4.3 Decision Tree

The purpose of this section is to analyze and compare the performance of decision tree classification algorithm for various values of maxDepth. Table 5-1 summarizes the results.

Table 5-1. Decision Tree Results 1

maxDepth	Accuracy
10	59.92
8	57.78
6	56.01
4	55.09
2	53.18

10. `maxDepth` represents the maximum depth of the decision tree.

11. A decision tree expands by making splits at each node based on different features. The depth of the tree refers to the length of the longest path from the root node to a leaf node.

12. Setting `maxDepth` to 10 means that the decision tree will continue splitting nodes until it reaches a depth of 10. Deeper trees can capture more complex patterns in the data, but they also increase the risk of overfitting, especially if the dataset is not large enough.

The results illustrate a notable trend in the accuracy of a decision tree model as the `maxDepth` parameter varies. Beginning with a `maxDepth` of 2, the accuracy starts at 53.18%. As `maxDepth` increases incrementally to 4, 6, 8, and then 10, there is a corresponding rise in accuracy, reaching its peak at 59.92% when `maxDepth` is set to 10. This uptick reflects the model's ability to capture intricate patterns and details within the training data, improving accuracy. However, as `maxDepth` exceeds 10, the accuracy begins to decline. This downturn occurs because the model, at higher depths, starts to overfit the training data, capturing noise and specifics that do not generalize well to new data.

The observed trend underscores the classic trade-off between model complexity and generalization. While increasing `maxDepth` enhances the model's fit to the training data, it often leads to reduced accuracy on unseen data, indicating decreased generalization. To determine the optimal `maxDepth`, it's crucial to pinpoint the point where accuracy on validation or test data is highest, striking a balance between capturing essential patterns and avoiding overfitting. In this scenario, the optimal depth seems to be around 10, where accuracy peaks before the decline, demonstrating the delicate balance necessary for effective decision tree model tuning. See Figure 5-9.

CHAPTER 5   POTABILITY ANALYSIS OF WATER USING MACHINE LEARNING

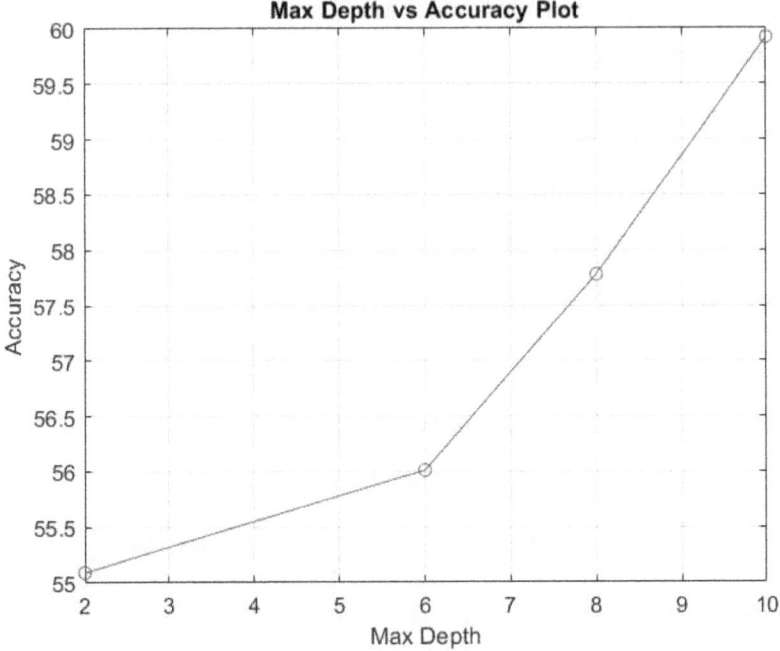

Figure 5-9. *Max depth versus accuracy plot*

Additionally, we analyze and compared the performance of decision tree classification algorithm for various values of minNumSamples. Table 5-2 summarizes the results.

Table 5-2. *Decision Tree Results II*

minNumSamples	Accuracy
3	61.92
6	59.60
9	56.79
12	61.09
15	58.28

CHAPTER 5   POTABILITY ANALYSIS OF WATER USING MACHINE LEARNING

The data provided reveals an intriguing pattern between the `minNumSamples` parameter and the accuracy of a decision tree model. As `minNumSamples` varies, the accuracy of the model demonstrates a nonlinear trend. Notably, the accuracy reaches its peak at specific intermediate values of `minNumSamples`, specifically at 3 (61.92%) and 12 (61.09%). These points represent the configurations where the model performs at its best, striking a balance between complexity and accuracy.

However, the trend takes a downturn as `minNumSamples` increases beyond these optimal points, notably at 9 and 15. At higher `minNumSamples`, the accuracy starts to decline. This decline occurs because larger `minNumSamples` values restrict the tree from making intricate splits, leading to oversimplified models incapable of capturing nuanced patterns in the data.

The observed pattern underscores a delicate balance. Lower `minNumSamples` values allow the model to capture fine-grained details in the training data, but if set too low, they risk overfitting. Conversely, higher values prevent overfitting by simplifying the tree, but if set excessively high, they oversimplify the model, leading to a decrease in accuracy.

In essence, the trend emphasizes the importance of selecting an optimal `minNumSamples` value. This value ensures that the decision tree strikes the right equilibrium between complexity and generalization, capturing crucial patterns while avoiding noise and thereby maximizing accuracy when making predictions on new, unseen data. See Figure 5-10.

CHAPTER 5   POTABILITY ANALYSIS OF WATER USING MACHINE LEARNING

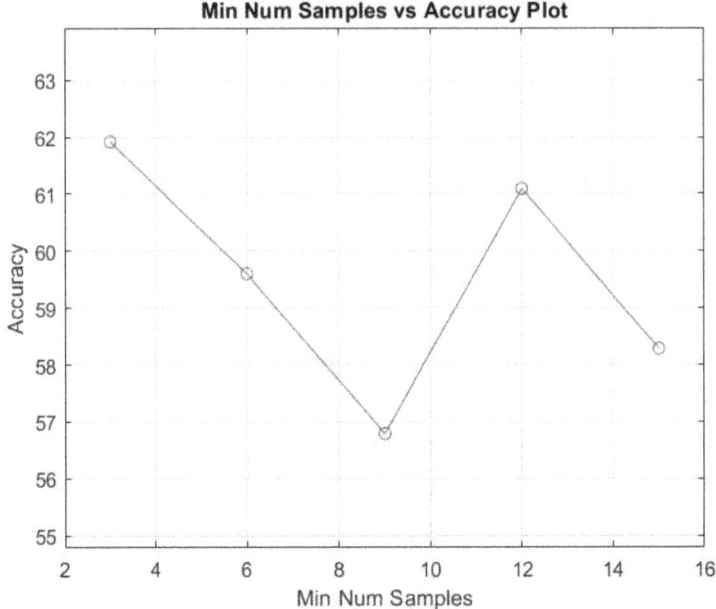

Figure 5-10. *Min num samples versus accuracy plot*

5.4.4 Random Forest

The purpose of this section is to analyze and compare the performance of random forest classification algorithm for various values of maxFeatures. Table 5-3 summarizes the results.

Table 5-3. *Random Forest Result I*

maxFeatures	Accuracy
0.8	58.44
0.6	62.58
0.4	59.93
0.2	58.61
0.1	58.00

CHAPTER 5 POTABILITY ANALYSIS OF WATER USING MACHINE LEARNING

maxFeatures determines the maximum fraction of features that are considered for splitting a node in a decision tree. In this case, 0.8 means that only 80% of the features are considered for each split. Randomly selecting a subset of features for each split can lead to more diverse and potentially better-performing trees. It helps in introducing diversity among the individual decision trees in the ensemble, enhancing the overall model's accuracy and robustness.

Analyzing the data, it becomes evident that the model attained its highest accuracy when maxFeatures was set to 0.6, reaching an impressive 62.58%. This finding suggests that considering 60% of the available features during each split resulted in the most accurate and robust predictions for the given dataset.

As maxFeatures decreased from 0.6 to 0.1, a consistent decline in accuracy was observed. This decline highlights the critical role of feature selection in model performance. Restricting the number of features considered for each split adversely affected the model's accuracy. Smaller maxFeatures values limited the diversity of trees within the ensemble, potentially leading to overfitting or the construction of less representative models for the underlying data.

The trend underscores the delicate balance required in feature selection. Too few features can yield overly specific trees that struggle to generalize, whereas too many features can result in overly complex models. The peak accuracy at maxFeatures = 0.6 indicates the successful equilibrium achieved for this specific dataset. It emphasizes the necessity of fine-tuning maxFeatures to optimize the random forest model's accuracy, ensuring that the chosen fraction of features fosters diversity, accuracy, and generalizability in the ensemble predictions. See Figure 5-11.

CHAPTER 5 POTABILITY ANALYSIS OF WATER USING MACHINE LEARNING

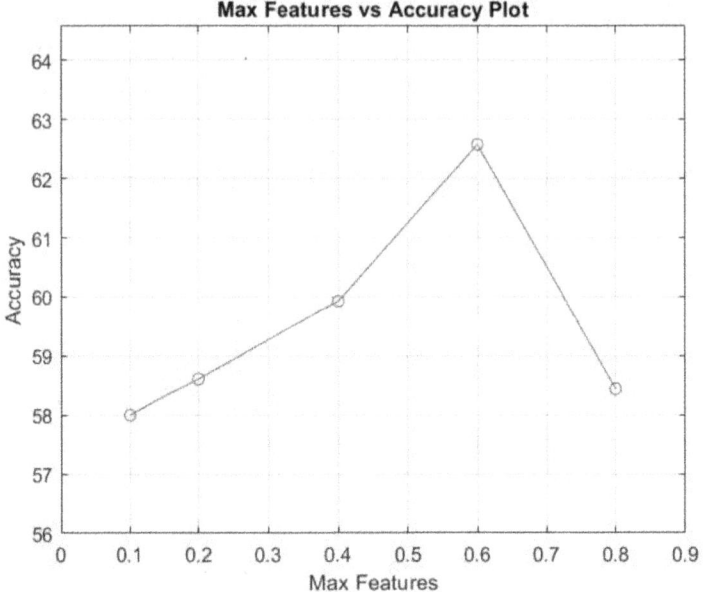

Figure 5-11. *Max features versus accuracy plot*

Additionally, we analyzed and compared the performance of random forest classification algorithm for various values of nEstimators. Table 5-4 summarizes the results.

Table 5-4. *Random Forest Results II*

nEstimators	Accuracy
20	58.01
25	59.78
30	64.24
35	60.10
40	58.77

CHAPTER 5   POTABILITY ANALYSIS OF WATER USING MACHINE LEARNING

nEstimators defines the number of trees in the random forest ensemble. Each tree is built independently and makes its own predictions. The predictions from all the trees are then combined (for classification, often by voting, and for regression, often by averaging) to produce the final output of the random forest model. Having a larger number of trees can improve the model's accuracy, up to a point. However, adding too many trees can lead to overfitting the training data, where the model memorizes the training set instead of learning the underlying patterns. The optimal number of estimators often depends on the specific dataset and problem.

Starting at 20 estimators, the accuracy stands at 58.01%. With an increase to 25 estimators, the accuracy improves significantly to 59.78%. Surprisingly, at 30 estimators, there is a substantial boost, resulting in an impressive accuracy of 64.24%. However, this high accuracy isn't sustained as the number of estimators continues to rise. With 35 estimators, the accuracy decreases slightly to 60.10%, and at 40 estimators, it further drops to 58.77%.

The trend suggests an optimal point for this specific dataset, and the problem lies around 30 estimators. Beyond this point, increasing the number of estimators doesn't yield proportional improvements in accuracy; instead, it appears to introduce noise or overfitting.

This observation aligns with the concept of diminishing returns in ensemble methods. Initially, adding more estimators enhances the model's predictive power, capturing more complex patterns in the data. However, after a certain point, the model becomes too specific to the training data, resulting in reduced accuracy on unseen data. Therefore, selecting an appropriate number of estimators is crucial, balancing computational efficiency with model accuracy. See Figure 5-12.

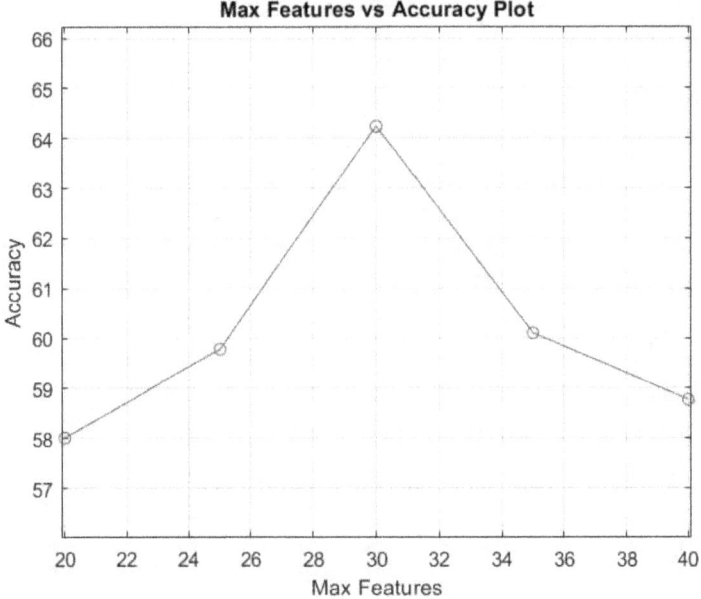

Figure 5-12. *Max features versus accuracy plot*

5.4.5 Naïve Bayes

Figure 5-13 illustrates the web application used to test water potability using the naïve Bayes algorithm. First, a table is generated to illustrate the values in the dataset.

CHAPTER 5   POTABILITY ANALYSIS OF WATER USING MACHINE LEARNING

Naive Bayes Classification

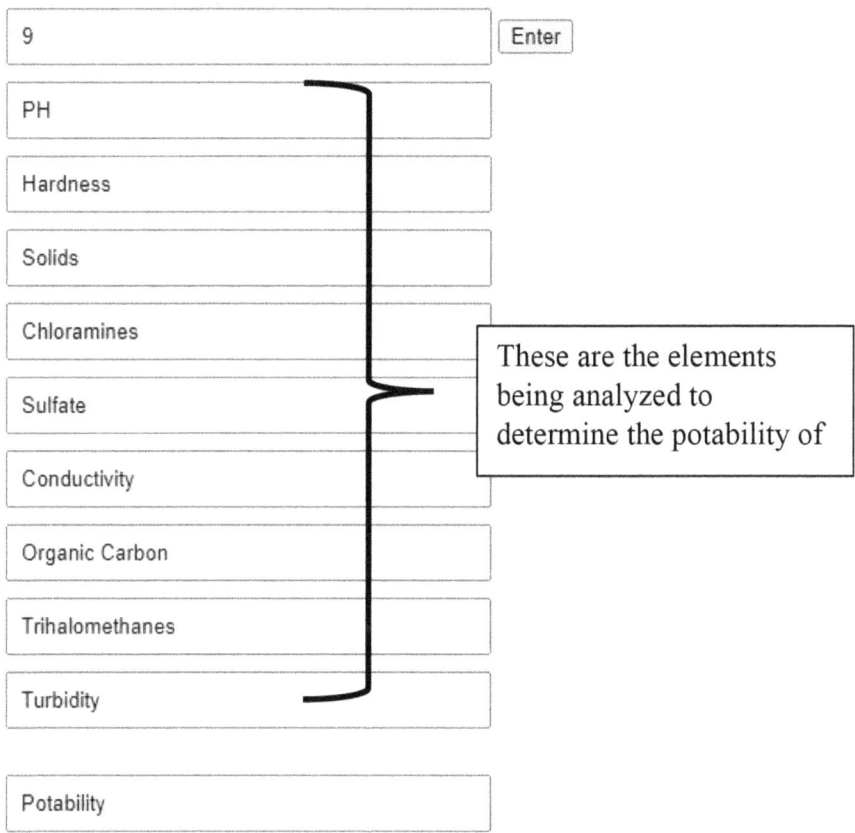

Figure 5-13.   Layout of naive Bayes classification

Then the CSV file is chosen to display the dataset. See Figure 5-14.

CHAPTER 5   POTABILITY ANALYSIS OF WATER USING MACHINE LEARNING

PH	Hardness	Solids	Chloramines	Sulfate	Conductivity	Organic Carbon	Trihalomethanes	Turbidity	Potability
8.316765884	214.3733941	22018.41744	8.059332377	356.8861356	363.2665162	18.4365245	100.3416744	4.628770537	0
9.092223456	181.1015092	17978.98634	6.546599974	310.1357375	398.4108134	11.55827944	31.99799273	4.075075425	0
5.584086638	188.3133238	28748.68774	7.544868789	326.6783629	280.4679159	8.39973464	54.91786184	2.559708228	0
10.22386216	248.0717353	28749.71654	7.513408466	393.6633955	283.6516335	13.78969532	84.60355617	2.672988737	0
8.635848719	203.3615226	13672.09176	4.563008686	303.3097712	474.6076449	12.3638167	62.79830896	4.401424715	0

Figure 5-14. *Dataset selection (naive Bayes)*

Figure 5-15 illustrates the computations performed for each element in the dataset. The computation is conducted on the number of instances chosen while displaying the dataset. (N/A illustrates the chosen values from the dataset for each of the elements.)

1. Figure 5-15 shows the computation of the pH value.

PH

N/A	0	P(0)
8.316765884	1	0.2
9.092223456	1	0.2
5.584086638	1	0.2
10.22386216	1	0.2
8.635848719	1	0.2
Total	5	100%

Figure 5-15. *Computation of pH value*

CHAPTER 5   POTABILITY ANALYSIS OF WATER USING MACHINE LEARNING

2. Figure 5-16 determines the computation for the hardness of the water.

Hardness

N/A	0	P(0)
214.3733941	1	0.2
181.1015092	1	0.2
188.3133238	1	0.2
248.0717353	1	0.2
203.3615226	1	0.2
Total	5	100%

Figure 5-16. *Computation of hardness*

3. Figure 5-17 shows the computation about the solids found in water.

Solids

N/A	0	P(0)
22018.41744	1	0.2
17978.98634	1	0.2
28748.68774	1	0.2
28749.71654	1	0.2
13672.09176	1	0.2
Total	5	100%

Figure 5-17. *Computation of solids*

4. Figure 5-18 illustrates the computation of chloramines in water.

CHAPTER 5   POTABILITY ANALYSIS OF WATER USING MACHINE LEARNING

Chloramines

N/A	0	P(0)
8.059332377	1	0.2
6.546599974	1	0.2
7.544868789	1	0.2
7.513408466	1	0.2
4.563008686	1	0.2
Total	5	100%

Figure 5-18. Computation of chloramines

Figure 5-19 illustrates the computation of sulfate in water.

Sulfate

N/A	0	P(0)
356.8861356	1	0.2
310.1357375	1	0.2
326.6783629	1	0.2
393.6633955	1	0.2
303.3097712	1	0.2
Total	5	100%

Figure 5-19. Computation of sulfate

Figure 5-20 illustrates the calculations of conductivity in water.

CHAPTER 5   POTABILITY ANALYSIS OF WATER USING MACHINE LEARNING

Conductivity

N/A	0	P(0)
363.2665162	1	0.2
398.4108134	1	0.2
280.4679159	1	0.2
283.6516335	1	0.2
474.6076449	1	0.2
Total	5	100%

Figure 5-20. Computation of conductivity

Figure 5-21 illustrates the calculations of organic compound in water.

Organic Carbon

N/A	0	P(0)
18.4365245	1	0.2
11.55827944	1	0.2
8.39973464	1	0.2
13.78969532	1	0.2
12.3638167	1	0.2
Total	5	100%

Figure 5-21. Computation of organic compound

Figure 5-22 illustrates the calculations of trihalomethanes in water.

CHAPTER 5　POTABILITY ANALYSIS OF WATER USING MACHINE LEARNING

Trihalomethanes

N/A	0	P(0)
100.3416744	1	0.2
31.99799273	1	0.2
54.91786184	1	0.2
84.60355617	1	0.2
62.79830896	1	0.2
Total	5	100%

Figure 5-22. *Computation of trihalomethanes*

Figure 5-23 illustrates the calculations of turbidity in water.

Turbidity

N/A	0	P(0)
4.628770537	1	0.2
4.075075425	1	0.2
2.559708228	1	0.2
2.672988737	1	0.2
4.401424715	1	0.2
Total	5	100%

Figure 5-23. *Computation of turbidity*

The tables show the probability calculated for each element in the dataset.

To test the potability of water, values need to be inserted for each element. See Figure 5-24.

CHAPTER 5   POTABILITY ANALYSIS OF WATER USING MACHINE LEARNING

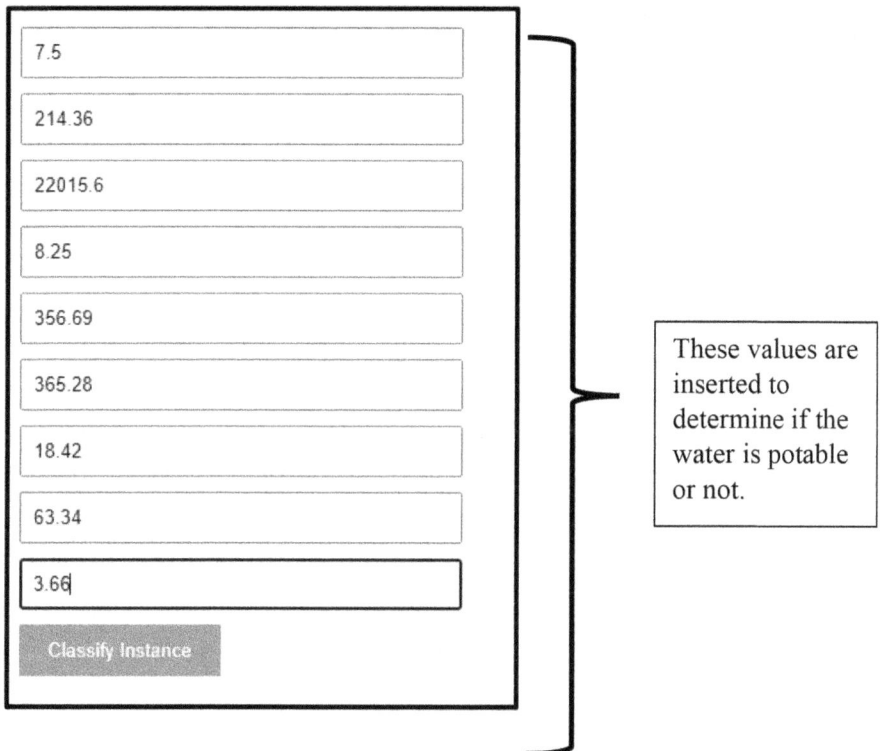

Figure 5-24. Testing of naïve Bayes classification

After clicking the Classify Instance button, the output is displayed. See Figure 5-25.

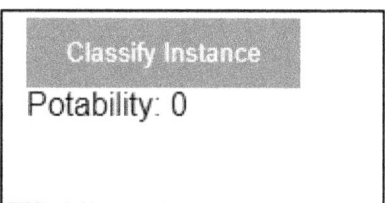

Figure 5-25. Output of naïve Bayes

Based on the output obtained, it can be determined that the water quality is not suitable for drinking.

5.5 Summary

The primary objectives of the chapter revolve around addressing SDGs 3, 6, and 12, which encompass good health and well-being, clean water and sanitation, and responsible consumption and production, respectively. To accomplish these objectives, an in-depth analysis of a dataset available from Kaggle related to water potability was conducted. The results highlighted significant variations in the performance of the four algorithms employed: decision tree, random forest, k-nearest neighbors (KNN) and naïve Bayes. Remarkably.

Essentially, a web page was designed in JavaScript and HTML whereby the user will be asked to enter the value of pH, hardness, solids, chloramines, sulfate, conductivity, organic carbon, trihalomethanes, and turbidity. Based on these values entered, it will predict whether the water is potable or not. Naïve Bayes emerged as the frontrunner with an exceptional accuracy rate of 99.95%. This remarkable performance suggests that naïve Bayes can be a robust choice for distinguishing between potable and nonpotable water. Decision tree, KNN, and random forest all had an accuracy of around 58%.

CHAPTER 6

Air Quality Monitoring: A Case Study for the Application of Machine Learning in Meeting SDGs 3 and 13

Chapter authors:
Aunowar Farhaan Mohammad Jeelany, farhaanaunowar@gmail.com
Munisamy Sodiyen, munisamysodiyen@gmail.com
Ragoo Navish Kumar, navishragoo@gmail.com
Kwok Hin John Darren Johsua, darrenkwok2000@gmail.com
Hawseea Mohammed Fayez, fayezunknown@gmail.com
Appadoo Sarvesh Sanjeevi, sarvesh.appadoo1@gmail.com
Department of Electrical and Electronic Engineering, University of Mauritius

CHAPTER 6 AIR QUALITY MONITORING: A CASE STUDY FOR THE APPLICATION OF MACHINE LEARNING IN MEETING SDGS 3 AND 13

The United Nations Sustainable Development Goals (SDGs) are dedicated to enhancing healthcare and education, reducing inequality, fostering economic growth, and addressing the challenges posed by climate change, among other initiatives beneficial for the planet and its inhabitants. Machine learning (ML) stands as a potent tool for harnessing vast amounts of data, making predictions, and uncovering patterns. This capability enables proactive decision-making, facilitating optimizations within core systems and distribution channels.

In this chapter, a web application was meticulously crafted to forecast air quality across multiple locations in Mauritius, aligning with the objectives of SDG 3 (Good Health and Well-Being) and SDG 13 (Climate Action). Leveraging the Weatherbit.io API, historical air quality data was procured to predict the Air Quality Index (AQI) and concentrations of key air pollutants, namely, O_3, CO, PM10, and PM25. Three ML algorithms were employed: simple linear regression (SLR), multilayer perceptron (MLP), polynomial regression (PR) and long short-term memory (LSTM).

Furthermore, various ML classification algorithms, namely, k-nearest neighbor (k-NN), decision tree (DT), and random forest (RF) were utilized to effectively classify the AQI levels. DT and RF have the highest accuracies of 99.5% and 98.9%, respectively. k-NN performed the least with an accuracy of 84.3%. The SLR, MLP, PR, and LSTM algorithms showcased varying accuracies in predicting air pollutant concentrations and AQI levels. The performance of these algorithms was thoroughly assessed using Mean Absolute Percentage Error (MAPE) as a performance metric. The MAPE for SLR ranged from 6.81% to 12.99%, while for PR it varied from 2.35% to 9.36%. The MAPE for MLP was between 1.48% and 2.31%, and for LSTM, it spanned from 1.20% to 1.91%. The MLP and LSTM algorithms stood out for their lower MAPE values, showing their ability to capture complex patterns in the data.

This research highlights the potential of ML methods for predicting air quality and improving public health. The web application offers real-time air quality predictions and insights for Mauritius, supporting global efforts toward the UN SDGs.

CHAPTER 6   AIR QUALITY MONITORING: A CASE STUDY FOR THE APPLICATION OF MACHINE LEARNING IN MEETING SDGS 3 AND 13

6.1 Introduction

The SDG framework is related to various human rights but can be distinguished by its focus on people, the planet, prosperity, peace, and partnership [1]. The three major pillars are environmental protection, social diversity, and economic growth. The significance of machine learning (ML) lies in its capacity to greatly impact the attainment of the UN SDGs. ML algorithms are powerful computational tools that enable computers to learn and make predictions without being explicitly programmed [1].

These algorithms are designed to analyze and extract patterns from vast amounts of data. By leveraging statistical techniques and iterative processes, ML algorithms can detect patterns and predict accurate results. Through the ability of ML algorithms to analyze vast and complex datasets, ML enhances decision-making, resource allocation, and predictive modeling, thus accelerating progress toward the SDGs. By optimizing processes, identifying patterns, and providing insights across various sectors, ML will contribute substantially to the global achievement of the SDGs by 2030 [2].

In this chapter, SDG 3, which aims at ensuring healthy lives and promoting well-being for all at all ages, and SDG 13 (climate action), which aims at taking urgent action to combat climate change and its impacts, have been targeted. A proposal has been put forward that involves a method to predict the level of air pollutants. This method aims to analyze how the concentration of air pollutants changes over time in real time for 10 different locations in Mauritius.

To achieve this, several regression algorithms of machine learning (ML) have been employed, which include simple linear regression (SLR), multiple linear regression (MLR), and polynomial regression (PR). Each of these algorithms provides an estimation of the air pollutant concentrations. Moreover, the objective of this work is to also assess the relationship between various factors and air pollutant levels, allowing for the creation of predictive models that can anticipate pollutant concentrations in real time. These models utilize regression algorithms to analyze historical data and output a predicted value for the number of days the user has input, thus offering valuable insights into air quality dynamics for the specified cities.

6.2 AI Use Cases for SDGs 3 and 13

6.2.1 SDG 3: Good Health and Well-Being

SDG 3 strives to ensure the well-being and good health of people of all ages. As a result, ML, a subset of artificial intelligence, has seen growing use in this domain to contribute to the attainment of this objective. In [3], some relevant literature concerning the use of ML tools and techniques in the field of drug discovery has been examined. These methods are employed at various stages of drug development to expedite research processes, mitigate risks, and reduce costs associated with clinical trials. ML techniques enhance decision-making by analyzing pharmaceutical data across different applications, including QSAR analysis, identifying potential drug candidates, and creating new drug designs, all with the aim of achieving more precise outcomes.

From [4], the use of deep learning approach (DLA) in medical image analysis has emerged as a rapidly advancing research domain where DLA is extensively applied in medical imaging to discern the presence or absence of diseases. This paper focuses on the evolution of artificial neural networks and conducts an extensive examination of DLA, which exhibits promising applications within the realm of medical imaging. In the work carried out in [5], an approach for distinguishing autism traits using machine learning is presented. An existing prediction model was enhanced by combining two different algorithms: CART and ID3 within random forest. They tested and evaluated the model using two datasets:

one called the Autism Spectrum Quotient (AQ10) dataset and the other containing 1,100 real-world data samples from individuals with and without autistic traits. The real-world dataset was obtained from hospital databases. The results showed an accuracy of 98% with only 2% false positive cases.

This study has the potential to reduce the diagnostic time of autism significantly. The use of a convolutional neural network (CNN) for the analysis of medical respiratory audio data related to obstructive pulmonary detection is presented in [6]. The Librosa machine learning library was utilized to analyze various audio features like MFCC, MEL-Spectrogram, Chroma, Chroma (Constant-Q), and Chroma CENS. The system can also determine the severity of the disease, categorizing it as mild, moderate, or severe. The results showed that this deep learning approach was effective and had a classification accuracy rate of 93% according to the ICBHI score. In [10], support vector machine (SVM) and the RF as conventional ML methods and CNN as deep learning (DL) methods were employed in a comparative analysis for the prediction and detection of diabetes in patients. RF achieved an accuracy of 83.67%, DL 76.81%, and SVM 65.38% in their experiment. In [7], Gabriel et al. applied logistic regression, random forest, support vector machine, K-nearest neighbor, naïve Bayes classifier, and feed-forward neural network to diagnose chronic kidney disease (CKD). A CKD dataset from the University of California Irvine was used. Random forest obtained a diagnosis accuracy of 99.75% and outperformed the other algorithms. In [8], Gabriel et al. introduced an approach leveraging ML, specifically neural networks and random forests. They developed two complementary models with the goal of estimating the likelihood of an individual succumbing to COVID-19. The training dataset encompassed demographic data and medical histories of two groups: one comprising individuals who unfortunately passed away due to COVID-19, and the other consisting of those who successfully recovered from the illness in Colombia during 2020.

CHAPTER 6   AIR QUALITY MONITORING: A CASE STUDY FOR THE APPLICATION OF MACHINE LEARNING IN MEETING SDGS 3 AND 13

6.2.2 SDG 13: Climate Action

In [9], the authors proposed a real-time, multistep, multi-output, multivariate ML model to forecast the concentrations of the different air pollutants in Ho Chi Minh City (HCMC) in Vietnam. The air pollutants include NO_2, SO_2, O_3, and CO. The model proposed by the authors took as input various parameters, including meteorological conditions and air quality data from urban, residential, and industrial areas as well as hourly NO_2, SO_2, O_3, and CO concentrations.

Moreover, the proposed ML model used an N-beats neural network with a deep stack of fully connected layers with both forward and backward links. Furthermore, the authors used data from six air quality monitoring sites in HCMC to generate several datasets that contain the concentrations of the pollutants from February 2021 to August 2022. The concentration of each air pollutant was predicted using the proposed model, and the results demonstrated that the MAPE value obtained, when predicting the concentration of each pollutant, ranged from 0.18 to 0.23.

The authors in [10] developed a robust method to forecast the AQI, crucial for industry pollution control and public health. They began by predicting PM2.5 and PM10 levels using an ANN. Building upon this, they extended their approach to predicting other significant air pollutants essential for estimating the AQI. They employed missForest, a machine learning–based technique utilizing the RF algorithm to fill in missing entries. RF was applied during the data pre-processing phase, enhancing accuracy. Validation in Kuwait's Al-Jahra city demonstrated an impressive 92.41% AQI prediction accuracy, surpassing previous methods.

In another work [11], various ML techniques were employed, including LR, SDG regression, RF, decision tree, SVR, ANN, Gradient Boost, and Ada Boost to predict the AQI for pollutants like PM2.5, PM10, CO, NO_2, SO_2, and O_3. SVR and ANNs emerged as the most accurate methods for forecasting air quality in New Delhi, displaying lower Mean Squared Error (MSE), Mean Absolute Error (MAE), and higher R^2 values.

Similarly, in [12], different ML algorithms were used to forecast the level of Particulate Matter, which is less than 2.5um in diameter in a specific region in Delhi, India. The authors also proposed a new model that combined two deep learning algorithms, namely, LSTM and GRU to predict the AQI. Two types of data were used; one consisted of different pollutant concentrations, and the other consisted of weather data. After preprocessing and feature extraction, the data was fed into the various algorithms such as LR, GRU, K-nearest neighbor (KNN), SVM, LSTM, and lastly the proposed hybrid model of LSTM-GRU. After evaluating all the results, it was found that the proposed model had the best performance among all the models with an MAE value of 36.11.

In [13], a deep learning approach for predicting the AQI in metropolitan cities is proposed. The AQI for Chennai city was forecasted by first gathering a dataset and performing pre-processing such as replacing missing values and eliminating redundant data. The AQI value is based on the level of pollutants such as particulate matter, ozone, and sulfur dioxide. The Grey Level Co-occurrence Matrix was used to compute statistical measures, namely, the mean, mean square error, and standard deviation from the dataset. SVM along with LSTM was used to classify the AQI value between six categories ranging from good to severe. The AQI value can be used to better plan sustainable metropolitan cities, control air pollution levels, encourage the plantation of trees, and convince people to use public transportation. Additionally, in [14], it discusses how ML methods have been used in the field of climate and numerical weather prediction. This article provides an introductory overview of DL and presents a preliminary summary of current methodologies for predicting extreme weather. These approaches leverage recurrent neural networks (RNNs) to forecast weather patterns and CNNs to predict extreme weather events. They automatically extract essential image features related to extreme weather, enabling predictions of extreme weather probabilities using a deep learning framework.

CHAPTER 6　AIR QUALITY MONITORING: A CASE STUDY FOR THE APPLICATION OF MACHINE LEARNING IN MEETING SDGS 3 AND 13

6.3 Data Processing and Application Design

This section describes the datasets used, the structure of the developed web application, and the preprocessing steps. Flowcharts and pseudocodes are also used to describe the different processes involved.

6.3.1 Data Collection Process and Dataset Description

The training data used for performing regression was obtained from the Weatherbit.io Air Quality API. This API allows users to access hourly historical air quality information such as the concentration of air pollutants and the AQI for any location on the planet. For this purpose, 10 locations were selected in Mauritius to retrieve the air quality information. General information about the selected locations is shown in Table 6-1.

Table 6-1. *Selected Locations*

Location	Surface Area (Km^2)	Population
Port Louis	61.50	145,793
Curepipe	24.10	78,256
Grand Baie	14.60	12,173
Flic En Flac	21.10	2,550
Quatres Bornes	21.10	77,084
Vacoas	107.0	105,688
Beau Bassin	20.10	103,452
Tamarin	47.90	4,371
Mahebourg	2.29	15,426
Flacq	20.3	16,175

CHAPTER 6 AIR QUALITY MONITORING: A CASE STUDY FOR THE APPLICATION OF MACHINE LEARNING IN MEETING SDGS 3 AND 13

The air pollutants that are monitored are shown in Table 6-2.

Table 6-2. Air Pollutants

Air Pollutant	Unit
PM_{10} – Particulate matter < 10 microns	$\mu g/m^3$
PM_{25} – Particulate matter < 2.5 microns	$\mu g/m^3$
CO – Carbon monoxide	$\mu g/m^3$
O_3 – Surface ozone	$\mu g/m^3$

To use the Air Quality API, a URL is created with the necessary parameters, and an HTTP GET request is sent to the API endpoint using the fetch() method. The parameters required are the city name, start date, end date, the time zone, and the API key. The response is obtained in the form of a JSON object containing an array of data. The extractFields() method is then used to retrieve the values of AQI, concentration of O_3, CO, PM_{10}, PM_{25} and the timestamp the values were measured. These values are stored in separate arrays to be used for performing regression. Figure 6-1 shows a flowchart illustrating the process for retrieving the air quality data.

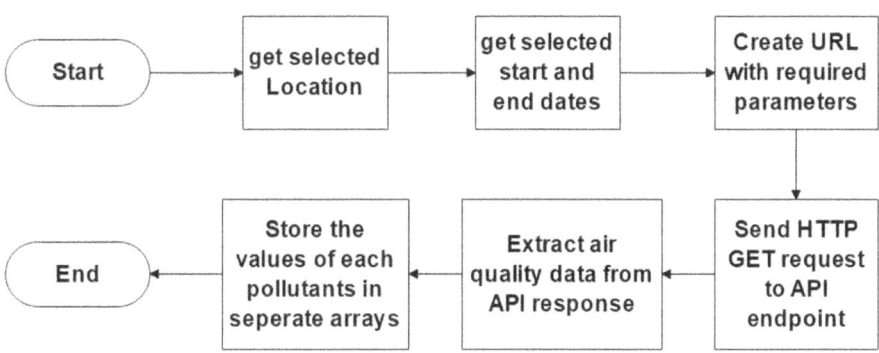

Figure 6-1. Process for retrieving the air quality data flowchart

CHAPTER 6   AIR QUALITY MONITORING: A CASE STUDY FOR THE APPLICATION OF MACHINE LEARNING IN MEETING SDGS 3 AND 13

6.3.2 Program Structure

Figure 6-2 shows the program structure. It is to be noted that all the code of this chapter can be found in the folder Chapter 6 - Codes hosted on the GitHub page of this book.

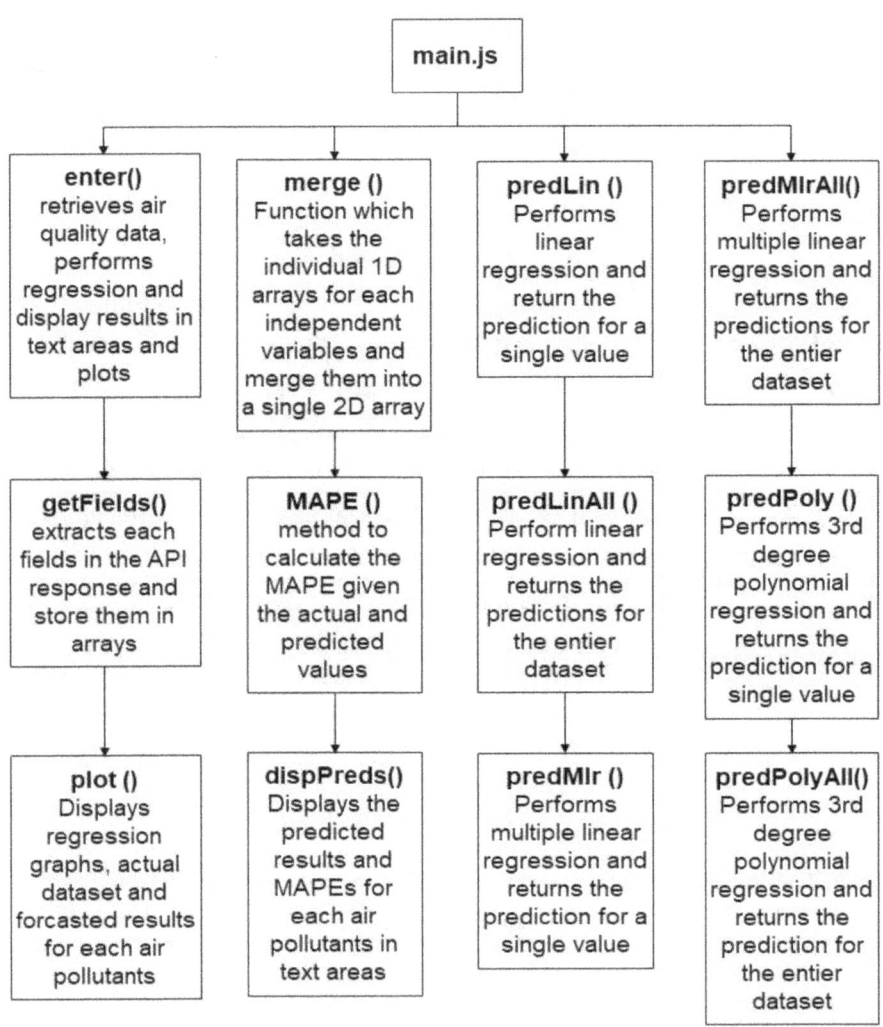

Figure 6-2. Program structure

CHAPTER 6   AIR QUALITY MONITORING: A CASE STUDY FOR THE APPLICATION OF MACHINE LEARNING IN MEETING SDGS 3 AND 13

6.3.3 Layout of Website

Figure 6-3 illustrates the main layout of the website.

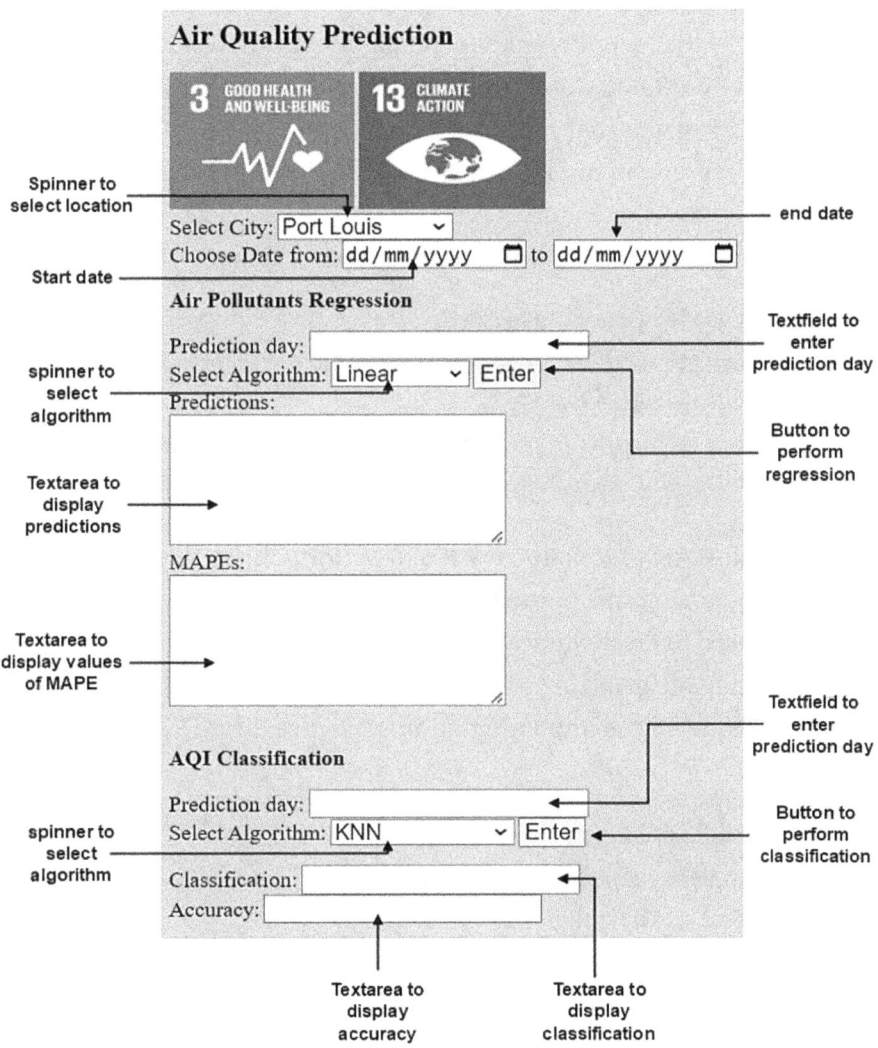

Figure 6-3. *Layout of website*

231

6.3.4 Implementation of Linear Regression

The predLin() function is used to perform linear regression for each air pollutant. It takes as input the dependant variable, which consists of the values of the air pollutant, the independent variable that is the recorded timestamps, and the prediction time in seconds. The SimpleLinearRegression() function from the ML.js library is used to create the regression model. The predict() function is then called to obtain the prediction before it is returned. The pseudocode for the implementation of the predLin() function is shown here:

Function predLin (x, y, xtarget)
       Create Linear regression model
       Get prediction from model
       Return prediction
End

The predLinAll() function is used to perform linear regression for each air pollutant on the entire dataset. The SimpleLinearRegression() function is used to create the regression model. Each entry in the dataset is predicted using the predict() function by iterating over the entire dataset. The pseudocode for the implementation of the predLinAll() function is shown here:

Function predLinAll (x, y)
       Create Linear regression model
       For i in range x:
          Get prediction for each entry in dataset
       End
       Return predictions
End

6.3.5 Implementation of Polynomial Regression

The predPoly() function is used to perform polynomial regression. It takes as input the dependent variable, independent variable, and prediction time. The 5th-degree polynomial regression is used. The regression model is then created using the PolynomialRegression() function from the ML.js library. The prediction at the prediction time is obtained using the predict() function. The prediction is then returned. The pseudocode for the implementation of the predPoly() function is shown here:

```
Function predPoly (x, y, xtarget)
        Set polynomial degree to 5
        Create polynomial regression model
        Get prediction from model
        Return prediction
End
```

The predPolyAll() function is used to perform polynomial regression on the entire dataset. The polynomial degree is set to 5. The PolynomialRegression() function is then used to create the regression model. Each entry in the dataset is predicted using the predict() function by iterating over the entire dataset. The predictions are then returned as shown by the following pseudocode:

```
Function predPolyAll (x, y)
        Set polynomial degree to 5
        Create polynomial regression model
        For i in range x:
            Get prediction for each entry in dataset
        End
End
```

6.3.6 Implementation of LSTM/MLP

```
MLP / LSTM Regression Algorithm
    Obtain window size from number of prediction days
    Create Perceptron / LSTM Object from Neataptic library
    Create sliding window for window-sized steps prediction
    Store all normalised input and output data in a 2D array
    Train the model with training data array and parameters
    Obtain prediction and de-normalised value
    Calculate MAPE.
End
```

6.3.7 Displaying Regression Graphs

The plot() function is used to display the original data, the regression graphs, and the predicted value at the prediction time. It takes as input the original data, the predicted data points for linear regression, MLR and polynomial regression, and the container for the plot. The timestamps are converted to days and shifted to begin at 0 days. Traces are created to contain the data points for the original data, linear regression, MLR, polynomial regression, and the predicted value at the prediction time in the y-axis. In the x-axis, the timestamps in days are used. In the layout, the unit and the title are set. The newPlot() function from the Plotly.js library is then used to display the traces in the container. The pseudocode for the implementation of the Plot() function is shown here:

```
Function Plot()
        Convert timestamps to days and shift to zero
        Create trace for original data
        Create trace for linear regression
        Create trace for polynomial regression
        Create trace for LSTM
```

CHAPTER 6   AIR QUALITY MONITORING: A CASE STUDY FOR THE APPLICATION OF MACHINE LEARNING IN MEETING SDGS 3 AND 13

```
Create trace for MLP
Create a SimpleLinearRegression / PolynomialRegression
3rd/5th Order Object from the ML library.
Create an LSTM/MLP Object from the ML library
Set unit and title of layour
Calculate MAPE.
```
End

6.3.8 AQI Classification

Figure 6-4 illustrates the operation of the Classify AQI button.

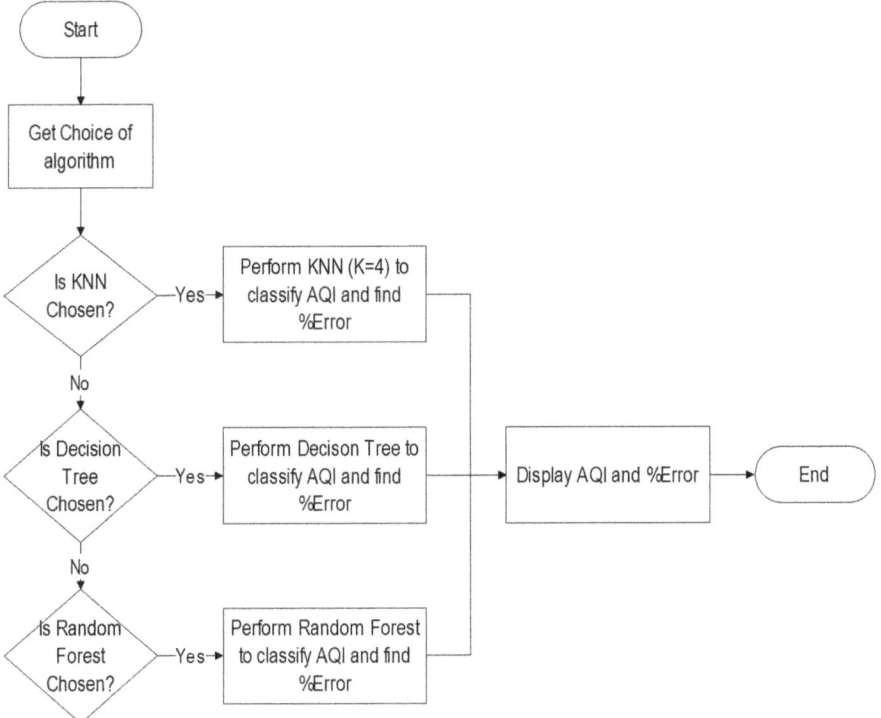

Figure 6-4. *Classify AQI button flowchart*

6.4 Application Testing and Analysis

6.4.1 Testing of Web Application

The features and functionalities of the web application are illustrated in this section. Figure 6-5 shows the web application after the user has entered all the necessary inputs for the regression part of the application. The location was set to Grand Baie. The dataset was selected to be seven days long. The PR algorithm was selected, and the prediction day was set to 2.

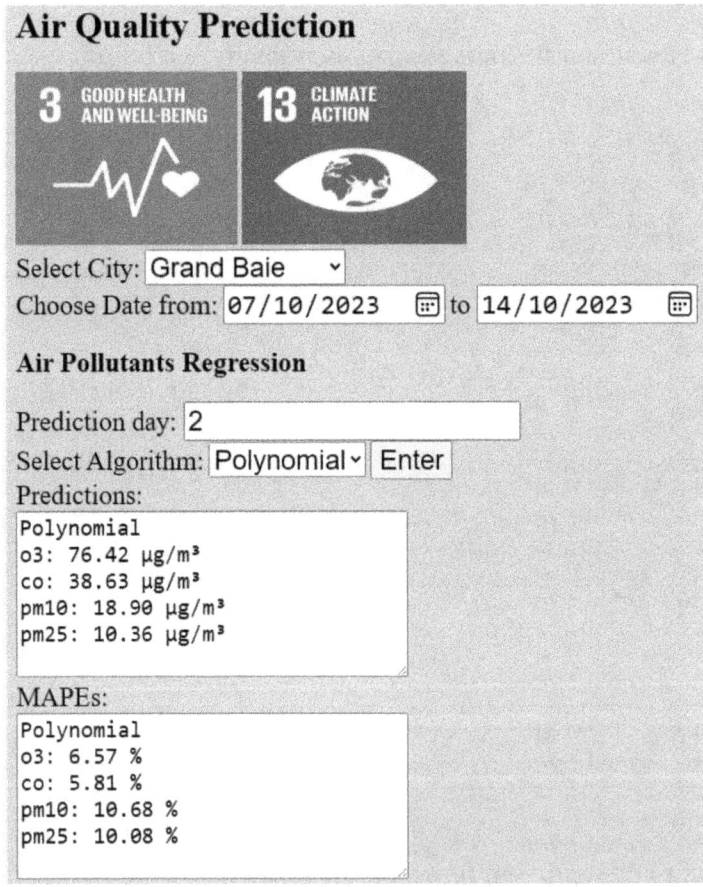

Figure 6-5. Regression part of web application

CHAPTER 6   AIR QUALITY MONITORING: A CASE STUDY FOR THE APPLICATION OF MACHINE LEARNING IN MEETING SDGS 3 AND 13

From the output obtained in Figure 6-5, it is seen that the predicted values for the air pollutants after 2 days in Grand Baie are as follows:

- O3 = 76.42 µg/m3
- CO = 38.63 µg/m3
- PM10 = 18.90 µg/m3
- PM25 = 10.36 µg/m3

The MAPE values and graphs were also displayed to illustrate how the algorithms accurately model the variation with time of each air pollutant. Figure 6-6 shows the graph of concentration of O3 against time.

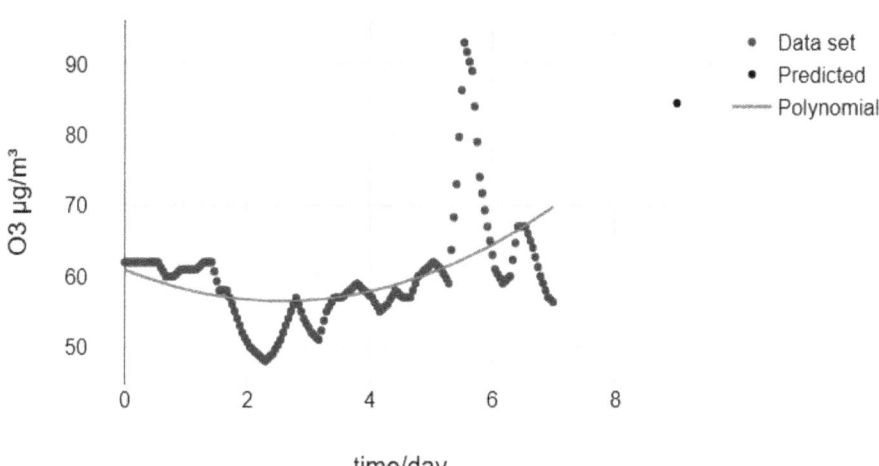

Figure 6-6. *Web application output for concentration of O3 against time*

CHAPTER 6   AIR QUALITY MONITORING: A CASE STUDY FOR THE APPLICATION OF MACHINE LEARNING IN MEETING SDGS 3 AND 13

Figure 6-7 shows the graph of concentration of CO against time.

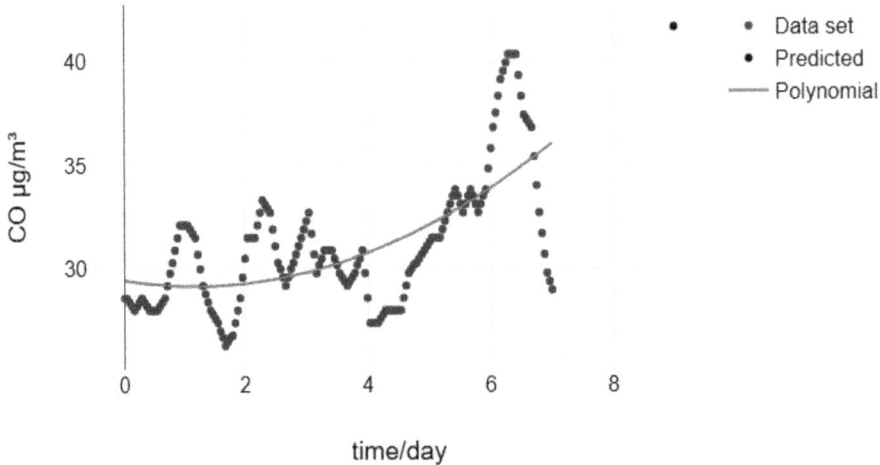

Figure 6-7. Web application output for concentration of CO against time

Figure 6-8 shows the graph of concentration of PM10 against time.

CHAPTER 6   AIR QUALITY MONITORING: A CASE STUDY FOR THE APPLICATION OF MACHINE LEARNING IN MEETING SDGS 3 AND 13

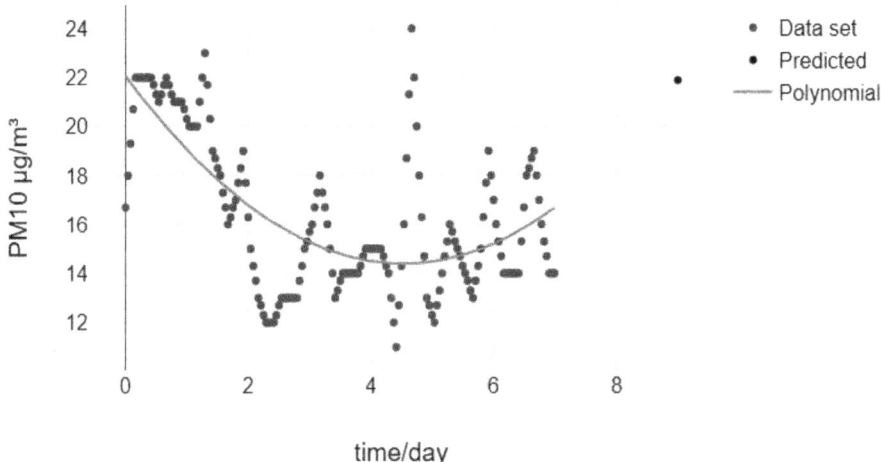

Figure 6-8. *Web application output for concentration of PM10 against time*

Figure 6-9 shows the graph of concentration of PM25 against time.

CHAPTER 6   AIR QUALITY MONITORING: A CASE STUDY FOR THE APPLICATION OF MACHINE LEARNING IN MEETING SDGS 3 AND 13

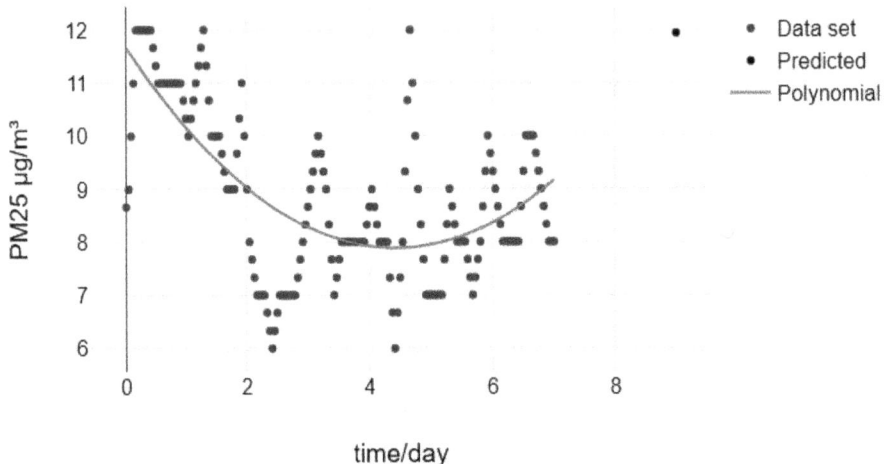

Figure 6-9. *Web application output for concentration of PM25 against time*

Figure 6-10 shows the web application after the user has entered the inputs for the classification part of the application. The location was set to Grand Baie. The dataset was selected to be 21 days long. The KNN algorithm was selected, and the prediction day was set to 2.

AQI Classification

Prediction day: 2
Select Algorithm: KNN   Enter

Classification: 1
Accuracy: 80.79207920792079%

Figure 6-10. *Classification part of web application*

From the output shown in Figure 6-10, the predicted AQI after 2 days is 1, and an accuracy of 80.79% was obtained for KNN for the selected dataset.

6.4.2 Performance of Regression Algorithms

The performance of each algorithm for predicting the concentration of air pollutants was evaluated by calculating the MAPEs for five locations out of the 10 selected ones and taking the average values. A sample size of 168, which is equivalent to 7 days, was used.

6.4.3 Performance of SLR

Figure 6-11 shows the graph of concentration of PM10 against time for SLR algorithm.

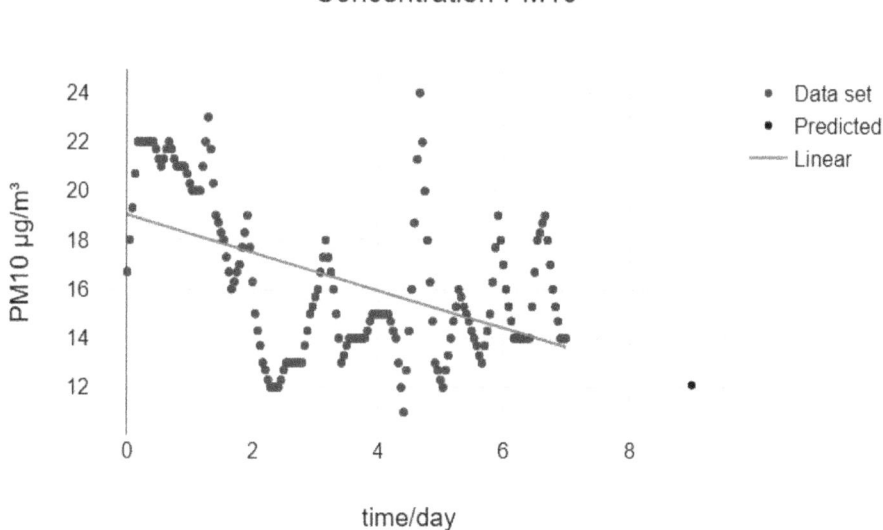

Figure 6-11. Web application output for SLR algorithm

CHAPTER 6   AIR QUALITY MONITORING: A CASE STUDY FOR THE APPLICATION OF MACHINE LEARNING IN MEETING SDGS 3 AND 13

Table 6-3 shows the MAPE values obtained for the SLR algorithm.

Table 6-3. *MAPE values for SLR algorithm*

Locations Air pollutants	Port Louis	Grand Baie	Quatre Bornes	Beau Bassin	Flacq	Average
O_3	6.64	7.00	7.08	6.89	6.43	6.81
CO	9.87	10.76	11.21	11.52	11.92	11.06
PM_{10}	12.33	12.65	12.99	12.80	14.16	12.99
PM_{25}	11.54	11.78	12.22	12.37	13.44	12.27

The SLR algorithm was selected as it can still be valuable when the relationship between a single predictor and a response variable is linear and well-suited for analysis using a simple linear model. However, it may not capture more complex relationships that PLR and MLP can handle. From the results obtained in Table 5-1, it can be observed that the MAPE is low ranging, from 6.81% to 12.99%. The MAPE for the concentration of O3 is the lowest at 6.81%. This could indicate that the concentration of O3 follows a predictable pattern, with low-magnitude fluctuations. For the other variables, the MAPE was relatively high, which could indicate that the air pollutants vary in a random manner, and it is difficult to obtain a line of best fit.

6.4.4 Performance of PR

The fifth-degree polynomial regression was used. Figure 6-12 shows the graph of concentration of PM10 against time for the PR algorithm.

CHAPTER 6   AIR QUALITY MONITORING: A CASE STUDY FOR THE APPLICATION OF MACHINE LEARNING IN MEETING SDGS 3 AND 13

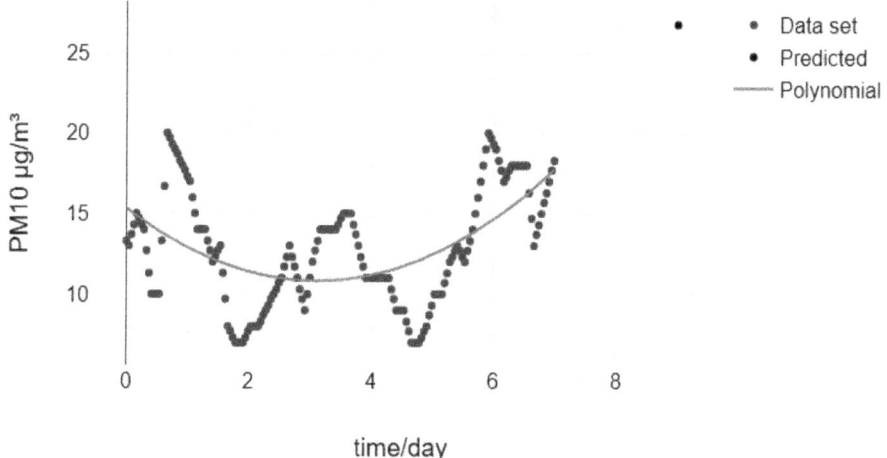

Figure 6-12. Web application output for PR algorithm

Table 6-4 shows the MAPE values obtained for the PR algorithm.

Table 6-4. MAPE values for PR algorithm

Locations Air pollutants	Port Louis	Grand Baie	Quatre Bornes	Beau Bassin	Flacq	Average
O_3	2.66	2.15	2.07	2.35	2.53	2.35
CO	11.75	8.39	8.67	9.96	8.04	9.36
PM_{10}	9.58	9.57	9.21	9.24	7.83	9.09
PM_{25}	9.45	9.44	9.05	9.09	8.02	9.01

The PR algorithm was selected as it is an extension of the concept of SLR to cases where predictors may be more accurately related to their responses using a polynomial function. The curvilinear relationship

CHAPTER 6   AIR QUALITY MONITORING: A CASE STUDY FOR THE APPLICATION OF MACHINE LEARNING IN MEETING SDGS 3 AND 13

between the predictor and the response is observed. From the results obtained in Table 5-3, it can be observed that the MAPE is low, ranging from 2.35% to 9.36%. The MAPE for the concentration of O3 is the lowest at 2.35%. The low values of MAPE indicate that the PR algorithm was able to model the variation of air pollutants with time accurately.

6.4.5 Performance of MLP

Table 6-5 shows the hyper parameters used for the MLP algorithm.

Table 6-5. Hyper Parameters of MLP Algorithm

Algorithm	Hyper Parameters
MLP	Window Size = 24 x prediction day
	Number of Epochs = 500
	Learning Rate = 0.001
	Momentum = 0.9
	Error = 0.001
	Number of hidden layers = 1
	Number of nodes in hidden layer = 24 x prediction day

Figure 6-13 shows the graph of concentration of PM10 against time for the MLP algorithm.

CHAPTER 6   AIR QUALITY MONITORING: A CASE STUDY FOR THE APPLICATION OF MACHINE LEARNING IN MEETING SDGS 3 AND 13

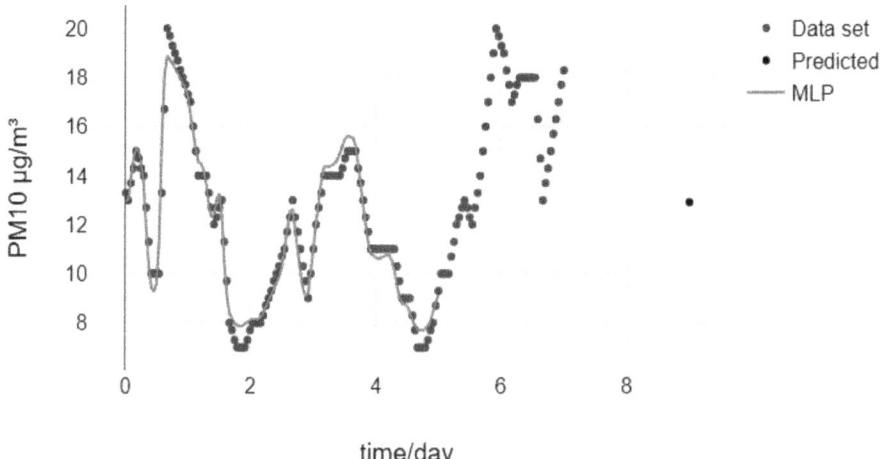

Figure 6-13. *Web application output for MLP algorithm*

Table 6-6 shows the MAPE values obtained for the MLP algorithm.

Table 6-6. *MAPE Values for MLP Algorithm*

Locations Air pollutants	Port Louis	Grand Baie	Quatre Bornes	Beau Bassin	Flacq	Average
O_3	1.89	1.51	2.88	2.12	1.56	1.99
CO	1.33	1.19	1.71	1.84	1.32	1.48
PM_{10}	2.35	1.73	2.12	2.89	2.45	2.31
PM_{25}	1.57	2.72	2.15	1.78	2.01	2.05

The MLP algorithm was selected as it has the ability to learn complex nonlinear relationships between input and output variables. It is also a universal approximator capable of approximating any continuous

CHAPTER 6 AIR QUALITY MONITORING: A CASE STUDY FOR THE APPLICATION OF MACHINE LEARNING IN MEETING SDGS 3 AND 13

function. From the results obtained in Table 6-6, the MAPE varies from 1.48% to 2.31%. The MAPE for concentration of CO is the lowest at 1.48%.

6.4.6 Performance of LSTM

Table 6-7 shows the hyper parameters for the LSTM algorithm.

Table 6-7. *Hyper Parameters of LSTM Algorithm*

Algorithm	Hyper Parameters
LSTM	Window Size = 24 x prediction day
	Number of Epochs = 500
	Learning Rate = 0.001
	Momentum = 0.9
	Error = 0.0001
	Clear = True
	Number of hidden layers = 1
	Number of nodes in hidden layer = 24 x prediction day

Figure 6-14 shows the graph of concentration of PM10 against time for the LSTM algorithm.

CHAPTER 6 AIR QUALITY MONITORING: A CASE STUDY FOR THE APPLICATION OF MACHINE LEARNING IN MEETING SDGS 3 AND 13

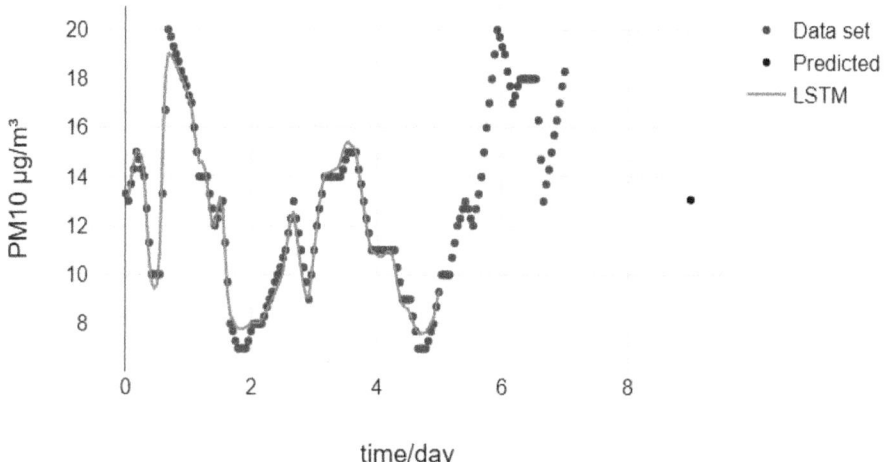

Figure 6-14. *Web application output for LSTM algorithm*

Table 6-8 shows the MAPE values obtained for the LSTM algorithm.

Table 6-8. *MAPE Values for LSTM Algorithm*

Locations Air pollutants	Port Louis	Grand Baie	Quatre Bornes	Beau Bassin	Flacq	Average
O_3	1.67	1.50	2.32	1.55	1.78	1.76
CO	1.22	0.96	0.99	1.45	1.37	1.20
PM_{10}	2.34	1.43	2.65	1.89	1.22	1.91
PM_{25}	1.67	1.58	2.04	2.22	1.83	1.87

The LSTM algorithm was selected as it is well suited for capturing temporal dependencies and patterns in sequential data. In regression tasks where the order of the input data is important such as time-series data,

LSTM can model the temporal relationship between observations. The results obtained in Table 6-8 shows that the MAPE values varies between 1.20% and 1.91%. The MAPE for the concentration of CO is lowest at 1.20%.

6.4.7 Performance of Classification Algorithms

The performance of the KNN, decision tree, and random forest algorithms for predicting the AQI based on the amount of air pollutants was evaluated by calculating the accuracy for five locations out of the ten selected ones and taking the average values. A sample size of 720, which is equivalent to 30 days was used. Table 6-9 shows the accuracy obtained for each algorithm.

Table 6-9. Accuracy for Classification Algorithms

Algorithm	Accuracy (%)
KNN	84.3
DT	99.5
RF	98.9

From the results obtained in Table 6-9, it can be observed that decision tree and random forest have the highest accuracies of 99.5% and 98.9%, respectively. KNN performed the least with an accuracy of 84.3%. Decision tree and random forest are more robust to noisy data and outliers, making it better at classifying AQI than KNN. Moreover, KNN is more susceptible to overfitting especially with small dataset.

Machine learning can be used to accurately predict air pollutant levels and categorize the AQI, which can be helpful to determine the long-term impacts of engineering activities on air quality. This can help to formulate new strategies and policies to improve the air quality for the public, contributing to the global achievements of SDGs 3 and 13.

CHAPTER 6   AIR QUALITY MONITORING: A CASE STUDY FOR THE APPLICATION OF MACHINE LEARNING IN MEETING SDGS 3 AND 13

6.5 Summary

In conclusion, this research focused on the development of a web application for predicting air pollutant levels and classifying the Air Quality Index using machine learning algorithms. The data collection process involved retrieving hourly historical air quality information from 10 selected locations in Mauritius through the Weatherbit.io Air Quality API. The selected air pollutants for monitoring included PM_{10}, PM_{25}, CO, and O_3.

The program structure of the web application was organized into different sections, including the layout of the website, implementation of linear and polynomial regression, as well as the use of LSTM/MLP algorithms for prediction. Additionally, classification algorithms (k-NN, decision tree, and random forest) were implemented to classify AQI based on air pollutant levels.

The testing of the web application demonstrated its functionality, providing users with accurate predictions of air pollutant concentrations and AQI classification. The regression algorithms, including simple linear regression (SLR), polynomial regression (PR), multilayer perceptron (MLP), and long short-term memory (LSTM), were evaluated for performance. Each algorithm exhibited varying levels of accuracy in predicting air pollutant concentrations, with the MAPE values indicating the effectiveness of the models. The MAPE for SLR ranged from 6.81% to 12.99%, while for PR it varied from 2.35% to 9.36%. The MAPE for MLP was between 1.48% and 2.31%, and for LSTM, it spanned from 1.20% to 1.91%. Notably, the MLP and LSTM algorithms demonstrated low MAPE values, suggesting their capability to capture complex nonlinear relationships in the data.

Furthermore, the classification algorithms were assessed for their accuracy in predicting AQI levels. Decision tree and random forest algorithms outperformed k-NN, achieving high accuracy percentages of 99.5% and 98.9%, respectively.

CHAPTER 6   AIR QUALITY MONITORING: A CASE STUDY FOR THE APPLICATION OF MACHINE LEARNING IN MEETING SDGS 3 AND 13

These results suggest the effectiveness of machine learning models in predicting both air pollutant concentrations and AQI levels, which are crucial for assessing air quality and making informed decisions for public health and environmental management. The findings of this research contribute to the understanding of how machine learning can be applied to predict and classify air quality indicators accurately. The web application developed in this study serves as a practical tool for users to obtain real-time predictions and classifications for air quality in Mauritius. This research aligns with the global Sustainable Development Goals, particularly SDG 3 (Good Health and Well-Being) and SDG 13 (Climate Action), by providing valuable insights for environmental monitoring and public health improvement.

CHAPTER 7

Clustering the Development of Worldwide Internet Connectivity for SDGs 7, 9, and 11

Chapter authors:
Lavesh Babooram, lavesh.babooram1@umail.uom.ac.mu
Tulsi Pawan Fowdur, p.fowdur@uom.ac.mu
Department of Electrical and Electronic Engineering, University of Mauritius

This chapter explores the global landscape of Internet connectivity development and its implications, with particular focus on Sustainable Development Goals (SDGs) 7, 9, and 11. These targets and indicators act as a measure for the success of the goals laid out by the United Nations (UN), which, in this chapter, revolve mainly around the expansion of technological infrastructure and increased access to information and communications technology. An interactive application capable of processing and visualizing worldwide Internet connectivity trends from 1980 to 2020 is thus developed using the K-means clustering algorithm. With the HTML, CSS, and JavaScript languages as the pillars of this web architecture, this unsupervised learning model presents users with a choropleth world map representing the development states of 187 countries among underdeveloped, emerging, developing, developed, and highly developed countries, making up a total of five clusters.

The components on the user interface allow the input of a dataset containing four main variables including cellular subscription, the percentage of Internet users, the number of Internet users, and broadband subscription. After data preprocessing on this dataset originally obtained from Kaggle, the end user is able to observe the digital divide and Internet penetration over the last four decades. The evolution of the Internet across the world is demonstrated, shedding light on geographical disparities, regions with limited connectivity, and underserved populations. The results indicate that by 2020 most countries had achieved either developed or highly developed status, with some African and Asian nations still facing an uphill battle.

This application can therefore serve as a tool toward making targeted interventions to address digital inequality. Moreover, this study contains discussions that delve into the implications of the findings for policymakers, investors, researchers, and international collaborators, thereby achieving the SDG targets 7.b, 9, and 11.c.

7.1 Introduction

The swift progress of technology, particularly in the field of machine learning (ML), has significantly transformed the approach of analyzing and tackling intricate global challenges in recent times. With its ability to sift through vast amounts of data and identify patterns, ML is extensively used to address urgent global complexities such as the uneven development of

CHAPTER 7   CLUSTERING THE DEVELOPMENT OF WORLDWIDE INTERNET CONNECTIVITY FOR SDGS 7, 9, AND 11

Internet connectivity around the world today [1]. These disparate levels of communication and connectedness are directly linked to socioeconomic growth and opportunities, given that the main backbone for instantaneous access to information today remains the colossal seepage of the Internet into daily human life.

The United Nations (UN) Sustainable Development Goals (SDGs) provide a comprehensive framework for navigating through labyrinths that surround global challenges, including the issue of unequal access to technology, known as the digital divide. As per the International Telecommunication Union (ITU), despite the accelerated progress in the deployment of Internet facilities around the world, at the end of 2023, about one-third of the global population, or 2.6 billion people, remain offline [2]. The organization, however, highlighted this enhancement in connectivity since it represents further progress toward inclusivity, in turn aligning with the UN SDGs, as stressed upon by the ITU Secretary-General Doreen Bogdan-Martin, who said that "We won't rest until we live in a world where meaningful connectivity is a lived reality for everyone, everywhere" [3].

The targets 7.b, 9, and 11.c directly pertain to the need for expanding infrastructure and technology, in turn promoting access to all, which would subsequently enhance scientific research and particularly help countries facing the uphill battle toward development. Target 7.b [4] aims to enhance the availability of cost-effective and enduring energy resources for developing countries, which can be partly achieved with the use of the Internet. The limited availability of electricity in developing regions presents a major obstacle to the adoption of the Internet due to the absence of a dependable energy infrastructure. As per the World Bank, sub-Saharan Africa's share of the global population with electricity jumped to 50.6% in 2021 from 46.3% in 2018, which still conveys that a major proportion of individuals do not have access to electricity, which hampers their capacity to utilize online resources and engage in the digital economy. Target 9 [5] seeks to develop resilient facilities to encourage a sustainable and equitable industrialization and drive innovation.

CHAPTER 7 CLUSTERING THE DEVELOPMENT OF WORLDWIDE INTERNET CONNECTIVITY FOR SDGS 7, 9, AND 11

Access to inexpensive and reliable Internet is a prerequisite for promoting economic expansion. According to research conducted by the World Economic Forum, raising Internet access to 75% of the world's population would increase the global collective GDP by $2 trillion and create 140 million new jobs [6]. Additionally, target 11.c [7] underscores the significance of building cities that are inclusive, safe, resilient, and sustainable. Access to high-speed Internet in urban areas is key for uplifting public services, optimizing communication networks, and promoting community involvement. For example, smart city Wi-Fi serves as a means of accessing the Internet and can potentially empower city residents to have a say in the advancement and enhancement of smart city initiatives, thereby enhancing the overall quality of life [8, 9].

This chapter focuses on the development and implementation of a web-based application designed to visualize and analyze the development of Internet connectivity across the globe, from 1980 to 2020. Powered with ML, the application uses a combination of the K-means algorithm, and an unlabeled dataset for unsupervised learning. The dataset was obtained from Kaggle and compiled from several sources across the Internet, in turn containing the cellular subscription per 100, Internet users per 100, number of Internet users, and broadband subscription per 100.

Upon data preprocessing, this dataset is fed into the application, which outputs five distinct clusters of countries, based on their levels of Internet connectivity over the past few decades. By visualizing these clusters on a world map, users can clearly identify regions that are highly developed, developed, developing, emerging, or underdeveloped in terms of Internet access. These insights can be beneficial to policymakers, researchers, and stakeholders who can steer the boat toward initiatives and progress. A simple glance at the end result can enable them to make well-informed decisions to address the digital divide and promote fair access to technology. Through the use of ML and data visualization, the overarching objectives of the SDG goals can be attained, with a clearer path toward a more interconnected and inclusive global community.

CHAPTER 7 CLUSTERING THE DEVELOPMENT OF WORLDWIDE INTERNET CONNECTIVITY FOR SDGS 7, 9, AND 11

7.2 AI Use Cases for SDGs 7, 9, and 11

A state-of-the-art review concerning related works performed by researchers is presented next.

In [10], Chinn and Fairlie investigated the determinants of the global digital divide in personal computer and Internet penetration by putting 161 countries under the microscope. The assessment metrics included economic parameters, demographic indicators, infrastructure variables, and telecommunications metrics such as telephone density and pricing.

The authors mentioned that these features, coupled with age dependency, pertain to patterns in Internet use and development. Through analysis of the Internet penetration rates, they revealed that the United States had the highest development rate, followed by the Nordic countries, i.e., Sweden, Denmark, Switzerland, and Norway. On the other side of the spectrum lies several countries from the sub-Saharan Africa, with reports showing computer penetration rates of less than two users per 1,000 individuals. The experiment concluded that the key determinant of Internet connectivity is income, which is directly tied to the demand for computers, in turn affecting the telecommunications infrastructure in a particular country. The paper also includes thorough analysis of reported metrics from the 1999–2001 era pertaining to Internet penetration rate.

In [11], Chen and Wellman addressed the global digital divide at both the international and national levels by evaluating socioeconomic, technological, and linguistic indicators. They first define the digital divide as the gap between individuals who have the ability to indulge in the information realm and those that do not. Although spread quickly across the globe, the prevalence of the Internet was concentrated in highly developed countries. The authors mentioned that the United States consisted of a major portion of individuals accessing the Internet, whereby in 2001, 60% of the country's total population was already using the Web. It was also stressed that for marginalized communities to be able to take part in the information age, it is necessary to have telecommunications

CHAPTER 7   CLUSTERING THE DEVELOPMENT OF WORLDWIDE INTERNET CONNECTIVITY FOR SDGS 7, 9, AND 11

policies, infrastructures, and education in place. The study concluded that disadvantaged communities face obstacles in using computers and even having access to the Internet due to the exorbitant expenses, low income, the overwhelming prevalence of the English language, the absence of pertinent material, and inadequate technological assistance.

On the same wavelength, a few years later, White et al. set out to assess the global digital divide through an empirical study involving three parameters [12]. It is mentioned that the gap that previously existed between highly developed and underdeveloped countries had broadened substantially. As such, the aim of the research was to create a comprehensive map representation of the current state of the digital divide, with countries being the focal point of analysis. An assessment of the current state of the global digital divide was conducted, which serves as a starting point for monitoring changes and conducting future research. As their information source, the authors used a dataset from the International Telecommunications Union (ITU), consisting of time-series data for almost 100 communications characteristics for 172 countries. Despite already having ample information regarding personal computers per 100 people and Internet users per 100 people, they emphasized the importance of also analyzing the quality of Internet access, in turn incorporating the third metric, i.e., the international Internet bandwidth per inhabitant. The method used to classify the countries among four tiers was the K-means clustering algorithm, allowing a clear demarcation of classified countries. The experiment concluded in the availability of a contemporary map representing the digital divide, as a baseline for further research.

In [13], De-Arteaga et al. examined the adoption of the ML sphere for real-world scenarios with particular attention to developing countries. The study is geared toward global development and mentions the lack of Internet accessibility, availability of data, and computational abilities in poor countries. The authors take the example of small communities in South Africa where niche languages are still spoken. They thus propose

CHAPTER 7 CLUSTERING THE DEVELOPMENT OF WORLDWIDE INTERNET CONNECTIVITY FOR SDGS 7, 9, AND 11

the implementation of natural language technologies, text-to-speech functionalities, and automated speech recognition techniques to bridge the gap between Internet connectivity.

Likewise, in [14], Alper and Miktus discussed the digital connectivity in sub-Saharan Africa, providing a comparative perspective by firstly confirming the existence of the global digital divide using the unsupervised ML K-means clustering algorithm on a dataset of 190 countries. The authors then used a composite digital connectivity index where the analysis revealed that the majority of countries in the sub-Saharan Africa region lagged behind in terms of digital connectivity, particularly in areas such as infrastructure, Internet access, and domain expertise. They also emphasize the fact that despite being heavily invested in information, communications, and technology (ICT) facilities, these countries still require a digital linkage to hop onto the technological train.

Additionally, the study also involved the relationship between 100 independent parameters to assess the weight of the digital divide. This was performed using logistic regression models, with some indicators concerning the SDGs. To conclude the experiment, the authors highlighted the significance of regulatory and business-facilitating environments, increased urbanization, and the availability of electrical power.

Further, Walelgne et al. proposed an effective approach to tackle the issue revolving around the data utilization patterns of mobile users, which ultimately dictates the optimal allocation of resources based on user traffic demand and behavior [15]. Using a dataset obtained from Netradar, which is a mobile network measurement infrastructure that collects information on a crowdsourcing basis, the study was focused on examining the patterns and behavior of users when it comes to using mobile data. Data was obtained from five different countries, and the primary factors considered were the users' mobility, subscription plan, network coverage, and network congestion. The approach involved the K-means method to categorize mobile users based on factors such as data consumption, network access type, number of user sessions, throughput, and mobility.

Thus, a clustering model was produced, revealing that the distribution of patterns among the five countries, namely, Finland, United Kingdom, Japan, Brazil, and Germany, is not uniform. In most cases, the high volume of data usage was due to a minority of users who consume a large amount of data. Heavy users have a tendency to install applications that require more traffic compared with regular and casual users.

The labeled dataset was then used to train three classification models including decision tree, gradient boosting classifiers, and random forest. The decision tree model offered the best performance accuracy of around 80%.

In [16], Mathrani et al. presented an analysis of the 2022 UN data report on the progress made toward achieving SDGs with respect to economic, social, environmental, and institutional factors. Ward's method was used as the clustering algorithm, to comprehend the degree of advancement of 45 Asian nations, together with their general patterns in attaining the SDGs. The findings indicated that East Asian nations exhibited subpar performance in the economic aspect, whereas certain countries in Southeast Asia and Central and West Asia demonstrated comparatively strong performance. In terms of social and institutional aspects, the results suggested that East and Central Asian nations exhibited comparatively superior performance compared to other countries. West and South Asian countries outperformed other Asian countries in the environmental dimension. The authors mentioned that policymakers can use these findings to track the progress of countries toward achieving SDGs.

In [17], Singh and Ru stated that the assessment of the SDG 9 targets is primarily based on indicators such as Internet and mobile broadband penetration, logistics performance index, university excellence and rankings, funding for research and development, industrial changes, emission management, and rural connectivity. They thus provide a systematic review of advancements, difficulties, and potential future outcomes in achieving SDG 9 targets. The paper mentions that the digital

CHAPTER 7   CLUSTERING THE DEVELOPMENT OF WORLDWIDE INTERNET CONNECTIVITY FOR SDGS 7, 9, AND 11

disparity in sub-Saharan Africa can be attributed to various factors including the ripple effect, GDP, income per capita, governance, laws, population, and state of the electrical infrastructure in the country.

It is also stated that the influence of Internet access on income inequality is more pronounced in developing regions compared to developed regions in Asia. The review indicated studies that demonstrated a decrease in inequality as a result of improved Internet penetration. Likewise, there is a correlation between the level of industrial activity and the extent to which the Internet is used, and these two factors can be used interchangeably. Finally, the authors mention that despite many countries having high mobile broadband subscriptions rates, the speed of the networks is of equal importance.

7.3 Data Processing and Application Design

This section dives into the implementation of the web application for clustering countries based on their development state using unsupervised learning. With a combination of HTML and CSS as the front end and JavaScript making up the back end, the architecture is broken down, together with the involvement of the K-means clustering algorithm, whose implementation is facilitated with ml.js [18]. As a whole, the application can be used on a dataset containing a list of countries with their Internet connectivity throughout decades, where a world map is then output to the user, showing each country's development. Moreover, the user can scroll through the years using a slider, showing clearly the phases where a country faced improvement or lagged behind with respect to other nations.

7.3.1 Collection and Description of Dataset

The dataset used in this work is obtained from Kaggle, a well-known source for datasets, typically used for ML projects. It can be found at [19] and was gathered from multiple sources and merged together, as stated by the author. The license attributed to this dataset is the Creative Commons designation CC0 1.0 Universal (CC0 1.0) license [20] stating that the work is dedicated to the public domain and is thus free of known restrictions under copyright law, allowing this dataset to be copied, modified, distributed, and used for commercial purposes.

With a collection of four columns of data for each country and its corresponding year ranging from 1980 to 2020, this dataset provides substantial information to extract meaningful insights. In ML terms, it is treated as an unsupervised learning problem since there are no labels associated with each row. The dataset thus consists of a total of eight columns, as shown in Figure 7-1 where the values are shown for the first country, i.e., Afghanistan.

CHAPTER 7   CLUSTERING THE DEVELOPMENT OF WORLDWIDE INTERNET CONNECTIVITY FOR SDGS 7, 9, AND 11

	Entity	Code	Year	Cellular Subscription	Internet Users(%)	No. of Internet Users	Broadband Subscription
1	Afghanistan	AFG	1980	0	0	0	0
2	Afghanistan	AFG	1981	0	0	0	0
3	Afghanistan	AFG	1982	0	0	0	0
4	Afghanistan	AFG	1983	0	0	0	0
5	Afghanistan	AFG	1984	0	0	0	0
6	Afghanistan	AFG	1985	0	0	0	0
7	Afghanistan	AFG	1986	0	0	0	0
8	Afghanistan	AFG	1987	0	0	0	0
9	Afghanistan	AFG	1988	0	0	0	0
10	Afghanistan	AFG	1989	0	0	0	0
11	Afghanistan	AFG	1990	0	0	0	0
12	Afghanistan	AFG	1991	0	0	0	0
13	Afghanistan	AFG	1992	0	0	0	0
14	Afghanistan	AFG	1993	0	0	0	0
15	Afghanistan	AFG	1994	0	0	0	0
16	Afghanistan	AFG	1995	0	0	0	0
17	Afghanistan	AFG	1996	0	0	0	0
18	Afghanistan	AFG	1997	0	0	0	0
19	Afghanistan	AFG	1998	0	0	0	0
20	Afghanistan	AFG	1999	0	0	0	0
21	Afghanistan	AFG	2000	0	0	0	0
22	Afghanistan	AFG	2001	0	0.004722568	930	0
23	Afghanistan	AFG	2002	0.1106157	0.004561395	958	0
24	Afghanistan	AFG	2003	0.844563544	0.087891251	19903	0
25	Afghanistan	AFG	2004	2.426528454	0.105809033	24922	0.000808843
26	Afghanistan	AFG	2005	4.677582741	1.224148035	298829	0.000857557
27	Afghanistan	AFG	2006	9.53490448	2.107123613	536114	0.001891571
28	Afghanistan	AFG	2007	17.22510529	1.899999976	492163	0.001844982
29	Afghanistan	AFG	2008	28.49300385	1.840000033	486261	0.001803604
30	Afghanistan	AFG	2009	36.97858429	3.549999952	972178	0.00352177
31	Afghanistan	AFG	2010	35.00312805	4	1127587	0.005139537
32	Afghanistan	AFG	2011	45.81362534	5	1462458	0.005139537
33	Afghanistan	AFG	2012	49.22797775	5.454545498	1661808	0.004813651
34	Afghanistan	AFG	2013	52.0835762	5.900000095	1860932	0.004648339
35	Afghanistan	AFG	2014	55.15951538	7	2290135	0.004494948
36	Afghanistan	AFG	2015	57.27106857	8.260000229	2788039	0.020535484
37	Afghanistan	AFG	2016	61.05463791	11	3809983	0.024873504
38	Afghanistan	AFG	2017	65.92913055	13.5	4811862	0.025297474
39	Afghanistan	AFG	2018	59.12084961	16.79999924	6163380	0.043040551
40	Afghanistan	AFG	2019	59.35601807	17.60000038	6647431	0.051740516
41	Afghanistan	AFG	2020	58.2558136	18.39999962	7170891	0.068253607

Figure 7-1. *Portion of the Internet dataset*

These columns are further described as follows:

- **Entity**: The name of the country corresponding to the data entry

- **Code**: The ISO 3166-1 alpha-3 country code representing the country

- **Year**: The year for which the data is recorded

- **Cellular Subscription**: The percentage of the population in the country with cellular subscription

- **Internet Users (%)**: The percentage of the population in the country using the Internet

- **No. of Internet Users**: The number of Internet users in the country

- **Broadband Subscription**: The percentage of the population in the country with broadband subscription

7.3.2 Data Preprocessing

Despite already containing the information needed for unsupervised learning when downloaded, this dataset consists of certain irregularities, as listed next:

- **Filtering regions**: The Code column contains several regions or collective entities such as East Asia and Pacific, Europe and Central Asia, and European Union, which were removed from the dataset. These entries do not represent individual countries and were thus excluded to focus specifically on country-level data.

- **Excluding sparse data**: Certain countries with incomplete data, such as American Samoa and Curacao, among a list of 14, were excluded from the dataset. Additionally, entities that are not member states of the UN such as Aruba, Bermuda, and British Virgin Islands are also removed. These decisions were made to ensure data reliability and to prevent potential misinterpretation of the visualization due to a large number of missing or misleading information over several years.

CHAPTER 7   CLUSTERING THE DEVELOPMENT OF WORLDWIDE INTERNET CONNECTIVITY FOR SDGS 7, 9, AND 11

- **Handling missing values**: In some instances, the values for a particular country and corresponding year might contain a zero value. This could arise due to some unavailable data rather than an actual zero value. This is addressed by replacing the value in question with that from the previous year. Likewise, the missing years for some countries are entered manually, by taking the values for the previous year. These adjustments help maintain data consistency and accuracy, ensuring that the visualization reflects the actual Internet development trends over time for each country. One such example before this change is depicted in Figure 7-2. In this case, it is simply assigned the value of 0.005139537.

29 Afghanistan	AFG	2009	36.97858429	3.549999952	972178	0.00352177
30 Afghanistan	AFG	2010	35.00312805	4	1127587	0.005139537
31 Afghanistan	AFG	2011	45.81362534	5	1462458	0
32 Afghanistan	AFG	2012	49.22797775	5.454545498	1661808	0.004813651
33 Afghanistan	AFG	2013	52.0835762	5.900000095	1860932	0.004648339

Figure 7-2. Before handling zero values

After the data preprocessing phase, the dataset contains 187 countries in total, out of the 195 member states of the UN, thereby making up a strong dataset.

7.3.3 Scatter Plots

In this section, the scatter plots containing all features of the dataset after data preprocessing are given. The columns are plotted against one another to clearly see the relationships between each parameter. Figures 7-3 to 7-6 show how the four main variables are laid out for the different countries.

CHAPTER 7 CLUSTERING THE DEVELOPMENT OF WORLDWIDE INTERNET CONNECTIVITY FOR SDGS 7, 9, AND 11

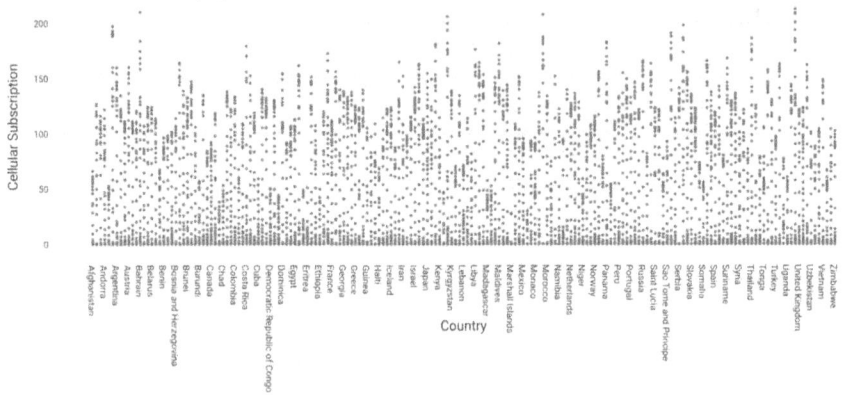

Figure 7-3. *Relationship between country and cellular subscription*

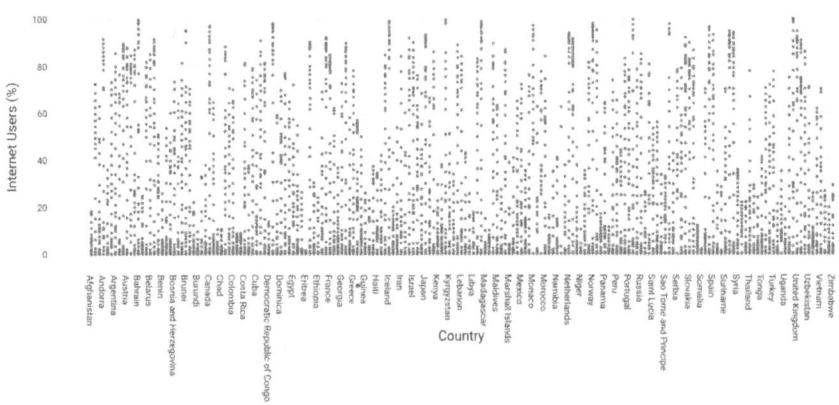

Figure 7-4. *Relationship between country and the percentage of Internet users*

CHAPTER 7 CLUSTERING THE DEVELOPMENT OF WORLDWIDE INTERNET CONNECTIVITY FOR SDGS 7, 9, AND 11

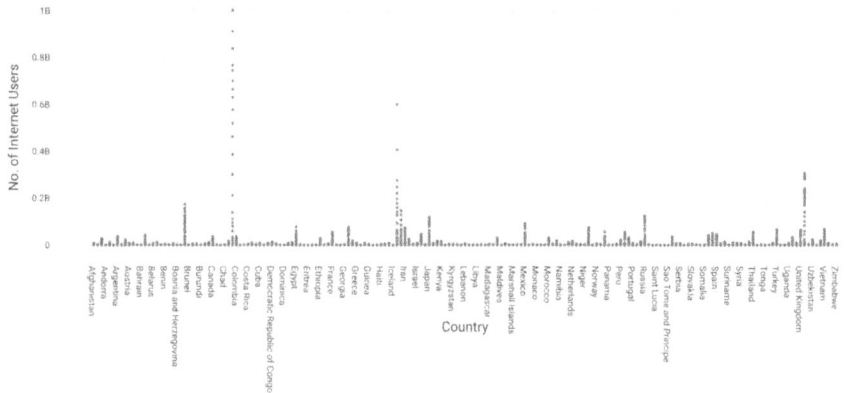

Figure 7-5. *Relationship between country and the number of Internet users*

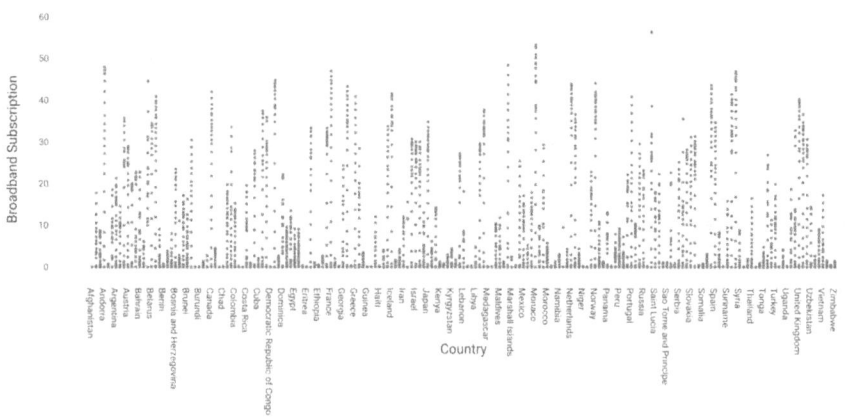

Figure 7-6. *Relationship between country and broadband subscription*

Likewise, the scatter plots that depict the relationship among each variable are depicted in Figures 7-7 to 7-10.

CHAPTER 7 CLUSTERING THE DEVELOPMENT OF WORLDWIDE INTERNET CONNECTIVITY FOR SDGS 7, 9, AND 11

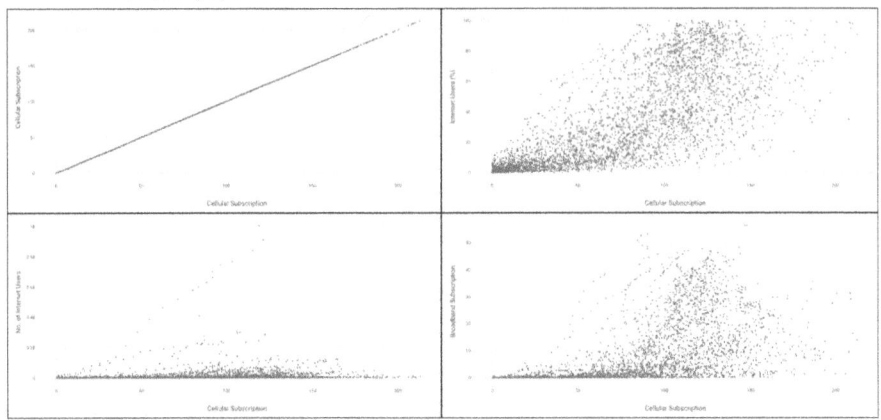

Figure 7-7. *Scatter plot of cellular subscription against all other variables*

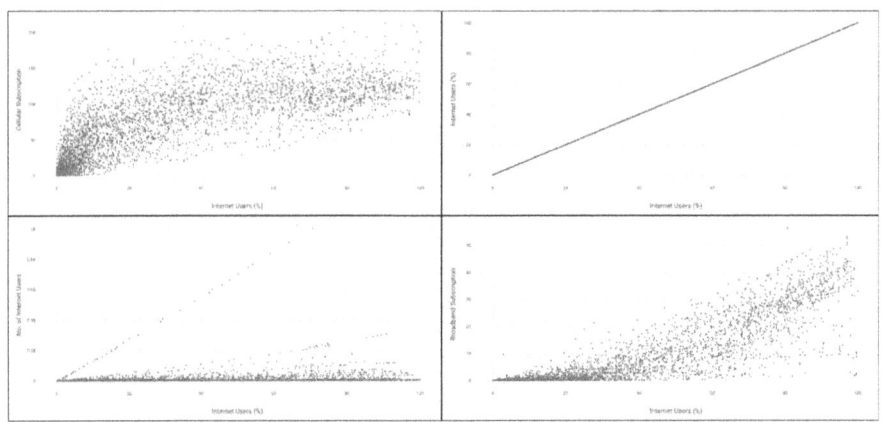

Figure 7-8. *Scatter plot of Internet users (%) against all other variables*

CHAPTER 7 CLUSTERING THE DEVELOPMENT OF WORLDWIDE INTERNET CONNECTIVITY FOR SDGS 7, 9, AND 11

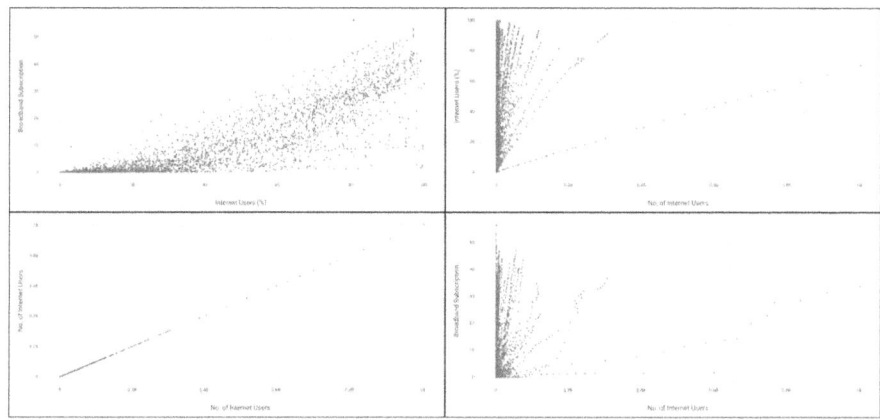

Figure 7-9. *Scatter plot of number of Internet users against all other variables*

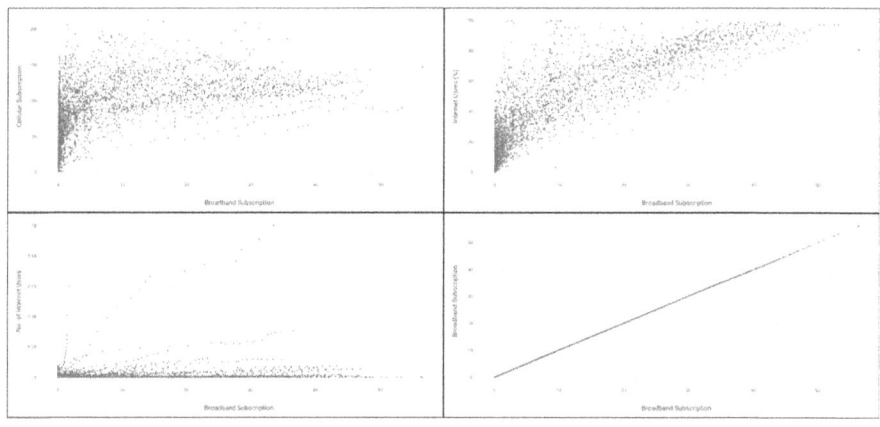

Figure 7-10. *Scatter plot of broadband subscription against all other variables*

7.3.4 Application System Model

In this section, the model for the web application is broken down into its components. The basic principle revolves around the web page taking as input the CSV dataset and performing K-means clustering to yield different levels of Internet connectivity development. The end user thus has a dashboard with the following capabilities:

1. Browse and select a CSV file as the dataset.
2. Select whether the clustered CSV file is downloaded locally.
3. Obtain a world map with five levels of worldwide Internet connectivity development.
4. Select the exact year ranging from 1980 to 2020 with a slider, to dynamically change the contents of the world map.

These functionalities are coded such that the dataset follows the same format as depicted in Figure 7-1. Once clustered, the resulting CSV file contains the Label and Category columns, which correspond to the numerical and informational labels, respectively. This application is coded with a blend of HTML and CSS as the front-end languages and JavaScript as the back-end pillar. Thus, client-side JavaScript allows ML to be performed within a few clicks inside of the web browser. It is to be noted that all the code of this chapter can be found in the folder `Chapter 7 - Codes` hosted on the GitHub page of this book.

Components and Functionalities

This web application, titled Worldwide Internet Connectivity Development, works with the combination of two files, as described next:

- **index.html**: This HTML file defines the structure and content of the user interface (UI), which contains several dashboard cards including the selection of the dataset, a legend, a slider, icons for the targeted SDGs, and a container for the world map. It also consists of a button that triggers the back end, i.e., the JavaScript code.

- **script.js**: This file acts as the logic for the index.html file, thereby containing the methods called when UI elements are interacted with. As the backend file, it handles tasks such as performing the clustering ML operation and updating the world map each time the slider is adjusted to select a different year.

On the same wavelength, the libraries and external frameworks associated with the development of this application are given in Table 7-1.

Table 7-1. Description of Libraries and Resources

Library/Resource	Purpose	Repository	Download Link	Location
Plotly.js	Provides interactive data visualizations in the web browser.	[21]		index.html
Papa Parse	Provides a simple interface for parsing CSV data and converting it into arrays or objects.	[22]		
bootstrap.min.css	Customized Bootstrap stylesheet for organizing row and columns.	[23]	[24]	
ml.js	Provides implementations for training and deploying ML algorithms.	[18]		

Clustering Worldwide Internet Connectivity Development

This section focuses on the process of clustering global Internet connectivity development. The objective of this procedure is to classify countries into five separate clusters according to their degree of Internet connectivity. Each cluster signifies a distinct phase or level of Internet advancement, which could be in the form of Internet access infrastructure, and takes into account both mobile and broadband subscriptions. The following are the five tiers of Internet connectivity that the application aims to determine:

CHAPTER 7 CLUSTERING THE DEVELOPMENT OF WORLDWIDE INTERNET CONNECTIVITY FOR SDGS 7, 9, AND 11

1. **Underdeveloped**: Countries categorized in this cluster demonstrate the lowest levels of Internet penetration and infrastructure development. They do not have extensive availability of the Internet, and its utilization may be restricted to urban regions or particular demographic categories.

2. **Emerging**: This cluster comprises countries where Internet usage is in the early stages of becoming mainstream but has not yet achieved widespread adoption. These nations might have undergone recent advancements in internet connectivity, propelled by factors like economic progress or governmental initiatives.

3. **Developing**: Nations that have made substantial progress in augmenting Internet facilities and accessibility fall in this category. The rates of Internet penetration are moderate, and access is increasingly becoming more prevalent.

4. **Developed**: Developed nations possess robust Internet systems and exhibit significant levels access. Internet connectivity is widespread in both urban and rural areas, and its usage is deeply ingrained in various facets of everyday life, such as education, commerce, and communication.

5. **Highly Developed**: This cluster represents countries with the most advanced Internet connectivity and infrastructure. These countries typically boast high-speed broadband networks, widespread access to digital technologies, and a thriving digital economy.

With a world map depicting countries with varying Internet connectivity categories, users can analyze the disparities in its adoption and ecosystems across various regions. This analysis is beneficial to policy makers, researchers, and stakeholders, helping them to identify patterns, obstacles, and prospects for enhancing the global reach of the Internet and work toward digital inclusion.

7.3.5 Application Layout

For this application, a single window contains all the components that facilitate the K-means clustering process, where the dataset is first input using the Browse button, before clicking Generate Clusters. The latter starts the process in the background before plotting the world map. The user can adjust the slider to select the exact year ranging from 1980 to 2020. On doing so, the colour indicators in the world map change according to their clustered Internet connectivity development. As a result, the user can draw certain conclusions in terms of worldwide Internet communications and infrastructure. The completed application is shown in Figure 7-11.

CHAPTER 7   CLUSTERING THE DEVELOPMENT OF WORLDWIDE INTERNET CONNECTIVITY FOR SDGS 7, 9, AND 11

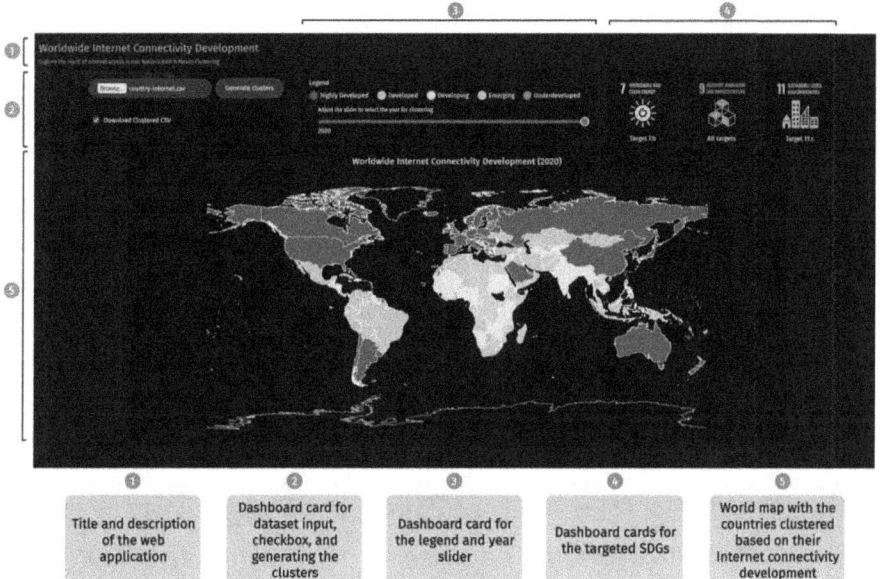

Figure 7-11. *Web application layout*

7.3.6 Program Structure

In this section, the index.html and script.js files are first described before diving into the functionalities of the methods implemented in JavaScript. An overview of the program structure is given in Figure 7-12.

CHAPTER 7 CLUSTERING THE DEVELOPMENT OF WORLDWIDE INTERNET CONNECTIVITY FOR SDGS 7, 9, AND 11

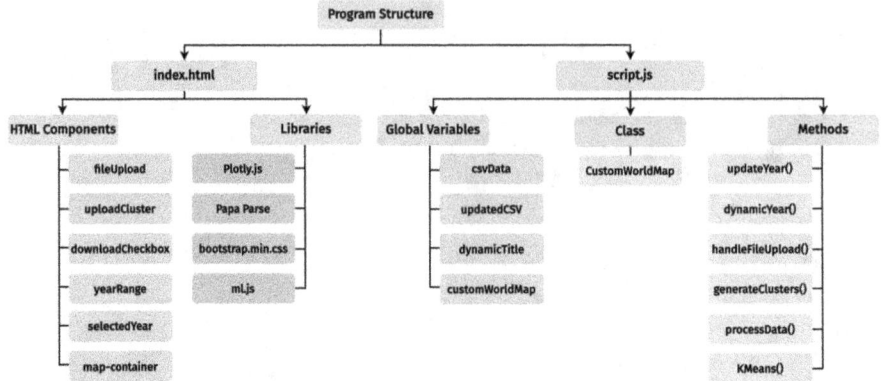

***Figure 7-12.** Web application program structure*

Additionally, the icons folder contains the necessary SDG icons and a favicon for the web page. Once the web page is opened, it awaits the input of the dataset through the Browse button. Figure 7-13 provides a general flowchart for this web application.

CHAPTER 7   CLUSTERING THE DEVELOPMENT OF WORLDWIDE INTERNET CONNECTIVITY FOR
           SDGS 7, 9, AND 11

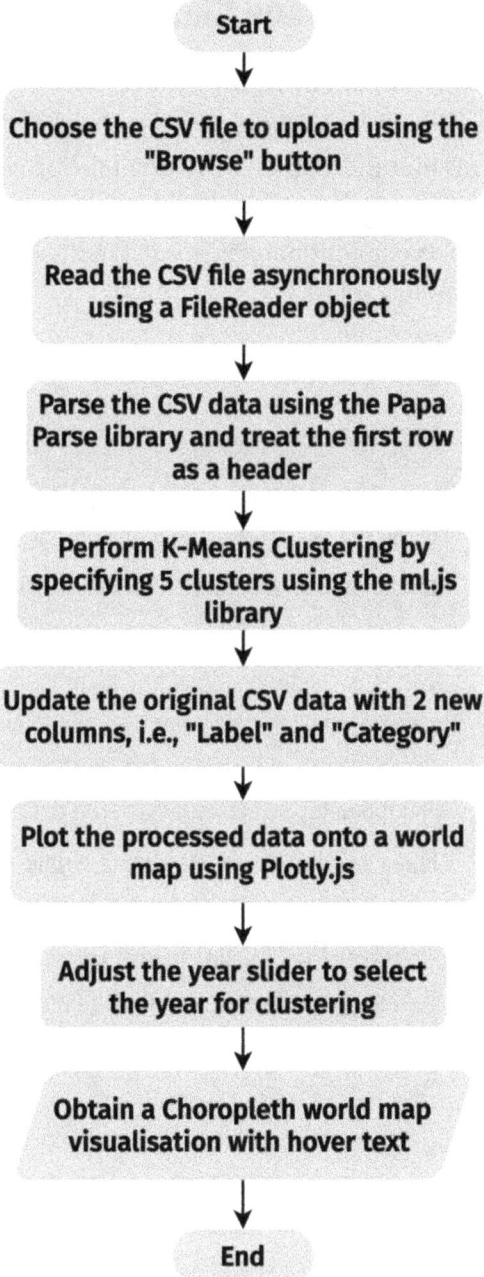

Figure 7-13. *Web application general flowchart*

CHAPTER 7 CLUSTERING THE DEVELOPMENT OF WORLDWIDE INTERNET CONNECTIVITY FOR SDGS 7, 9, AND 11

Description of Methods and Classes

After handling the CSV dataset using the `handleFileUpload()` method, the `generateClusters()` method is triggered once the user clicks the Generate Clusters button. This method acts as the heart of the program, dictating which other methods and classes are called, as well as when they are called. A summary of the functionalities of each method and class in the `script.js` file is given in Table 7-2.

Table 7-2. Description of Methods and Classes

Method/Class	Description
`handleFileUpload()`	Handles the file upload event triggered when a user selects a CSV file. It reads the uploaded file asynchronously, parses it, and initiates the data processing workflow.
`generateClusters()`	Generates clusters from the parsed CSV data using the K-means clustering algorithm. It computes centroids, assigns labels to data points, and updates the data accordingly. Additionally, it handles the option to download the updated CSV file with clustered data.
`ML.KMeans()`	Takes as input the normalized CSV data, as well as the number of clusters to perform K-means clustering.
`processData()`	Processes the CSV data by extracting relevant features, from each row and storing them in an array, which it passes to the `CustomWorldMap` object for plotting on the world map.
`CustomWorldMap`	Is a class representing a custom template for creating a world map object. It encapsulates the functionality to plot data onto a world map using `Plotly.js`, with customizable configurations for the map layout and styling.

(continued)

Table 7-2. (*continued*)

Method/Class	Description
dynamicYear()	Dynamically updates the selected year displayed on the UI as the user adjusts the year slider. It provides real-time feedback to the user regarding the selected year for data visualization. This helps the user know which year is being selected before releasing the slider.
updateYear()	Responsible for updating the selected year when the user adjusts and releases the year slider. It updates the selected year value on the UI and triggers the data processing workflow with the updated year filter.

K-means Clustering Algorithm

Next, Figure 7-14 elaborates upon the steps involved in the generateClusters() method for the K-means clustering process.

CHAPTER 7   CLUSTERING THE DEVELOPMENT OF WORLDWIDE INTERNET CONNECTIVITY FOR SDGS 7, 9, AND 11

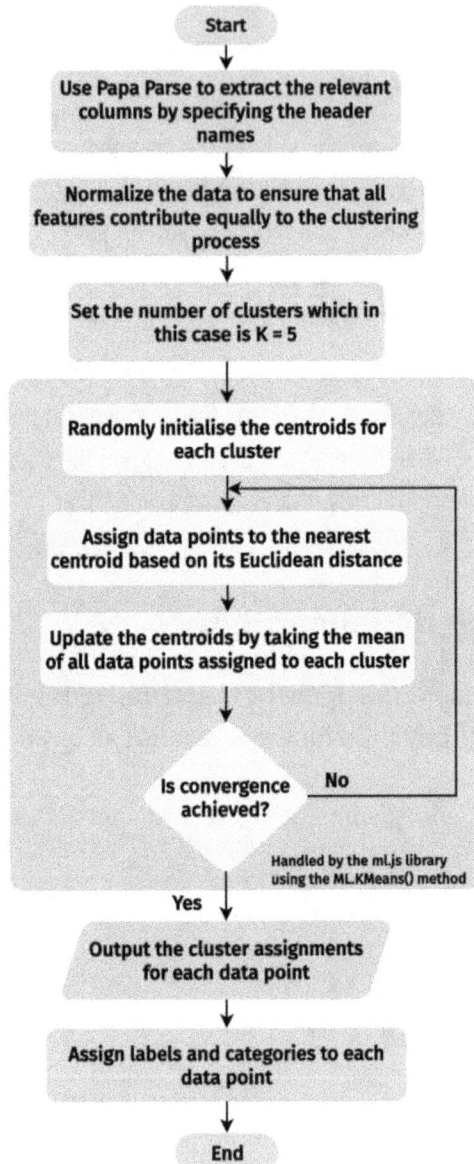

Figure 7-14. *Flowchart for the K-means clustering process*

CHAPTER 7   CLUSTERING THE DEVELOPMENT OF WORLDWIDE INTERNET CONNECTIVITY FOR SDGS 7, 9, AND 11

The clustering process is handled by the ml.js library where it is stopped when convergence occurs. This denotes the point where the centroids no longer change significantly or after a specified number of iterations. In this application, it is the former.

7.4 Application Testing and Analysis

With the front-end and back-end built, the web application is ready to be run. This section thus concerns snapshots of the application, as well as a discussion on the results obtained.

7.4.1 Application Testing

Figures 7-15 to 7-21 demonstrate the choropleth maps for different years as selected using the slider, together with a description of the progress of North America, South America, Europe, Africa, Asia, and Australia.

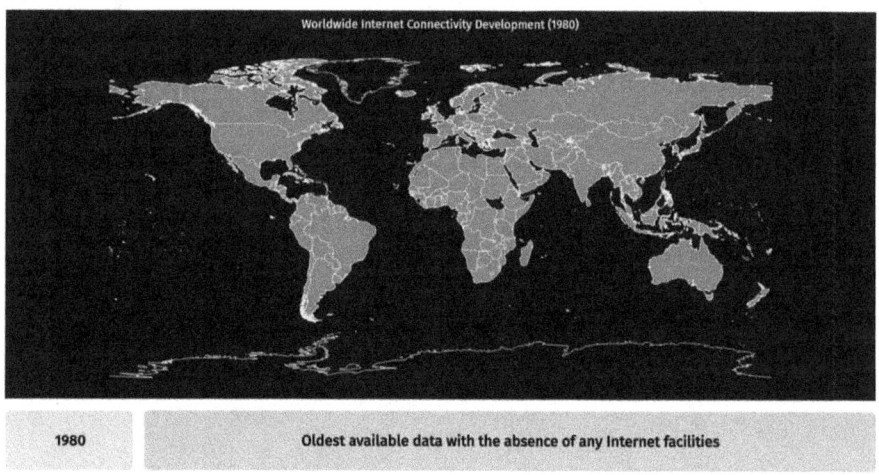

Figure 7-15. Results for 1980

CHAPTER 7   CLUSTERING THE DEVELOPMENT OF WORLDWIDE INTERNET CONNECTIVITY FOR
              SDGS 7, 9, AND 11

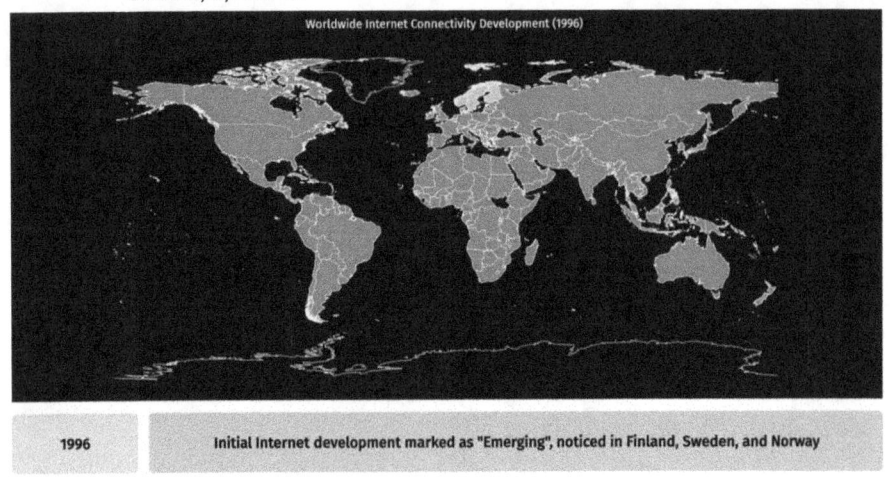

Figure 7-16. Results for 1996

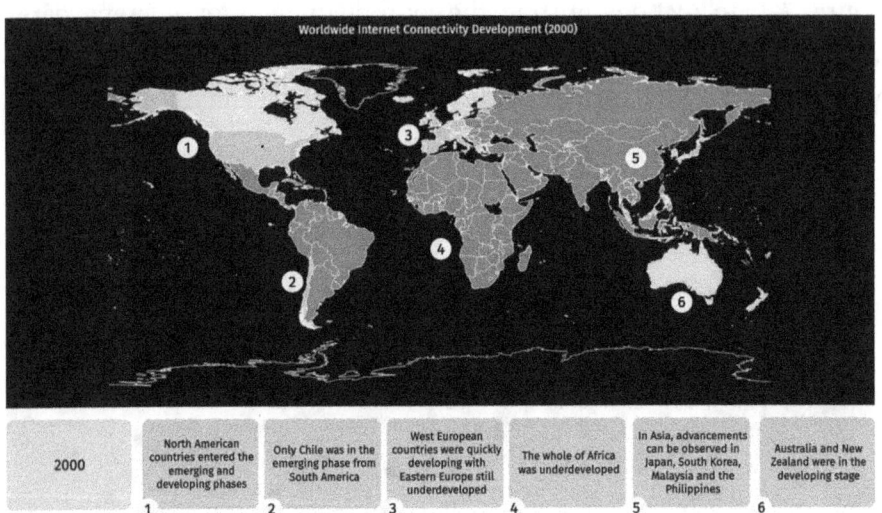

Figure 7-17. Results for 2000

CHAPTER 7   CLUSTERING THE DEVELOPMENT OF WORLDWIDE INTERNET CONNECTIVITY FOR SDGS 7, 9, AND 11

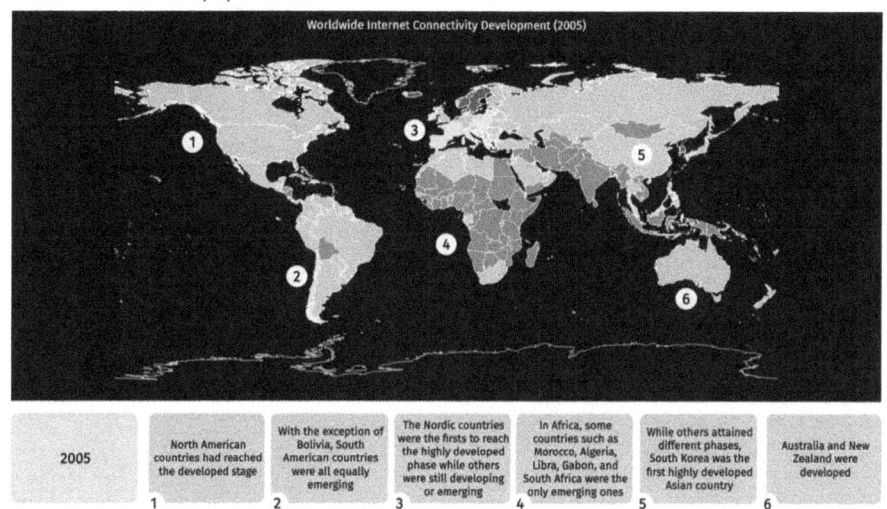

Figure 7-18. *Results for 2005*

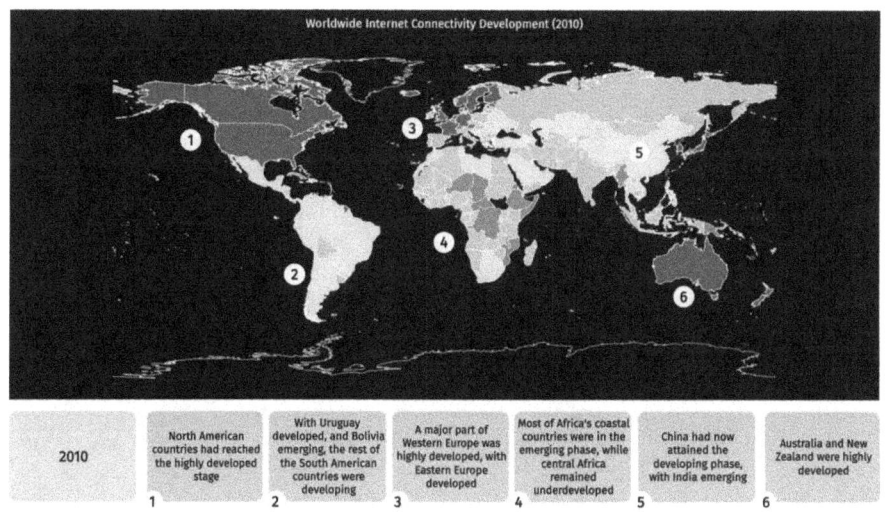

Figure 7-19. *Results for 2010*

CHAPTER 7   CLUSTERING THE DEVELOPMENT OF WORLDWIDE INTERNET CONNECTIVITY FOR SDGS 7, 9, AND 11

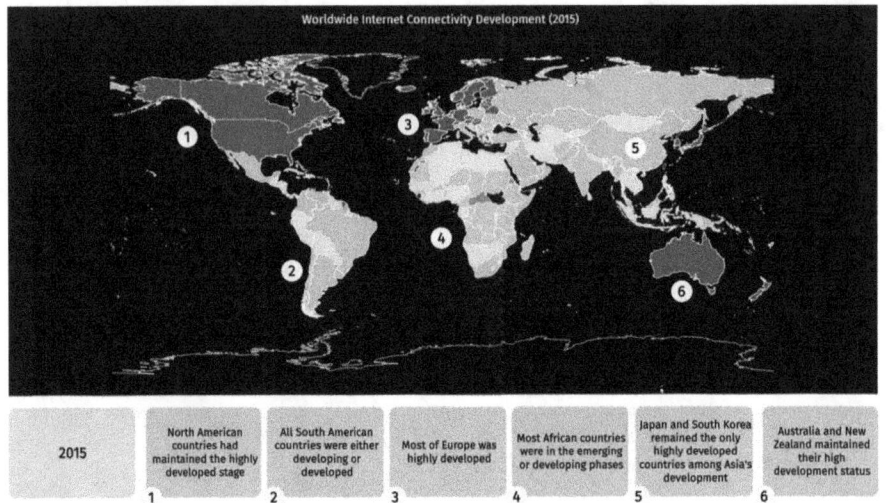

Figure 7-20. *Results for 2015*

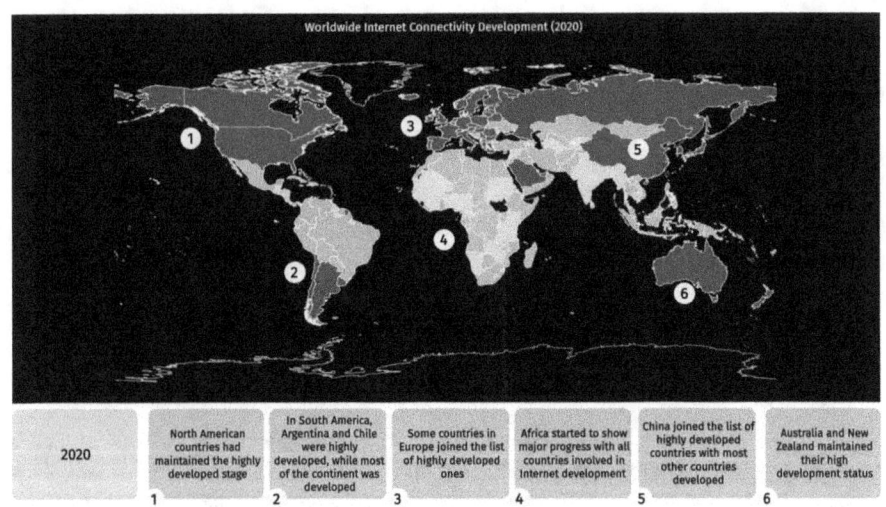

Figure 7-21. *Results for 2020*

CHAPTER 7 CLUSTERING THE DEVELOPMENT OF WORLDWIDE INTERNET CONNECTIVITY FOR SDGS 7, 9, AND 11

7.4.2 Discussions

This section consists of noteworthy insights inferred from the maps obtained, by simply adjusting the slider and observing the trend in worldwide Internet adoption.

Comparison with Historical Trends

The application's visualizations offer valuable insights into the progression of Internet connectivity over time, enabling comparisons with past trends. An in-depth comprehension of the course of global connectivity and its consequences can be obtained by analyzing the patterns and fluctuations in Internet penetration. Some key observations are given next:

- **Early Adoption and Expansion**: The maps illustrate the initial embrace of web technology in areas including North America, some parts of Asia, and the Nordic countries of Europe. Historical data from the 1990s to the early 2000s shows a swift growth of infrastructure and access in these areas, propelled by technological progress and rising demand [25]. This is shown in Figure 7-16 where despite the fact that the Internet originated from the United States of America, the first "Emerging" countries were Finland, Sweden, and Norway. This is due to the smaller population of the Nordic countries.

- **Emergence in Developing Regions**: Conversely, underdeveloped regions like Africa, certain areas of the Asian continent, and South America demonstrate a postponed yet consistent growth in Internet accessibility [26]. The application's visualizations showcase the expansion of Internet infrastructure in these regions starting from the early 2000s, indicating a progressive reduction in the digital divide. This is highly visible in the case of African countries, which struggled from the Underdeveloped state to the Emerging phase in 2010, and a majority of Developing countries in 2020.

- **Differential Growth Rates**: An examination of past patterns indicates varying rates of expansion in Internet usage across different regions and countries. While certain countries witnessed rapid and significant growth in their level of connectivity, others encountered obstacles such as inadequate infrastructure, economic limitations, and regulatory impediments.

- **Regional Disparities**: The visualizations highlight the ongoing regional differences in Internet access and development. Developed regions possess elevated levels of connectivity and sophisticated digital infrastructure, whereas under-resourced regions persistently fall behind, intensifying socioeconomic disparities.

Geographical Disparities

Through the analysis of disparities in Internet access and its degrees of expansion, areas of concern can be identified and treated as high priority for focused interventions. Some observations are as follows:

- **Regional Variations**: Developed regions, such as North America and Europe, generally have higher rates of consumption and more sophisticated facilities in comparison to developing economies in Africa, Asia, and Latin America. This is highly visible in Figure 7-21, where data for 2020 shows the clear demarcation between Africa and Asia, and the rest of the world.

- **Urban-Rural Divide:** Urban areas generally exhibit superior connectivity and technology owing to their higher population densities and greater economic advancement, whereas rural communities often face challenges in accessing reliable Internet services due to inadequate investment in equipment and geographical obstacles This can be seen in the case of India for 2020, in Figure 7-21 where despite having stable Internet infrastructure, rural areas contribute to the country being classified as Developing.

- **Economic Factors:** Economic factors are pivotal in determining regional variations in access to the Web. More affluent countries and urban areas typically possess greater financial means to allocate toward digital infrastructure and the expansion of broadband networks. Conversely, countries with lower income levels and remote areas may face difficulties in financing and executing essential infrastructure improvements. As shown in Figures 7-18 and 7-19, from 2005 to 2010, Africa struggled to have most of its countries in the Emerging category. By that time, some parts of Europe, the United States of America, and Australia were already in the Highly Developed stage

- **Policy and Regulatory Environment:** Countries that implement favourable policies, such as offering incentives for investment from the private sector, establishing regulatory frameworks that encourage concurrence, and launching initiatives to extend broadband coverage to underprivileged regions, generally achieve superior connectivity results.

7.5 Benefits of Global Internet Connectivity Analysis

This section highlights the importance of the Internet in driving socio-economic development, fostering innovation, and promoting digital inclusion in our interconnected world, especially with the recent surge in new trends such as artificial intelligence (AI) [27]. These new technologies necessitate the fundamental backbone of the Internet for proper functioning, especially with constant client demands for ultra-low latencies, owing to the nature of refined applications such as gaming, remote medical operations, videoconferencing, and augmented reality use cases. As countries aim to use the revolutionary potential of digital technologies, it is crucial to have a comprehensive understanding of global Internet connectivity trends. This section highlights the various advantages of using ML-based applications, as presented in this chapter, for the analysis of worldwide Internet connectivity. This application informs strategic decision-making, fosters international collaboration, and supports the achievement of the UN SDGs. Some of the benefits are elaborated upon next:

- **Empowering Policy Decision-Makers**: This application provides government officials and policymakers with valuable insights to create and enforce effective policies that aim to improve Internet accessibility and infrastructure. Decision-makers can pinpoint regions or communities that lack sufficient access and allocate resources accordingly. For example, they have the ability to allocate funds toward the construction of broadband infrastructure in areas that lack adequate service or to carry out programmes aimed at reducing the gap in digital access. Instead of using datasets that comprise countries at global level, they can simply replace the dataset with regional data, such as for districts, or states within a country. Furthermore, policymakers can use the data from the application to track the effectiveness of their interventions over a period of time. This allows them to make decisions based on evidence and ensures that their efforts are focused on the areas that require the most attention.

- **Enabling Strategic Investments**: Businesses and investors may benefit from the application's extensive data on universal online access to identify lucrative possibilities for strategic investments. Emerging markets that offer substantial opportunities for growth can be identified. This information is extremely valuable for making well-informed decisions regarding investments in telecommunications infrastructure, technology startups, and e-commerce initiatives. Moreover, businesses may use the application's analytics to customize their advertising approaches and product offerings for precise demographics, thus optimizing their return on investment.

- **Supporting Research and Development**: The application functions as a valuable tool for researchers and academics who are interested in examining different facets of the Internet. The application promotes cooperation and information exchange among researchers, fostering interdisciplinary research endeavors focused on tackling intricate issues pertaining to Internet connectivity.

- **Fostering International Collaboration:** Effective resolution of global Internet connectivity challenges necessitates partnership among governments, organizations, and stakeholders. The application functions as a platform for the dissemination of data, optimal methods, and tactics for its global expansion. The application promotes collaboration and knowledge sharing allowing stakeholders to use shared expertise to overcome obstacles. The adoption of this cooperative approach is crucial for the successful implementation of sustainable solutions that can significantly contribute to the attainment of universal Internet access.

- **Addressing Digital Inequality:** By identifying regions with limited or unequal access to the Internet, stakeholders can develop focused strategies to enhance connectivity and narrow the gap in digital access. For instance, governments and organizations may leverage infrastructure improvements, collaborations between the public and private sectors, and grassroots campaigns to enhance accessibility for communities that currently lack sufficient access. By prioritizing the reduction of digital inequality, stakeholders can guarantee that every individual and community has equitable access to the advantages of the digital revolution.

7.6 Summary

The aim of this chapter was to develop a web-based application that takes as input a CSV dataset containing information about global Internet connectivity, before performing K-means clustering as an unsupervised ML model, to generate five different levels of Internet development. With the unlabeled and preprocessed dataset consisting of 187 countries among the 195 member states of the UN, each country is categorized among Underdeveloped, Emerging, Developing, Developed, and Highly Developed.

This indicates the degree of Internet facilities and access in that country, which is then plotted onto a choropleth world map using Plotly.js, along with the option to select the year from 1980 to 2020. By simply viewing the map, a number of observations can be made with respect to historical trends, geographical disparities, digital inequality, and the quest for narrowing the digital divide. The K-means algorithm, built using the `ml.js` framework, thus proved to be effective in clustering global Internet connectivity since the observations tally with known historical occurrences. For instance, the application showed that in 1996 Finland, Sweden, and Norway were the first countries to embark on the Internet era, with the progress to improve Internet facilities apparent in the early 2000s. The Nordic countries were the firsts to reach the Highly Developed phase with the United States closely behind.

By 2020, most countries around the world had reached the Developed or the Highly Developed stages, with Africa and Asia on the verge of adequate Internet infrastructure. This application acts as a catalyst for collaboration, innovation, and collective action among policymakers, investors, researchers, and grassroot organizations with the purpose of promoting reliable universal Internet access. In the future, further progress and improvement of the application show potential for discovering new knowledge, making a significant difference, and promoting the worldwide goals of sustainable development and digital transformation.

References

Chapter 1

[1] UNDP, "Background on the goals" [Online]. Available at: https://www.undp.org/sdg-accelerator/background-goals#:~:text=The%20Sustainable%20Development%20Goals%20(SDGs,economic%20challenges%20facing%20our%20world [Accessed: September 21, 2023].

[2] Pekmezovic, A. The UN and goal setting: From the MDGs to the SDGs. In Sustainable Development Goals: Harnessing Business to Achieve the SDGs through Finance, Technology, and Law Reform; Walker, J., Pekmezovic, A., Walker, G., Eds.; John Wiley & Sons Ltd: West Sussex, UK, 2019; Volume 1.

[3] Gabriel, I.; Gauri, V. Towards a new global narrative for the sustainable development goals. In Sustainable Development Goals: Harnessing Business to Achieve the SDGs through Finance, Technology, and Law Reform; Walker, J., Pekmezovic, A., Walker, G., Eds.; John Wiley & Sons Ltd: West Sussex, UK, 2019; Volume 3.

[4] https://sdgs.un.org/goals/goal1

REFERENCES

[5] DAIA, Artificial Intelligence and Global Challenges — No Poverty | by DAIA | DAIA | Medium. Available at: https://medium.com/daia/artificial-intelligence-and-global-challenges-a-plan-for-progress-fecd37cc6bda [Accessed: September 2023].

[6] Mhlanga, D. Artificial Intelligence (AI) and Poverty Reduction in the Fourth Industrial Revolution (4IR). Preprints 2020, 2020090362 (doi: 10.20944/preprints202009.0362.v1). https://www.preprints.org/manuscript/202009.0362/v1.

[7] The Borgen Project, "Artificial Intelligence and Poverty." Available at: https://borgenproject.org/tag/artificial-intelligence-and-poverty/ [Accessed: September 2023].

[8] https://sdgs.un.org/goals/goal2 [Accessed: September 2023].

[9] https://www.tomra.com/en/food [Accessed: September 2023].

[10] N. Saranya and A. Mythili, "Classification of Soil and Crop Suggestion using Machine Learning Techniques," March 5, 2020. [Online]. Available at: https://www.ijert.org/classification-of-soil-and-crop-suggestion-using-machine-learning-techniques [Accessed: September 15, 2023].

[11] V. Pandith, H. Kour, S. Singh, J. Manhas and V. Sharma, "Performance Evaluation of Machine Learning Techniques for Mustard Crop Yield

REFERENCES

Prediction from Soil Analysis," 2020. [Online]. Available at: https://www.researchgate.net/profile/Haneet-Kour-2/publication/343219111_Performance_Evaluation_of_Machine_Learning_Techniques_for_Mustard_Crop_Yield_Prediction_from_Soil_Analysis/links/5f1d42a792851cd5fa489406/Performance-Evaluation-of-Machine-Learning-T [Accessed: September 21, 2023].

[12] S. A. Z. Rahman, K. C. Mitra and S. M. Islam, "Soil Classification Using Machine Learning Methods and Crop Suggestion Based on Soil Series," February 3, 2019 [Online]. Available at: https://ieeexplore.ieee.org/document/8631943 [Accessed: September 21, 2023].

[13] O. Folorunso, O. Oluwafolake, M. Busari, A. Muftau, J. Adejumobi, F. Daniel, C. O. Ugwunna, O. Olufemi and O. Olabanjo, "Exploring Machine Learning Models for Soil Nutrient Properties Prediction: A Systematic Review," 08 June 2023. [Online]. Available at: https://www.mdpi.com/2504-2289/7/2/113 [Accessed: September 21, 2023].

[14] U. Nations, "United Nations," 2023 [Online]. Available at: https://unric.org/en/sdg-3/ [Accessed: September 21, 2023].

[15] Puttagunta, M., Ravi, S. Medical image analysis based on deep learning approach. *Multimed Tools Appl* **80**, 24365–24398 (2021). https://doi.org/10.1007/s11042-021-10707-4.

REFERENCES

[16] G. Srividhya, "Sustainable Development of Green Healthcare Communities for Prediction of Autism Spectrum Disorder using Machine Learning Approach," Journal of Green Engineering, vol. 10, no. 9, 2020.

[17] https://sdgs.un.org/goals/goal6 [Accessed: September 21, 2023].

[18] Dogo, E. M., Nwulu, N. I., Twala, B., & Aigbavboa, C. (2019). A survey of machine learning methods applied to anomaly detection on drinking-water quality data. *Urban Water Journal, 16*(3), 235-248. https://doi.org/10.1080/1573062X.2019.1637002.

[19] Ambel, A.A., Bain, R., Degefu, T.B. *et al.* Addressing gaps in data on drinking water quality through data integration and machine learning: evidence from Ethiopia. *npj Clean Water* **6**, 63 (2023). https://doi.org/10.1038/s41545-023-00272-8.

[20] P. Qian *et al.*, "Multi-Target Deep Learning for Algal Detection and Classification," *2020 42nd Annual International Conference of the IEEE Engineering in Medicine & Biology Society (EMBC)*, Montreal, QC, Canada, 2020, pp. 1954-1957, doi: 10.1109/EMBC44109.2020.9176204.

[21] Kaddoura, S. Evaluation of Machine Learning Algorithm on Drinking Water Quality for Better Sustainability. *Sustainability* **2022**, *14*, 11478. https://doi.org/10.3390/su141811478.

REFERENCES

[22] Küfeoğlu, S. (2022). SDG-7 Affordable and Clean Energy. In: Emerging Technologies. Sustainable Development Goals Series. Springer, Cham. https://doi.org/10.1007/978-3-031-07127-0_9.

[23] Carl Elkin and Sims Witherspoon, "Machine learning can boost the value of wind energy," DeepMind 2019. Available at: https://deepmind.com/blog/article/machine-learning-can-boost-value-wind-energy [Accessed: September 23, 2023].

[24] United Nations, "Goal 9 | Department of Economic and Social Affairs" [Online]. Available at: https://sdgs.un.org/goals/goal9 [Accessed: September 23, 2023].

[25] UNDP, "Sustainable Development Goals | United Nations Development Programme" [Online]. Available at: https://www.undp.org/sustainable-development-goals/industry-innovation-and-infrastructure [Accessed: September 23, 2023].

[26] Triki, R.; Maâloul, M.H.; Bahou, Y.; Kadria, M. The Impact of Digitization to Ensure Competitiveness of the Ha'il Region to Achieve Sustainable Development Goals. *Sustainability* **2023**, *15*, 1661. https://doi.org/10.3390/su15021661.

[27] Jaber M (2023) IoT and machine learning for enabling sustainable development goals. *Front. Comms. Net* 4:1219047. doi: 10.3389/frcmn.2023.1219047.

[28] https://sdgs.un.org/goals/goal11 [Accessed: September 23, 2023].

REFERENCES

[29] United Nations. "World's population increasingly urban with more than half living in urban ar-eas." Available at: http://www.un.org/en/development/desa/news/population/world-urbanization-prospects-2014.html [Accessed: September 23, 2023].

[30] INTELLIGENT CONNECTIVITY - HOW THE COMBINATION OF 5G, AI AND IOT IS SET TO CHANGE THE AMERICAS, GSMA. Available at: https://itig-iraq.iq/wp-content/uploads/2019/05/21494-MWC-Americas-report.pdf [Accessed: September 23, 2023].

[31] https://sdgs.un.org/goals/goal12 [Accessed: September 23, 2023].

[32] A. Antunes, A. Andrade-Campos, A. Sardinha-Lourenço, M. S. Oliveira, "Short-term water demand forecasting using machine learning techniques" Journal of Hydroinformatics (2018) 20 (6): 1343-1366. https://doi.org/10.2166/hydro.2018.163.

[33] Rajnish Rakholia, Quan Le, Bang Quoc Ho, Khue Vu, Ricardo Simon Carbajo, "Multi-output machine learning model for regional air pollution forecasting in Ho Chi Minh City, Vietnam," Environment International, Volume 173, 2023,107848, ISSN 0160-4120, https://doi.org/10.1016/j.envint.2023.107848 (https://www.sciencedirect.com/science/article/pii/S0160412023001216).

REFERENCES

[34] Ghaffarian, S.; Emtehani, S. Monitoring Urban Deprived Areas with Remote Sensing and Machine Learning in Case of Disaster Recovery. *Climate* **2021**, 9, 58. https://doi.org/10.3390/cli9040058.

[35] Copeland, J. (2000). *What is Artificial Intelligence?* AlanTuring.net. http://www.alanturing.net/turing_archive/pages/Reference%20Articles/What%20is%20AI.html [Accessed: September 2023].

[36] Deloitte. (2018). *Artificial Intelligence White paper.* delloite.com. https://www2.deloitte.com/content/dam/Deloitte/nl/Documents/deloitte-analytics/deloitte-nl-data-analytics-artificial-intelligence-whitepaper-eng.pdf [Accessed: September 2023].

[37] Tulsi Pawan Fowdur, Satyadev Rosunee, Robert T. F. Ah King, Pratima Jeetah and Mahendra Gooroochurn (eds) "Artificial Intelligence, Engineering Systems and Sustainable Development: Driving the UN SDGs," Emerald Publishing Limited, ISBN: 9781837535415, January 18, 2024. https://books.emeraldinsight.com/book/detail/artificial-intelligence-engineering-systems-and-sustainable-development/?k=9781837535415.

[38] Rahman, W. (2020). *AI and machine learning.* New Delhi: SAGE Publications India Pvt Ltd, 2020, p. 11.

[39] Goertzel, B., & C, Pennachin. (2007). *Artificial general intelligence.* 1st ed. Berlin: Springer, 2007.

[40] Yampolskiy, R. (2017). *Artificial Super intelligence.* CRC Press, 2017.

REFERENCES

[41] Khan, S., Rahmani, H., Shah, S and Bennamoun, M. (2018). A guide to convolutional neural networks for computer vision. Morgan & Claypool, ISBN: 978-3-031-01821-3, https://link.springer.com/book/10.1007/978-3-031-01821-3.

[42] Hintze, A. (2016). *Understanding the Four Types of Artificial Intelligence.* govtech.com. https://www.govtech.com/computing/understanding-the-four-types-of-artificial-intelligence.html [Accessed: September 2023].

[43] Phil Kim, "MATLAB Deep Learning With Machine Learning, Neural Networks and Artificial Intelligence," Apress 2017, DOI 10.1007/978-1-4842-2845-6.

[44] Alex Smola and S.V.N. Vishwanathan, "Introduction to Machine Learning," Cambridge University Press 2008, ISBN 0 521 82583 0 hardback.

[45] Fowdur, T.P., Babooram, L., Nazir Rosun, M.N.I., & Indoonundon, M. (2021). *REAL-TIME CLOUD COMPUTING AND MACHINE LEARNING APPLICATIONS.* Nova Science Publishers, July 2021, Computer Science, Technology and Applications Book Series, ISBN: 978-1-53619-813-3.

[46] Russell, S.J., & Norvig, P. (2020). Artificial Intelligence - A Modern Approach. Pearson Series in Artificial Intelligence, 4th Edition. ISBN: 978-0134610993.

REFERENCES

[47] Sutton, R., Bach, F., and Barto, A. (2018). Reinforcement Learning: An Introduction. Massachusetts: MIT Press, 2nd ed. ISBN: 978-0-262-19398-6.

[48] Zhang, C., & Ma, Y. (2012). *Ensemble Machine Learning.* 1st ed. Boston, MA: Springer US, 2012.

[49] Boštjan Kaluža, "Machine Learning in Java," Copyright © 2016 Packt Publishing, ISBN 978-1-78439-658-9.

[50] IBM, "What is Data Integration?" https://www.ibm.com/topics/data-integration [Accessed: September 2023].

[51] https://cdn.jsdelivr.net/npm/papaparse@5.4.1/papaparse.min.js [Accessed: January 2023].

[52] https://cdn.plot.ly/plotly-latest.min.js [Accessed: January 2023].

[53] https://cdnjs.cloudflare.com/ajax/libs/mathjs/12.4.1/math.js [Accessed: January 2023].

[54] https://www.lactame.com/lib/ml/6.0.0/ml.min.js [Accessed: January 2023].

[55] https://www.kaggle.com/datasets/saurabh00007/diabetescsv [Accessed: January 2023].

REFERENCES

Chapter 2

[1] Anastasiadou, M., Santos, V. and Dias, M.S. (2021). Machine Learning Techniques Focusing on the Energy Performance of Buildings: A Dimensions and Methods Analysis. Buildings, 12(1), p. 28. doi:https://doi.org/10.3390/buildings12010028.

[2] Asadikia, A., Rajabifard, A. and Kalantari, M. (2020). Systematic prioritisation of SDGs: Machine learning approach. World Development, 140, p. 105269. doi:https://doi.org/10.1016/j.worlddev.2020.105269.

[3] Boza, P. and Evgeniou, T. (2021). Artificial intelligence to support the integration of variable renewable energy sources to the power system. Applied Energy, 290, p. 116754. doi:https://doi.org/10.1016/j.apenergy.2021.116754.

[4] Brázdil, S.B.K., Pinto, F.M. and Oliveira, J.M., 2019. The role of wind power forecasting in grid operation and optimization. *Energy Policy*, [online] 129, pp. 359-370. Available at: https://www.sciencedirect.com/science/article/pii/S0301421519301096 [Accessed: August 22, 2024].

[5] Chen, C., Sun, J., Qian, J., Chen, X., Hu, Z., Jia, G., Xing, X. and Wei, S. (2022). Indirect Assessment of Watershed SDG7 Development Process Using Nighttime Light Data—An Example of the Aral Sea Watershed. Remote Sensing, [online] 14(23), p. 6131. doi:https://doi.org/10.3390/rs14236131.

REFERENCES

[6] Chen, C., Hu, Y., Karuppiah, M. and Kumar, P.M. (2021). Artificial intelligence on economic evaluation of energy efficiency and renewable energy technologies. Sustainable Energy Technologies and Assessments, 47, p. 101358. doi:https://doi.org/10.1016/j.seta.2021.101358.

[7] Chiang, M. and Zhang, T. (2016). Fog and IoT: An Overview of Research Opportunities. IEEE Internet of Things Journal, 3(6), pp. 854–864. doi:https://doi.org/10.1109/jiot.2016.2584538.

[8] Dataset Source: https://www.kaggle.com/code/qusaybtoush1990/texas-wind-turbine-accuracy-99/notebook

[9] De Las Heras, A., Luque-Sendra, A. and Zamora-Polo, F. (2020). Machine Learning Technologies for Sustainability in Smart Cities in the Post-COVID Era. Sustainability, 12(22), p. 9320. doi:https://doi.org/10.3390/su12229320.

[10] Esapour, Khodakhast; Moazzen, Farid; Karimi, Mazaher; Dabbaghjamanesh, Morteza; Kavousi-Fard, Abdollah (2022) A novel energy management framework incorporating multi-carrier energy hub for smart city, IET Generation, Transmission & Distribution, Vol.17, Issue(3) DOI:10.1049/gtd2.12500.

REFERENCES

[11] Foley, A.M., Leahy, P.G., Marvuglia, A. and McKeogh, E.J. (2012). Current methods and advances in forecasting of wind power generation. Renewable Energy, [online] 37(1), pp. 1-8. doi:https://doi.org/10.1016/j.renene.2011.05.033.

[12] Gupta, A.K., Patel, M.S. and Garcia, L.V., 2021. Economic impacts of wind power forecasting on power system operations. *Energy Economics*, [online] 94, p. 105042. Available at: https://www.sciencedirect.com/science/article/pii/S0140988320302725 [Accessed: August 22, 2024].

[13] Hannan, M.A., Al-Shetwi, A.Q., Ker, P.J., Begum, R.A., Mansor, M., Rahman, S.A., Dong, Z.Y., Tiong, S.K., Mahlia, T.M.I. and Muttaqi, K.M. (2021). Impact of renewable energy utilization and artificial intelligence in achieving sustainable development goals. Energy Reports, 7, pp. 5359-5373. doi:https://doi.org/10.1016/j.egyr.2021.08.172.

[14] Kufeoglu, S., 2022. SDG-7 Affordable and Clean Energy. Emerging Technologies, pp. 305-330. Sustainable Energy for All | SEforALL. (n.d.). *Renewable energy* [Online]. Available at: https://www.seforall.org/goal-7-targets/renewable-energy.

[15] Larson, E.M., Smith, R.J. and Wong, T.Y., 2023. Optimizing energy infrastructure through predictive wind power models. *Renewable and Sustainable Energy Reviews*, [online] 176, p. 113215. Available at: https://www.sciencedirect.com/science/article/pii/S1364032123000348 [Accessed: August 22, 2024].

REFERENCES

[16] Le Blanc, D. (2015). Towards Integration at Last? The Sustainable Development Goals as a Network of Targets. Sustainable Development, 23(3), pp. 176–187. doi:https://doi.org/10.1002/sd.1582.

[17] Liu, X., Zhang, X. and Baziar, A. (2023). Hybrid Machine Learning and Modified Teaching Learning-Based English Optimization Algorithm for Smart City Communication. Sustainability, [online] 15(15), p. 11535. doi:https://doi.org/10.3390/su151511535.

[18] Mwitondi, K.S., Munyakazi, I. and Gatsheni, B.N. (2020). A robust machine learning approach to SDG data segmentation. Journal of Big Data, 7(1). doi:https://doi.org/10.1186/s40537-020-00373-y.

[19] Nathans, L., Oswald, F. and Nimon, K. (2019). Interpreting Multiple Linear Regression: A Guidebook of Variable Importance. *Practical Assessment, Research, and Evaluation*, [online] 17(1). doi:https://doi.org/10.7275/5fex-b874.

[20] Nwokolo, S.C., Obiwulu, A.U. and Ogbulezie, J.C. (2023). Machine learning and analytical model hybridization to assess the impact of climate change on solar PV energy production. Physics and Chemistry of the Earth, Parts A/B/C, 130, p. 103389. doi:https://doi.org/10.1016/j.pce.2023.103389.

REFERENCES

[21] Rashid, H., Haider, W. and Batunlu, C. (2020). Forecasting of Wind Turbine Output Power Using Machine learning. 2020 10th International Conference on Advanced Computer Information Technologies (ACIT). doi:https://doi.org/10.1109/acit49673.2020.9208852.

[22] Salih Mohammed Salih, M. Q. T. M. K. A., 2012. Performance analysis of wind turbine systems under different parameters effect. *INTERNATIONAL JOURNAL OF ENERGY AND ENVIRONMENT,* 3(6), pp. 895-904.

[23] Sarkodie, S.A., Ackom, E., Bekun, F.V. and Owusu, P.A. (2020). Energy-Climate-Economy-Population Nexus: An Empirical Analysis in Kenya, Senegal, and Eswatini. Sustainability, 12(15), p. 6202. doi:https://doi.org/10.3390/su12156202.

[24] Shahzad, U., Sengupta, T., Rao, A. and Cui, L. (2023). Forecasting carbon emissions future prices using the machine learning methods. Annals of Operations Research. doi:https://doi.org/10.1007/s10479-023-05188-7.

[25] Singh, A., Anurag Kanaujia, Vivek Kumar Singh and Vinuesa, R. (2023). Artificial intelligence for Sustainable Development Goals: Bibliometric patterns and concept evolution trajectories. Sustainable Development. doi:https://doi.org/10.1002/sd.2706.

[26] Thomas, J.D., Ruiz, P.M. and Johnson, A.S., 2022. Managing grid stability with wind power forecasting techniques. *IEEE Transactions on Power Systems*, [online] 37(4), pp. 3156-3166. Available at: https://ieeexplore.ieee.org/document/9720434 [Accessed: August 22, 2024].

[27] Verhoef, D., de Vries, H.J.N. and van der Meer, A., 2020. Short-term wind power forecasting using classification models. *Renewable Energy* [Online]. Available at: https://www.sciencedirect.com/science/article/pii/S0960148120300302 [Accessed: August 22, 2024].

[28] Yiannis A. Katsigiannis, G. S. S. C. P., 2013. *Effect of Wind Turbine Classes on the Electricity Production of Wind Farms in Cyprus Island.* s.l., Hindawi.

[29] Zhang, Y., Wang, J. and Wang, X. (2014). Review on probabilistic forecasting of wind power generation. Renewable and Sustainable Energy Reviews, 32, pp. 255–270. doi:https://doi.org/10.1016/j.rser.2014.01.033.

Chapter 3

[1] P. T. Fowdur, M. Indoonundon, M. A. Hosany, D. Milovanovic and Z. Bojkovic, "Achieving Sustainable Development Goals Through Digital Infrastructure for Intelligent Connectivity," January 31, 2022 [Online]. Available at: https://link.springer.com/chapter/10.1007/978-3-030-90618-4_1 [Accessed: September 20, 2023].

REFERENCES

[2] E. Elbasi, Z. Chamseddine, T. E. Ahmet, A. Wiem, Z. I. Aymen, C. Elda, S. Ahmed and S. Louai, "Crop Prediction Model Using Machine Learning Algorithms," August 16, 2023 [Online]. Available at: https://www.mdpi.com/2076-3417/13/16/9288#B17-applsci-13-09288. [Accessed: September 18, 2023].

[3] V. Pandith, H. Kour, S. Singh, J. Manhas and V. Sharma, "Performance Evaluation of Machine Learning Techniques for Mustard Crop Yield Prediction from Soil Analysis," 2020 [Online]. Available at: https://www.researchgate.net/profile/Haneet-Kour-2/publication/343219111_Performance_Evaluation_of_Machine_Learning_Techniques_for_Mustard_Crop_Yield_Prediction_from_Soil_Analysis/links/5f1d42a792851cd5fa489406/Performance-Evaluation-of-Machine-Learning-T [Accessed: September 21, 2023].

[4] S. A. Z. Rahman, K. C. Mitra and S. M. Islam, "Soil Classification Using Machine Learning Methods and Crop Suggestion Based on Soil Series," February 3, 2019 [Online]. Available at: https://ieeexplore.ieee.org/document/8631943 [Accessed: September 21, 2023].

[5] O. Folorunso, O. Oluwafolake, M. Busari, A. Muftau, J. Adejumobi, F. Daniel, C. O. Ugwunna, O. Olufemi and O. Olabanjo, "Exploring Machine Learning Models for Soil Nutrient Properties Prediction: A Systematic Review," June 8, 2023 [Online]. Available at: https://www.mdpi.com/2504-2289/7/2/113 [Accessed: September 21, 2023].

REFERENCES

[6] N. Efremova, D. Zausaev and G. Antipov, "Prediction of soil moisture content based on satellite data and sequence-to-sequence networks," *arXiv preprint arXiv,* p. doi: 1907.03697, 2019.

[7] B. Ferreira, I. Muriel and R. G. Silva, "Monitoring sustainable development by means of earth observation data and machine learning: a review," *Environmental Sciences Europe,* vol. 32, no. 1, pp. 1-17, doi: https://doi.org/10.1186/s12302-020-00397-4, 2020.

[8] AlKhereibi, A. Hasan, W. G. Tadesse, K. Murat and N. C. Onat, "Predictive Machine Learning Algorithms for Metro Ridership Based on Urban Land Use Policies in Support of Transit-Oriented Development," *Sustainability,* vol. 15, no. 2, p. 1718, doi: https://doi.org/10.3390/su15021718, 2023.

[9] V. Sberveglieri, E. N. Carmona and M. Abbatangelo, "How Nanotechnology Can Help the "Zero Hunger" Goal," 2021 [Online]. Available at: https://iopscience.iop.org/article/10.1149/MA2021-01571535mtgabs/meta#back-to-top-target [Accessed: 16 September 2023].

[10] A. Wahid, K. Mason and I. Faiud, "Integrating Renewable Energy in Agriculture: A Deep Reinforcement Learning-based Approach," August 16, 2023 [Online]. Available at: https://arxiv.org/abs/2308.08611 [Accessed: 16 September 2023].

REFERENCES

[11] M. Subhadra, M. Debahuti and S. H. Gour, "Applications of Machine Learning Techniques in Agricultural Crop Production: A Review Paper," *Indian Journal of Science and Technology*, vol. 9, no. 38, pp. 1-14 doi: 10.17485/ijst/2016/v9i38/95032, 2016.

[12] M. Kalimuthu, V. P and K. M, "Crop prediction using machine learning," *2020 third international conference on smart systems and inventive technology (ICSSIT)*, pp. 926–932, doi: 10.1109/ICSSIT48917.2020.9214190, 2020.

[13] R. Kumar, P. Kumar, M. P. Singh and J. P. Singh, "Crop Selection Method to maximize crop yield rate using machine learning technique," August 27, 2015 [Online]. Available at: Crop Selection Method to maximize crop yield rate using machine learning technique [Accessed: September 15, 2023].

[14] N. Saranya and A. Mythili, "Classification of Soil and Crop Suggestion using Machine Learning Techniques," March 5, 2020 [Online]. Available at: https://www.ijert.org/classification-of-soil-and-crop-suggestion-using-machine-learning-techniques [Accessed: September 15, 2023].

[15] M. Paul, A. Verma and S. K. Vishwakarma, "Analysis of Soil Behaviour and Prediction of Crop Yield Using Data Mining Approach," August 18, 2016 [Online]. Available at: https://ieeexplore.ieee.org/abstract/document/7546199 [Accessed: September 15, 2023].

REFERENCES

[16] A. Ingle, "Crop Recommendation Dataset," Kaggle, 2020 [Online]. Available at: https://www.kaggle.com/datasets/atharvaingle/crop-recommendation-dataset [Accessed: September 15, 2023].

[17] Google, "Google," Google, [Online]. Available at: https://research.google.com/colaboratory/faq.html [Accessed: September 15, 2023]

[18] M. Holt, "Papa Parse," papaparse, 11, 2023 [Online]. Available at: https://www.papaparse.com/ [Accessed: September 15, 2023].

[19] mljs, "Github - ml," github, 12, 2023 [Online]. Available at: https://github.com/mljs/ml [Accessed: September 15, 2023].

[20] TensorFlow, "TensorFlow," TensorFlow [Online]. Available at: https://www.tensorflow.org/js [Accessed: September 15, 2023].

[21] I. Mike Bostock and Observable, "D3," Observable, [Online]. Available at: https://d3js.org/ [Accessed: September 15, 2023].

[22] J. Singh and R. Banerjee, "A Study on Single and Multi-layer Perceptron Neural Network," August 29, 2019 [Online]. Available at: https://ieeexplore.ieee.org/abstract/document/8819775/authors#authors [Accessed: 17 September 2023].

[23] Shiksha Online, "What is Multilayer Perceptron (MLP) Neural Networks?," February 9, 2023 [Online]. Available at: https://www.shiksha.com/online-courses/articles/understanding-multilayer-perceptron-mlp-neural-networks/ [Accessed: September 17, 2023].

REFERENCES

[24] N. K. Kain, "Understanding of Multilayer perceptron (MLP)," Medium, November 21, 2018 [Online]. Available at: https://medium.com/@AI_with_Kain/understanding-of-multilayer-perceptron-mlp-8f179c4a135f [Accessed: September 17, 2023].

[25] UNESCO, "UNESCO and Sustainable Development Goals," UNESCO, [Online]. Available at: https://en.unesco.org/sustainabledevelopmentgoals [Accessed: September 15, 2023].

[26] L. S. Cedric, W. Y. H. Adoni, R. Aworka, J. T. Zoueu, M. Krichen, C. L. M. Kimpolo and F. K. Mutombo, "Crops yield prediction based on machine learning models: Case of West African countries," 2 December 2022 [Online]. Available at: https://www.sciencedirect.com/science/article/pii/S2772375522000168 [Accessed: September 20, 2023].

[27] UNDP, "Background on the goals" [Online]. Available at: https://www.undp.org/sdg-accelerator/background-goals#:~:text=The%20Sustainable%20Development%20Goals%20(SDGs,economic%20challenges%20facing%20our%20world [Accessed: September 21, 2023].

[28] B. Mahesh, "Machine Learning Algorithms -A Review," January 2019 [Online]. Available at: https://www.researchgate.net/publication/344717762_Machine_Learning_Algorithms_-A_Review [Accessed: September 21, 2023].

[29] S. Miteva, "How Can AI Help in Achieving the Sustainable Development Goals?," March 22, 2022 [Online]. Available at: https://www.valuer.ai/blog/how-can-ai-help-in-achieving-the-sustainable-development-goals [Accessed: September 22, 2023].

[30] IBM, "What is random forest?," IBM [Online]. Available at: https://www.ibm.com/topics/random-forest [Accessed: September 22, 2023].

Chapter 4

[1] UNDP, "What are the Sustainable Development Goals?," 2021 [Online]. Available at: https://www.undp.org/sustainable-development-goals [Accessed: September 19, 2023].

[2] WHO, "Sustainable Development Goals," 2021 [Online]. Available at: https://www.who.int/europe/about-us/our-work/sustainable-development-goals#:~:text=Section%20navigation&text=The%20Sustainable%20Development%20Goals%20(SDGs,enjoy%20health%2C%20justice%20and%20prosperity [Accessed: September 19, 2023].

[3] UN, "THE 17 GOALS," 2022 [Online]. Available at: https://sdgs.un.org/goals [Accessed: September 19, 2023].

REFERENCES

[4] S. S. Gill and D. S. K. Singh, "The Combination between Machine Learning and Sustainable Development Goal (SDG)," 2022 [Online]. Available at: https://insights2techinfo.com/the-combination-between-machine-learning-and-sustainable-development-goal-sdg/#:~:text=Machine%20learning%20plays%20a%20vital,classifiers%20such%20as%20decision%20trees [Accessed: September 19, 2023].

[5] M. S. U. Miah, J. Sulaiman, M. I. Islam, M. Masuduzzaman, N. C. Giri, S. Bhattacharyya, G. F. Segbedji and L. Mrsic, "Predicting Short-Term Energy Demand in the Smart Grid: A Deep Learning Approach for Integrating Renewable Energy Sources in Line with SDGs 7, 9, and 13," *Energy Reports*, p. 38, 20 July 2023, 10.2139/ssrn.4534111.

[6] P. R. Pandurangan and B. S. Kumar, "A Study on Sustainable Development Goals in South India Using Data Mining and Machine Learning Approaches," *Journal of Data Acquisition and Processing*, vol. 38, 2023, 10.5281/zenodo.9854907.

[7] S. Lee and S. Tae, "Development of a Decision Support Model Based onMachine Learning for Applying Greenhouse GasReduction Technology," MDPI, Korea, 2020, 10.3390/su12093582.

[8] P. Asha, M. Kasiprasad, R. Khilar, N. Subbulakshmi, R. Dhanalakshmi, V. Tripathi, V. Mohanavel, R. Sathyamurthy and M. Sudhakar, "Role of machine learning in attaining environmental sustainability," in *Energy report*, Elsevier, Ed., China, Science Direct, 2022, pp. 863–871, 10.1016/j.egyr.2022.09.206.

REFERENCES

[9] S. Madeh Piryonesi and T. El-Diraby, "Climate change impact on infrastructure: A machine learning solution for predicting pavement condition index," *Construction and Building Materials,* vol. 306, 2021, 10.1016/j.conbuildmat.2021.124905.

[10] A. Asadikia, A. Rajabifard and M. Kalantari, "Systematic prioritisation of SDGs: Machine learning approach," *World Development,* April 2021, 10.1016/j.worlddev.2020.105269.

[11] A. H. AlKhereibi, T. G. Wakjira, M. Kucukvar and N. C. Onat, "Predictive Machine Learning Algorithms for Metro Ridership Based on Urban Land Use Policies in Support of Transit-Oriented Development," *Sustainability,* vol. 15, no. 2, p. 1718, January 13, 2023, 10.3390/su15021718.

[12] A. Rao, A. Talan, S. Abbas, D. Dev and F. Taghizadeh-Hesary, "The role of natural resources in the management of environmental sustainability: Machine learning approach," *Resources Policy,* vol. 82, p. 103548, May 1, 2023, 10.1016/j.resourpol.2023.103548.

[13] K. N. Sami, Z. M. A. Amin and R. Hassan, "Waste Management Using Machine Learning and Deep Learning Algorithms," *International Journal on Perceptive and Cognitive Computing,* vol. 6, no. 2, pp. 97–106, December 14, 2020, 10.31436/ijpcc.v6i2.165.

REFERENCES

[14] Z. Liu, Y. Zhang, X. Ni, M. Dong, J. Zhu, Q. Zhang and J. Wang, "Climate action may reduce the risk of unemployment: An insight into the city-level interconnections among the sustainable development goals," *Resources Conservation and Recycling,* vol. 194, p. 107002, July 1, 2023, 10.1016/j.resconrec.2023.107002.

[15] L. Gaur, G. Singh, A. Solanki, N. Zaman Jhanjhi, U. Bhatia, S. Sharma, S. Verma, Kavita, N. Petrović, M. Fazal Ijaz and K. Wonjoon, "Disposition of Youth in Predicting Sustainable Development Goals Using the Neuro-fuzzy and Random Forest Algorithms," *Human-Centric Computing and Information Sciences,* vol. 11, July 2021, 10.22967/HCIS.2021.11.024.

[16] K. Parvin, M. S. Hossain Lipu, M. A. Hannan, M. A. Abdullah, P. Jern Ker, B. Rawshan Ara, M. Mansor, K. Muttaqi, T. M. Indra Mahlia, and Z. Yang Dong, "Intelligent Controllers and Optimization Algorithms for Building Energy Management Towards Achieving Sustainable Development: Challenges and Prospects," *IEEEAccess,* vol. 9, 2021, 10.1109/ACCESS.2021.3065087.

[17] S. Ghaffarian and S. Emtehani, "Monitoring Urban Deprived Areas with Remote Sensing and Machine Learning in Case of Disaster Recovery," *Climate,* vol. 9, p. 58, 2021, 10.3390/cli9040058.

REFERENCES

[18] Our World in Data, "Greenhouse gas emissions by sector, World," 2020 [Online]. Available at: https://ourworldindata.org/grapher/ghg-emissions-by-sector [Accessed: September 20, 2023].

[19] Our World in Data, "CO_2 emissions by sector, World," 2020 [Online]. Available at: https://ourworldindata.org/grapher/co-emissions-by-sector [Accessed: September 20, 2023].

[20] The World Bank, "GDP growth (annual %)-Mauritius," 2022 [Online]. Available at: https://data.worldbank.org/indicator/NY.GDP.MKTP.KD.ZG?end=2019&locations=MU&start=1990&view=chart [Accessed: September 20, 2023].

[21] The World Bank, "Population, total-Mauritius," 2022 [Online]. Available at: https://data.worldbank.org/indicator/SP.POP.TOTL [Accessed: September 20, 2023].

[22] "ml.js" [Online]. Available at: https://www.lactame.com/lib/ml/6.0.0/ml.min.js [Accessed: August 20, 2023].

[23] "Papa Parse" [Online]. Available at: https://cdnjs.cloudflare.com/ajax/libs/PapaParse/5.4.1/papaparse.min.js [Accessed: August 20, 2023].

[24] "plotly.js" [Online]. Available at: https://cdnjs.cloudflare.com/ajax/libs/plotly.js/2.24.2/plotly.min.js [Accessed: August 20, 2023].

[25] "math.js" [Online]. Available at: https://cdnjs.cloudflare.com/ajax/libs/mathjs/11.8.2/math.js [Accessed: August 20, 2023].

REFERENCES

[26] EPA, "Mandatory Reporting of Greenhouse Gases (40 CFR part 98)," 2011 [Online]. Available at: https://www.ecfr.gov/current/title-40/chapter-I/subchapter-C/part-98?toc=1 [Accessed: September 23, 2023].

[27] EIA, "Energy and the environment explained," August 22, 2023 [Online]. Available at: https://www.eia.gov/energyexplained/energy-and-the-environment/where-greenhouse-gases-come-from.php#:~:text=In%20the%20United%20States%2C%20most,and%20petroleum%E2%80%94for%20energy%20use [Accessed: September 24, 2023].

[28] SOS, "POVERTY IN AFRICA - THE INDICATORS," 2023 [Online]. Available at: https://www.sos-usa.org/about-us/where-we-work/africa/poverty-in-africa#:~:text=Africa%20is%20considered%20the%20poorest,society%2C%20their%20children%20and%20women [Accessed: September 24, 2023].

Chapter 5

[1] Surjeet Dalal, Edeh Michael Onyema, Carlos Andres Tavera Romero, Lauritta Chinazaekpere Ndufeiya-Kumasi, "Machine learning-based forecasting of potability of drinking water through adaptive boosting model," *Open Chemistry*, vol. 20, no. 1, pp. 816–828 doi: 10.1515/chem-2022-0187, 2022.

REFERENCES

[2] Sunday tunmibi, David O. Okhakhu, Machine Learning for Sustainable Development, Nigeria: Research Gate, 2022, pp. 4-6 doi: 10.1109/IDAACS58523.2023.10348888.

[3] Hamid Mehmood, Danielle Liao, Kimberly Mahadeo, "A review of Artificial Intelligence Applications to achieve water-related Sustainable Development Goals," IEEE, Geneva, Switzerland, 2020.

[4] E. Dogo, "A survey of machine learning methods applied to anomaly detection on drinking-water quality data," *Urban Water Journal*, vol. 16, no. 1, pp. 1-14; doi: 10.1080, 2019.

[5] P. Qian, "Multi-Target Deep Learning for Algal Detection and Classification," *Annual International Conference of the IEEE Engineering in Medicine and Biology Society (EMBC)*, vol. 1, pp. 1-8; doi: 10.1109/EMBC44109.2020.9176204, 2020.

[6] A. Antunes, "Short-term water demand forecasting using machine learning techniques," *Journal of Hydroinformatics*, pp. 1-8; doi: 20.6, 2018.

[7] K. N. Sami, Z. M. A. Amin and R. Hassan, "Waste management using machine learning and deep learning algorithms," *International Journal on Perceptive and Cognitive Computing*, vol. 6, no. 2, pp. 97-106 ;doi:10.31436/ijpcc.v6i2.165, 2020.

[8] E. K. Siabi, Y. T. Dile, A. T. Kabo-Bah, M. AmoBoateng, G. K. Anornu and K. Akpoti, "Machine learning based groundwater prediction in a data-scarce basin of Ghana," *Applied Artificial Intelligence*, vol. 36, no. 1, p. doi:10.1080/08839514.2022.2138130, 2022.

REFERENCES

[9] J. Castaneda, J. F. Cardona, L. d. C. Martins and A. A. Juan, "Supervised Machine Learning Algorithms for Measuring and Promoting Sustainable Transportation and Green Logistics," vol. 58, pp. 455–462; doi:10.1016/j.trpro.2021.11.061, 2021.

[10] Jiangtao Ren, Sau Dan Lee, Xianlu Chen, Ben Kao, Reynold Cheng, David Cheung, "Naive Bayes classification of uncertain Data," IEEE, Miami Beach, FL, USA, 2009.

Chapter 6

[1] T. P. Fowdur, I. Madhavsingh, M. A. Hosany, B. Zoran and M. Dragorad, "Achieving Sustainable Development Goals Through Digital Infrastruture for Intelligent Connectivity," *Lecture notes on data engineering and communications technologies,* pp. 3-26, 2022, doi: https://doi.org/10.1007/978-3-030-90618-4_1.

[2] O. Theobald, "What is Machine Learning?," *Machine Learning for absolute beginners,* pp. 4-10, 2017, ISBN: 9781549617218. Accessed: Aug. 13, 2021 [Online]. Available at: https://books.google.mu/books?id=PGNzswEACAAJ.

[3] D. Suresh, D. Swetha, S. J. Surender, M. B. CH and J. A. Mohamed, "Machine Learning in Drug Discovery: A Review," *Artificial Intelligence Review,* vol. 55, no. 3, 2021, doi: https://doi.org/10.20944/preprints202110.0242.v1.

REFERENCES

[4] P. Muralikrishna and R. S., "Medical image analysis based on deep learning approach," *Multimedia Tools and Applications,* vol. 80, pp. 24365–24398, 2021, https://doi.org/10.1007/s11042-021-10707-4.

[5] G. Srividhya, "Sustainable Development of Green Healthcare Communities for Prediction of Autism Spectrum Disorder using Machine Learning Approach," *Journal of Green Engineering,* vol. 10, no. 9, 2020, https://doi.org/10.3389/fninf.2020.575999.

[6] S. Arpan, J. Sonakshi, M. Ryan, P. Shruti, P. Sharnil and K. Ketan, "Deep-learning based respiratory sound analysis for detection of chronic obstructive pulmonary disease," *PeerJ Computer Science,* vol. 7, 2021, https://doi.org/10.7717/peerj-cs.369.

[7] R. V. M. Gabriel, M. M. Sergio, P. M. G. and A. G. Juan, "Explainable Prediction of Chronic Renal Disease in the Colombian Population Using Neural Networks and Case-Based Reasoning," 2019, https://doi.org/10.1109/ACCESS.2019.2948430.

[8] R. V. M. Gabriel, M. M. M. Sergio, A. R. G. Juan and M. G. Pablo, "Explainable Machine Learning Prediction for COVID-19 Mortality in the Colombian Population," 2021, https://doi.org/10.21203/rs.3.rs-828089/v1

[9] N. Bhoj and R. S. Bhadoria, "Time-series based prediction for energy consumption of a smart home data using hybrid convolution-recurrent neural network," *Telematics and Informatics,* vol. 75, p. 101907, 2022, https://doi.org/10.1016/j.tele.2022.101907.

REFERENCES

[10] M. Miah, J. Sulaiman, M. Islam and Masuduzzaman, "Predicting Short-Term Energy Demand in the Smart Grid: A Deep Learning Approach for Integrating Renewable Energy Sources in Line with SDGs 7.9 and 13," *arXiv,* 2023, https://doi.org/10.48550/arXiv.2304.03997.

[11] C. Srivastava, S. Singh and A. P. Singh, "Estimation of Air Pollution in Delhi Using Machine Learning Techniques," in *2018 International Conference on Computing Power and Communication Technologies (GUCON),* India, 2018, https://doi.org/10.1109/GUCON.2018.8675022.

[12] H. Alkabbani, A. Ramadan, Q. Zhu and A. Elkamel, "An Improved Air Quality Index Machine Learning-Based Forecasting with Multivariate Data Imputation Approach," *Atmosphere,* vol. 13, no. 7, pp. 1144–2022, https://doi.org/10.3390/atmos13071144.

[13] R. Janarthanan, P. Partheeban, K. Somasundaram and P. E. Navin, "A deep learning approach for prediction of air quality index in a metropolitan city," *Sustainable Cities and Society,* vol. 67, 2021, https://doi.org/10.1016/j.scs.2021.102720.

[14] F. Wei, X. Qiongying, S. Liang and S. Victor, "Survey on the Application of Deep Learning in Extreme Weather Prediction," *Atmosphere,* vol. 12, no. 6, p. 661, 2021, https://doi.org/10.3390/atmos12060661.

Chapter 7

[1] S. Akter, S. Sultana, Angappa Gunasekaran, R. J. Bandara, and S. J. Miah, "Tackling the global challenges using data-driven innovations," Annals of Operations Research, vol. 333, no. 2-3, pp. 517-532, February 2024, doi: https://doi.org/10.1007/s10479-024-05875-z.

[2] International Telecommunication Union (ITU), "Population of global offline continues steady decline to 2.6 billion people in 2023," ITU, September 12, 2023. https://www.itu.int/en/mediacentre/Pages/PR-2023-09-12-universal-and-meaningful-connectivity-by-2030.aspx [Accessed: April 15, 2024].

[3] "One Third of Global Population Remains Offline: ITU Study," Telecom Review, September 13, 2023. https://www.telecomreview.com/articles/reports-and-coverage/7331-one-third-of-global-population-remains-offline-itu-study [Accessed: April 15, 2024].

[4] United Nations, "Goal 7 | Department of Economic and Social Affairs," sdgs.un.org, 2023. https://sdgs.un.org/goals/goal7#targets_and_indicators [Accessed: April 15, 2024].

[5] United Nations, "Goal 9 | Department of Economic and Social Affairs," sdgs.un.org, 2023. https://sdgs.un.org/goals/goal9#targets_and_indicators [Accessed: April 15, 2024].

REFERENCES

[6] D. Broom, "These are the places in the world where internet access is still an issue – and why," World Economic Forum, September 5, 2023. https://www.weforum.org/agenda/2023/09/broadband-no-luxury-basic-necessity/ [Accessed: April 15, 2024].

[7] United Nations, "Goal 11 | Department of Economic and Social Affairs," sdgs.un.org, 2023. https://sdgs.un.org/goals/goal11#targets_and_indicators [Accessed: April 15, 2024].

[8] C. Louw and B. Von Solms, "Free Public Wi-Fi Security in a Smart City Context—An End User Perspective," Elsevier eBooks, pp. 113–127, January 2019, doi: https://doi.org/10.1016/b978-0-12-815032-0.00009-3.

[9] S. Kumar Bhoda, "Public Wi-Fi Networks and Digital Inclusion in Smart Cities," LinkedIn, February 14, 2024. https://www.linkedin.com/pulse/public-wi-fi-networks-digital-inclusion-smart-cities-bhoda-bggie/?trk=article-ssr-frontend-pulse_more-articles_related-content-card [Accessed: April 15, 2024].

[10] M. D. Chinn and R. W. Fairlie, "The determinants of the global digital divide: a cross-country analysis of computer and internet penetration," Oxford Economic Papers, vol. 59, no. 1, pp. 16–44, June 2006, doi: https://doi.org/10.1093/oep/gpl024.

[11] W. Chen and B. Wellman, "The Global Digital Divide - Within and Between Countries," IT & Society, vol. 1, no. 7, pp. 39–45, Mar. 2004, Accessed: April 15, 2024. [Online]. Available at: https://www.ec.tuwien.ac.at/~dieter/teaching/GmA/Chen2004.pdf

[12] D. S. White, A. Gunasekaran, T. P. Shea, and G. C. Ariguzo, "Mapping the global digital divide," International Journal of Business Information Systems, vol. 7, no. 2, p. 207, 2011, doi: https://doi.org/10.1504/ijbis.2011.038512.

[13] M. De-Arteaga, W. Herlands, D. B. Neill, and A. Dubrawski, "Machine Learning for the Developing World," ACM Transactions on Management Information Systems, vol. 9, no. 2, pp. 1–14, September 2018, doi: https://doi.org/10.1145/3210548.

[14] Mr. Emre. Alper and M. Miktus, Digital Connectivity in sub-Saharan Africa: A Comparative Perspective. International Monetary Fund, 2019. Accessed: April 15, 2024. [Online]. Available at: https://www.elibrary.imf.org/doc/IMF001/28404-9781513514604/28404-9781513514604/Other_formats/Source_PDF/28404-9781513515939.pdf.

[15] E. A. Walelgne, A. S. Asrese, J. Manner, V. Bajpai, and J. Ott, "Clustering and predicting the data usage patterns of geographically diverse mobile users," Computer Networks, vol. 187, p. 107737, March 2021, doi: https://doi.org/10.1016/j.comnet.2020.107737.

REFERENCES

[16] A. Mathrani, J. Wang, D. Li, and X. Zhang, "Clustering Analysis on Sustainable Development Goal Indicators for Forty-Five Asian Countries," Sci, vol. 5, no. 2, p. 14, March 2023, doi: https://doi.org/10.3390/sci5020014.

[17] S. Singh and J. Ru, "Goals of sustainable infrastructure, industry, and innovation: a review and future agenda for research," Environmental Science and Pollution Research, vol. 30, January 2023, doi: https://doi.org/10.1007/s11356-023-25281-5.

[18] "ml.js - Machine learning tools in JavaScript," GitHub, May 12, 2022, https://github.com/mljs/ml [Accessed: April 15, 2024].

[19] "Global Internet users," www.kaggle.com. https://www.kaggle.com/datasets/ashishraut64/internet-users [Accessed: April 16, 2024].

[20] Creative Commons, "Creative Commons — CC0 1.0 Universal," Creativecommons.org, 2019. https://creativecommons.org/publicdomain/zero/1.0/.

[21] "plotly/plotly.js," GitHub, June 13, 2022. https://github.com/plotly/plotly.js [Accessed: April 16, 2024].

[22] M. Holt, "mholt/PapaParse," GitHub, April 15, 2024. https://github.com/mholt/PapaParse [Accessed: April 16, 2024].

[23] M. Otto, "Bootstrap," Getbootstrap.com, 2022. https://getbootstrap.com/ [Accessed: April 16, 2024].

REFERENCES

[24] "bootstrap - Libraries - cdnjs - The #1 free and open source CDN built to make life easier for developers," cdnjs. https://cdnjs.com/libraries/bootstrap/5.0.0 [Accessed: April 16, 2024].

[25] S. Kemp, "Internet use in 2024," DataReportal – Global Digital Insights, January 31, 2024. https://datareportal.com/reports/digital-2024-deep-dive-the-state-of-internet-adoption [Accessed: April 16, 2024].

[26] C. Van Wyk, "The role of artificial intelligence in improving internet speed and reliability in Africa," Open Nettest, July 23, 2023. https://nettest.com/de/articles/the-role-of-artificial-intelligence-in-improving-internet-speed-and-reliability-in-africa [Accessed: April 15, 2024].

[27] S. Muniraj, "Accessibility and Artificial Intelligence: A More Diverse Future?," IEEE Computer Society, June 7, 2023. https://www.computer.org/publications/tech-news/trends/artificial-intelligence-and-accessibility [Accessed: April 16, 2024].

Index

A

ACCESS-CM2, *see* Australian Community Climate and Earth System Simulator (ACCESS-CM2)
accuracy() function, 199
Accuracy trend, 203
Adaptive neuro-fuzzy inference system (ANFIS), 146, 147
AI, *see* Artificial intelligence (AI)
AIEM, *see* Artificial intelligence-based useful evaluation model (AIEM)
Air Quality Index (AQI), 222, 249
Air quality monitoring
    application testing and analysis
        classification algorithm, 248
        LSTM algorithm, 246, 247
        MLP algorithm, 244, 245
        PR performance, 242–244
        regression algorithms performance, 241
        SLR performance, 241, 242
        web application, 236–241
    data processing and application design
        AQI classification, 235
        data collection process, 228, 229
        display regression graphs, 234, 235
        linear regression, 232
        LSTM/MLP implementation, 234
        polynomial regression, 233
        program structure, 230
        website layout, 231
    SDG 3: good health and well-being, 224, 225
    SDG 13: climate action, 226, 227
ANFIS, *see* Adaptive neuro-fuzzy inference system (ANFIS)
ANNs, *see* Artificial neural networks (ANNs)
Application layout, 112, 119, 120, 272, 273
Application system model
    capabilities, 268
    client-side JavaScript, 268
    clustering global Internet connectivity development developed, 271

INDEX

Application system model (*cont.*)
  developing, 271
  emerging, 271
  highly developed, 271
  phase/level, 270
  tiers, 270
  underdeveloped, 271
 components and functionalities
  index.html, 269
  libraries and resources, 269, 270
  script.js, 269
 functionalities, 268
 principles, 268
Application testing, 82–86, 119–120, 200–201, 279–282
AQI, *see* Air Quality Index (AQI)
AQ10, *see* Autism Spectrum Quotient (AQ10)
Aral Sea Basin's GDP, 66
Arduino UNO, 106
Artificial intelligence (AI), 2, 286
 affordable and clean energy, 8–10
 capabilities and functionalities, 16
 classifications, 15, 16
 clean water and sanitation, 6–8
 climate action, 14, 15
 defined, 15
 good health and well-being, 4–6
 industry, innovation, and infrastructure, 10, 11
 no poverty, 3, 4
 responsible consumption and production, 12, 13
 sustainable cities and communities, 12
 WQAD, 7
 zero hunger, 4
Artificial intelligence-based useful evaluation model (AIEM), 67
Artificial neural networks (ANNs), 19, 146, 186
Australian Community Climate and Earth System Simulator (ACCESS-CM2), 65
Autism Spectrum Quotient (AQ10), 225
Automated waste classification system, 186

B

Backup power sources, 62, 67
Bagging, 26
BEMS, *see* Building Energy Management System (BEMS)
Boosted regression trees model, 64, 143, 145
Boosting, 26, 66, 105, 106, 183

INDEX

Building Energy Management System (BEMS), 147

C

CART algorithm, 6, 126, 127
Classification algorithms, 2, 19, 103, 128, 187, 201, 206, 208, 210, 222, 248, 249
Classification analysis, 19
Classification-based wind power predictions, 62, 67
Classification models
  cost reduction, 62
  warnings and insights, 62
Classify Instance button, 219
Clean energy technologies, 9, 60
Climate change, 144
Cloud-to-Things continuum, 68
CMIP6, *see* Coupled Model Intercomparison Project Phase 6 (CMIP6)
CNNs, *see* Convolutional neural networks (CNNs)
CO_2 emission, 49, 66, 67, 140, 145, 148, 155, 160, 163, 165, 169, 170, 176
Colab, 110
Confusion matrix, 117–119, 123–125, 127, 128, 130, 132, 133
  decision trees, 127, 128
  k-NN
    with k = 3, 124
    with k = 4, 125
    with k = 5, 126
  K-NN model, 123
  ML.js dependency, 117
  MLP, 132, 133
  random forest, 130
  TensorFlow.js, 117
Conventional and intelligent control methods, 146
Conventional time-series analysis techniques, 185
Convolutional neural networks (CNNs), 22, 23, 146, 183, 186
Coupled Model Intercomparison Project Phase 6 (CMIP6), 65
Crop dataset, 102, 103, 109, 136
Crop production, 103, 106
Crop recommendation method, 107
Crop recommendation system, algorithms, ML
  accuracy, 134
  AI use cases
    SDG 2, 104–107
    SDG 9, 104–107
    SDG 12, 104–107
  application layout, 119, 120
  application test, 119
  confusion matrix, 118
  confusion matrix, k-NN
    with k = 3, 124
    with k = 4, 124, 125
    with k = 5, 125, 126

Crop recommendation system, algorithms (*cont.*)
  data processing and application design
    data collection process, 108, 109
    data preprocessing steps, 110, 111
    datasets description, 108, 109
    program structure, 111, 112
  decision trees
    classification results
      CART algorithm, 126, 127
      confusion matrix, 127, 128
      k-NN algorithm, 126
    K-NN classification results
      confusion matrix, 123
      k = 3, 121
      k = 4, 122
      k = 5, 122
    k-NN model, 135
    MLP, 130–133, 135
    predict soil qualities, 103
    rainfall factor, 135
    random forest, 128–130, 134
    SDG 2, 102, 103
    SDG 9, 102, 103
    SDG 12, 102, 103
    SDGs 2 and 12, 135
    web application, 102, 103, 134
    web application layout, 113–117
Crop selection method (CSM), 106

Crop yield rate, 106
CSM, *see* Crop selection method (CSM)
CSV dataset, 268, 289
CSV file, 194, 213

D

DAIA, *see* Decentralized AI Alliance (DAIA)
Data cleaning, 34, 149, 150, 190
Data cleansing/data scrubbing
  fill missing values, 30, 31
  formatting data, 32
  parsing data, 32
  remove outliers, 31
Data integration, 33
Data preprocessing, 110, 262, 263
  data integration, 33
  data reduction, 34
  data transformation, 32, 33
  dimensionality reduction, 34
  JavaScript program
    DataCollection.html, 36
    data cleaning, 34
    dataset, 35
    Display Data and Analyse, 36
    and HTML, 35, 36
    and layout of data collection, 37
    original temperature dataset *vs.* corrected dataset, 37–39

INDEX

Data preprocessing stages
   data cleaning, 149
   missing data, 150
   noisy data, 150
Data processing
   application layout, 272, 273
   application system model, 268–272
   data preprocessing, 262, 263
   dataset, 259–262
   HTML and CSS, 259
   K-means clustering algorithm, 259
   program structure, 273–279
   scatter plots, 263–266
Data reduction, 23, 34
Dataset, 176
   collection and description, 259–262
Data transformation, 32, 33
Data types
   attribute-values, 27
   interval, 28
   measurement scales, 27
   nominal, 27
   ordinal, 27
   ratio, 28
   semi-structured data, 29
   structured data, 27, 28
   unstructured data, 28
Decentralized AI Alliance (DAIA), 3
Decision-makers, 286
Decision-making, 175, 223
Decision trees, 126–128

Deep learning approach (DLA), 6, 224
Deep learning (DL), 7, 22, 23, 184
Deep Q-network (DQN), 105
Digital connectivity, 257
Digital disparity, 258
Digital divide, 252–257, 284, 289
Digital economy, 253
Digital environment, 33
Digital inequality, 252, 288
Digital revolution, 288
Digital technologies, 286
Dimensionality reduction, 34
DL, *see* Deep learning (DL)
DLA, *see* Deep learning approach (DLA)
DL-ELM hybrid technique, 184
DQN, *see* Deep Q-network (DQN)

E

Econometric techniques, 66
EE, *see* Energy efficiency (EE)
EKC, *see* Environmental Kuznets Curve (EKC)
Energy efficiency (EE), 66
Energy performance (EP), 65
Ensemble learning, 25, 26
Environmental factors, 60
Environmental Kuznets Curve (EKC), 66
Environmental sustainability, 144
EP, *see* Energy performance (EP)
Euclidean distance, 55

331

INDEX

extractFields() method, 229
Extreme Gradient Boosting (XGBoost), 7
Extreme learning machines (ELM), 184, 186
Extreme poverty, 3

F

Feedforward Neural Network with Multilayer Perceptron (FNN-MLP), 186
FileReader dependency, 113
Final CSV file, 72
fit method, 199
FNN-MLP, *see* Feedforward Neural Network with Multilayer Perceptron (FNN-MLP)
Fog computing, 68
for loop, 114

G

Gaussian distribution, 32
getAccuracy method, 117
getKNNRegression() function, 76
GHG emissions, 140
GHG reduction technologies, 144
Global energy efficiency, 9
Global goals, 141
global_variables.js files, 112
Google Colab, 110
Grey Level Co-occurrence Matrix, 227

Grid operators, 62, 96
Grid stability, 97
Groundwater (GW), 186
Gumbel probabilistic functional model, 64
GW, *see* Groundwater (GW)

H

Heuristic strategy, 63
Hierarchical clustering, 20
Hybrid model, 64

I

ID3, 6
Intelligent approach, 147
International Telecommunications Union (ITU), 253, 256
Internet of Things, Fifth Generation (5G), 68
Internet of Things (IoT), 11, 68
IoT, *see* Internet of Things (IoT)
ITU, *see* International Telecommunications Union (ITU)

J

JavaScript language, 60

K

Kaggle, 98, 108, 180
K closest neighbors, 55

INDEX

Kernel Regularized Least Squares (KRLS), 66
K-means algorithm, 254
K-means clustering algorithm, 252, 256, 259
K-means clustering process, 279–281
K-Nearest Neighbor (k-NN), 7, 8, 60, 61
    categorizes, 55
    classification program, 57
    CO_2 and GHG emissions, 159
    Diabetes.csv dataset, 55–57
    Euclidean distance, 55
    flowchart, 160, 161
    improvements, 175
    Plotly.js library, 160
    prediction and plot
        CO_2 emissions, 169, 170
        GHG emissions, 171, 172
    pseudocode Upload() Function, 162
    text field, 160
    Upload() function, 159
KNN classification, 83, 90, 92, 121–125
KNN.html program, 169
KNN machine learning algorithm, 74
k-NN model, 135
KNN regression model, 84, 88
KRLS, *see* Kernel Regularized Least Squares (KRLS)
K-Values, 203

K-Value *vs.* MAPE, KNN regression, 89

L

Land database, 107
Learning methods, 147
Least squares method, 40, 46, 50
Linear regression methods, 66
Logistic regression models, 257
LSTM algorithm, 247
LSTM/MLP algorithms, 249

M

Machine-learning-based predictive modeling approach, 104
Machine learning (ML), 2, 252
    advantages, 180
    affordable and clean energy, 8–10
    and AI interrelationship, 17, 18
    aim, 60
    algorithms, 60, 179, 180
    clean water and sanitation, 6–8
    climate action, 14, 15
    data, 17
    dataset processing, 61
    data's suitability, 29
    decision trees, 4
    defined, 16
    and DL, 22, 23
    energy industry, 60
    ensemble learning, 25, 26

INDEX

Machine learning (ML) (*cont.*)
  good health and well-being, 4–6
  industry, innovation, and
    infrastructure, 10, 11
  investigation, 64
  k-NN, 4
  mathematical models, 17
  multivariate logistic
    regression, 4
  no poverty, 3, 4
  optimized/trained model, 16, 17
  optimizing resource
    utilization, 180
  potability analysis (*see* Water
    potability testing)
  random forest, 4
  regression and classification
    algorithms, 39–57
  responsible consumption and
    production, 12, 13
  RL, 23–25
  shallow learning, 21, 22
  significance, 223
  supervised learning, 18, 19
  sustainable cities and
    communities, 12
  technologies, 63
  unsupervised learning, 20, 21
  wind power prediction, 61
  zero hunger, 4
Machine learning (ML) algorithms
  example, 141
  greenhouse gas (GHG)
    reduction, 143
  innovative solutions, sustainable
    development, 141
  manufacturing emissions with
    SDGs 9 and 13 (*see*
    Manufacturing emissions
    with SDGs 9 and 13)
  SDG 7, 141
  SDG 9, 13, 141
  sustainable development, 139
main.js file, 77
main.js class, 76, 77
Manufacturing emissions with
  SDGs 9 and 13
  application, ML Algorithms, 140
  application testing and analysis
    k-NN, 169–171
    MLP, 165–167
    SLR, 162–165
  data collection process and
    datasets description
    CO_2 emissions, 148
    data points, 149
    GHG emissions, 148
  data preprocessing steps
    attributes removal, 150
    data preprocessing stage,
      149, 150
    feature selection, 150
    ML model, 149
  improvements, 175
  in Mauritius, GHG
    emissions, 172
  Mauritius's compliance, EPA
    threshold, 173

INDEX

ML algorithms accuracy
    CO_2 emissions, 174
    GHG emissions, 174
  Other Gases, 173
  policymakers and
    stakeholders, 174
  program structure, models, ML
    functions and methods, 154
    general layout, MLR website,
      152, 153
    HTML files, 152
    k-NN, 159–162
    libraries, 151
    methodologies, 151
    MLR, 157–159
    SLR, 155, 156
  recommendations, 174
  research questions, 143
  use cases, 143–147
Manufacturing industries, 173
map() method, 111
mAP, *see* Mean average
    precision (mAP)
MDGs, *see* Millennium
    Development Goals (MDGs)
Mape *vs.* degree polynomial, 88
math.js, 151
maxDepth parameter, 205
Max depth *vs.* accuracy plot, 206
maxFeatures parameter, 209, 210
Max features *vs.* accuracy plot, 210
Mean absolute percentage error
    (MAPE), 14, 42, 48, 49, 61,
    78, 82, 96, 98, 145, 222

Mean average precision (mAP), 185
Millennium Development Goals
    (MDGs), 2
minNumSamples parameter, 207
ML, *see* Machine learning (ML)
ML-based applications, 286
ML classification algorithms, 222
ML classifications methods, 107
ML.js, 151
MLP, *see* Multilayer
    perceptron (MLP)
ML model, 289
MLP algorithm, 244, 245
MLR, *see* Multiple linear
    regression (MLR)
MLR.html program, 165
ML terms, 260
Model accuracy, 117
Model selection
    considerations, 204
Multilayer perceptron (MLP)
  architecture, 136
  confusion matrix, 132, 133
  deep networks, 136
  nonlinear relationships,
    data, 135
  number of epochs, 131, 132
  results, 130
Multiple linear regression (MLR),
    80, 81, 84, 90
  calculates MAPE, CO_2 and GHG
    predictions, 157
  characteristics, 50
  CO_2 and GHG emissions, 157

Multiple linear regression (MLR) (cont.)
  coefficients, 50
  CO_2 emission, 140
  dataset, 53
  flowchart, 158
  functions, 154
  GHG emission, 140
  improvements, 175
  inputs and outputs, 51–54
  JavaScript implementation, 51
  least squares method, 50
  matrix form, 50
  methods, 154
  multiple variables, 49
  prediction and plot
    CO_2 emissions, 165, 166
    GHM emissions, 167, 168
  pseudocode Upload() function, 159
  regression plots, 52–55
  Upload() function, 157

N

Naïve Bayes classifier, 106
Naïve Bayes (NB), 198, 199, 212–219
National Renewable Energy Laboratory software, 68
Natural language processing, 181
NB, see Naïve Bayes (NB)
NBAcc() function, 199
NB classifier class, 199

nEstimators parameter, 211
Neural and Bayesian network models, 141
new ML.DecisionTree Classifier(options) constructor, 197
Nonlinear dynamics, 64

O

Other Gases, 140, 171, 173, 176
Other Gases value, 155, 157, 165, 167

P, Q

Pandas, 110
Pandemics, 5
PapaParse, 113, 151
Plot() function, 234
Plotly.js library, 151, 155, 158, 160
Policymakers, 287
Polynomial regression, 85–87
Polynomial regression (PLR), 78, 79, 85–87, 242–244
  inputs and outputs, 47, 48
  JavaScript implementation, 46
  least square method, 46
  and MAPE, 48, 49
  predictor and response, 45
  regression curve, 47
  Regression_Weather.csv., 48
PolynomialRegression() function, 233

PowerCategory, 70
Power classification, 72
PR, *see* Polynomial regression (PR)
PR algorithm, 241-244
predict() function, 232
Prediction process, 155
predict method, 199
predLin() function, 232
predLinAll() function, 232
predPoly() function, 233
predPolyAll() function, 233
PRISMA guidelines, 65
Program structure, 230
    description of methods and classes, 276, 277
    flowchart, 274, 275
    HTML and JavaScript files, 72
    K-means clustering process, 279-281
    KNN, 74-78
    layout, 73
    multiple linear regression, 80, 81
    PR, 78, 79
    SDG icons, 274
    web application, 274
    web application layout, 73, 74
Python library, 110

R

Random forest (RF), 7, 128-130, 134, 136
panda's read_csv() method, 110

Recognition system, 183
Recurrent neural networks (RNNs), 227
Regression algorithms, 223, 249
Regression analysis, 19, 164, 165
Regression and classification algorithms
    k-NN, 55-57
    MLR, 49-55
    PLR, 45-49
    SLR, 39-45
Regression models, 93, 142
Regression techniques
    CO_2 and GHG emissions prediction, 142
Regression_Weather-outliers, 36
Reinforcement learning (RL)
    actions, 24
    agent, 24
    environment, 24
    objectives, 23
    policy, 25
    reward, 25
    state, 24
    training dataset, 23
    training environment, 23
    value, 25
Renewable energy technology, 67
RF ML models, 147
Risk mapping algorithms, 7
RL, *see* Reinforcement learning (RL)
RMSE, *see* Root mean square error (RMSE)

INDEX

RNNs, *see* Recurrent neural networks (RNNs)
Root mean square error (RMSE), 65, 145

S

Scatter plots
    broadband subscription against all other variables, 267
    cellular subscription against all other variables, 266
    Internet users (%) against all other variables, 266
    number of Internet users against all other variables, 267
    parameter, 263
    relationship between country and broadband subscription, 265
    relationship between country and cellular subscription, 264
    relationship between country and the number of Internet users, 265
    relationship between country and the percentage of Internet users, 264
    variables, 265
SDG 2, 102
SDG 9, 102
SDG 12, 102
SDG 13 (Climate Action), 65
SDG framework, 223
SDGs, *see* Sustainable Development Goals (SDGs)
SDGs 2 and 12, 105
SDGs 7, 255–259
SDGs 7 and 9, 105
SDGs 9, 255–259
SDGs 11, 255–259
Semi-structured data, 29
Shallow learning, 21, 22
shuffleDataset() function, 196
SimpleLinearRegression() function, 232
Simple linear regression (SLR), 49
    CO_2 and GHG emissions prediction, 155
    datasets, 40
    flowchart, 155, 156
    functions, 154
    GHG *vs.* CO_2 emissions, 155
    improvements, 175
    independent dependent variables, 39
    inputs and outputs, 41, 44
    JavaScript implementation, 40
    least squares method, 40
    and MAPE, 45
    MAPE, 42
    methods, 154
    prediction and plot
        CO_2 emissions, 163, 164
        GHG emissions, 164, 165
    prediction process, 155

INDEX

quantitative and dependent variables, 39
regression analysis, 164, 165
Regression_Weather.csv, 43
pseudocode Upload() function, 156, 157
weather dataset, 43
SLR, *see* Simple linear regression (SLR)
SLR algorithm, 241, 242
SLR.html program, 162
Small and medium-sized enterprises (SMEs), 11
Smart city communication, 63
SMEs, *see* Small and medium-sized enterprises (SMEs)
Socio-economic concerns, 12
Soil fertility categories, 107
Soil fertility technique, 107
Solar PV energy generation, 65
Strategic investments, 287
Structured data, 28
Supervised learning, 18, 19, 23
Supervised learning algorithm, 55
Support vector machine (SVM), 8, 146, 184
Sustainable development, 104
Sustainable Development Goal (SDGs)
  zero hunger, 104
Sustainable Development Goals (SDGs), 2, 60, 179, 222
Sustainable transport planning, 104

SVM, *see* Support vector machine (SVM)
SVM classification method, 147

T

TDS, *see* Total Dissolved Solids (TDS)
TexasTurbine.csv, 69
The 17 UN SDGs, 102
The European Green Deal, 65
TOMRA Sorting Solutions, 4
Total Dissolved Solids (TDS), 188
Trihalomethanes, 218
2030 Agenda for Sustainable Development, 6, 141

U

UI elements, 269
UN SDGs
  AI *see* Artificial intelligence (AI)
  community development aspects, 2
  future and quality of life, 2
  ML *see* Machine learning (ML)
  SDG 1: no poverty, 3, 4
  SDG 2: zero hunger, 4
  SDG 3: good health and well-being, 4–6
  SDG 6: clean water and sanitation, 6–8
  SDG 7-affordable and clean energy, 8–10

339

UN SDGs (*cont.*)
    SDG 9: industry, innovation, and infrastructure, 10, 11
    SDG 11: sustainable cities and communities, 12
    SDG 12: responsible consumption and production, 12, 13
    SDG 13–climate action, 14, 15
Unstructured data, 28
Unsupervised learning, 20, 21, 23
UN Sustainable Development Goals (SDGs)
    global goals, 141
    SDG 13, 141
    SDGs 9, 141
    social, economic, and environmental challenges, 139
Upload() function, 155, 157, 159, 194
U.S. Environmental Protection Agency (EPA), 140
User interface components, 252

V

VRE, *see* Variable renewable energy (VRE)
Variable renewable energy (VRE), 67

W

Ward's method, 258
Waste management, 185
water_potability.csv file, 188
Water potability testing, 13
    automated waste classification system, 186
    CNN, 183
    consumption analysis, 181
    forecasting technique, 185
    groundwater (GW), 186
    Kaggle, 183
    modified Faster R-CNN architecture, 184
    multitarget deep learning framework, 185
    primary research questions, 182
    SVM, 184, 187
    transparency and interpretability, 182
    transportation operations, 186
    water_potability.csv file, 182
    WQAD, 184
    WSS, 185
Water quality, 7
Water quality anomaly detection (WQAD), 7, 184
Water quality classification
    data collection process, 188, 189
    data preprocessing steps, 190
    decision tree performance testing, 204–207

general layout, web application, 190, 191
K-NN performance testing, 201–204
ML algorithms
  application testing, 200, 201
  KNN, 193–195
  Naïve Bayes (NB), 198, 199
  random forest and decision tree, 195–198
NB performance testing, 212–219
random forest performance testing, 208–211
water potability system, 192
Water supply systems (WSS), 185
Weatherbit.io API, 222
Weather dataset, 43
Web application flowchart, 274, 275
Web application layout, 113
  accuracy, methods, 118
  classification, 114
  confusion matrix object, 117
  FileReader dependency, 113
  for loop, 114
  machine learning model, 115
  methods, classification, 115
  model accuracy, 117
  PapaParse, 113
"What-if" analysis, 64
Wind energy management, 10
Wind power generation prediction and classification
  advantages
    accurate energy generation forecasting, 96
    cost reduction, 97
    enhanced energy planning, 97
    grid stability, 97
    optimized energy distribution, 96
  application testing and analysis
    KNN classification, 83, 90, 92
    KNN regression model, 84, 88
    multiple linear regression, 84, 90
    polynomial regression, 85–87
    regression techniques, 82
    test values, 82
  comparative analysis, 93–96
  data processing and application design
    data collection process, 68, 69
    data processing steps, 70
    program structure, 72–81
    wind turbine modeling, 71, 72
Wind turbine modeling, 71, 72
World Economic Forum, 254
Worldwide Internet Connectivity
  addressing digital inequality, 288
  application testing, 279–282
  benefits, 286

341

Worldwide Internet Connectivity (*cont.*)
  data processing (*see* Data processing)
  dataset, 257
  data utilization patterns of mobile users, 257
  digital connectivity, 257
  digital disparity, 259
  digital divide, 253, 255
  digital economy, 253
  digital technologies, 286
  empowering policy decision-makers, 286
  enabling strategic investments, 287
  fostering international collaboration, 288
  geographical disparities
    economic factors, 285
    policy and regulatory environment, 285
    regional variations, 284
    urban-rural divide, 285
  vs. historical trends
    differential growth rates, 284
    early adoption and expansion, 283
    emergence in developing regions, 283
    regional disparities, 284
  Internet penetration rates, 255
  ITU, 253, 256
  K-means algorithm, 254
  K-means clustering algorithm, 256
  logistic regression models, 257
  ML, 252
  mobile users, 257
  research and development support, 287
  SDGs 7, 9, and 11, 255–259
  targets 7.b, , and 11.c, 9, 253
  Ward's method, 258
  World Economic Forum, 254
WQAD, *see* Water quality anomaly detection (WQAD)

X, Y

XGBoost, *see* Extreme Gradient Boosting (XGBoost)
XGBoost model, 66

Z

Zero hunger, 4, 104

GPSR Compliance
The European Union's (EU) General Product Safety Regulation (GPSR) is a set of rules that requires consumer products to be safe and our obligations to ensure this.

If you have any concerns about our products, you can contact us on

ProductSafety@springernature.com

In case Publisher is established outside the EU, the EU authorized representative is:

Springer Nature Customer Service Center GmbH
Europaplatz 3
69115 Heidelberg, Germany

www.ingramcontent.com/pod-product-compliance
Lightning Source LLC
LaVergne TN
LVHW010335260326
834688LV00036B/718